A Beginner's Guide to Tibetan Buddhism

A Beginner's Guide
to Tibetan Buddhism

Practice, Community,
and Progress on the Path

BRUCE NEWMAN

Revised edition

SHAMBHALA

Shambhala Publications, Inc.
2129 13th Street
Boulder, Colorado 80302
www.shambhala.com

Cover art: Courtesy of Robert Beer
Cover design: Daniel Urban-Brown
Interior design: Kat Ran Press

9 8 7 6 5 4 3 2 1

Second edition
Printed in the United States of America

⊖This edition is printed on acid-free paper that meets the
American National Standards Institute z39.48 Standard.

♻This book is printed on 30% postconsumer recycled paper.
For more information please visit www.shambhala.com.

Shambhala Publications is distributed worldwide by
Penguin Random House, Inc., and its subsidiaries.

LIBRARY OF CONGRESS CATALOGING-IN-PUBLICATION DATA
Names: Newman, Bruce, 1950- author.
Title: A beginner's guide to Tibetan Buddhism: practice, community,
and progress on the path / Bruce Newman.
Description: Boulder: Shambhala, 2022. | Includes bibliographical references.
Identifiers: LCCN 2021036917 | ISBN 9781559395038 (trade paperback)
Subjects: LCSH: Buddhism—China—Tibet Autonomous Region. |
Spiritual life—Buddhism.
Classification: LCC BQ7805 .N348 2022 | DDC 294.3/923—dc23
LC record available at https://lccn.loc.gov/2021036917

Dedication

The book is humbly and devotedly dedicated to the long life and enlightened activities of my two primary teachers, Venerable Chökyi Nyima Rinpoche and Venerable Gyatrul Rinpoche.

Contents

Foreword to the First Edition

Bruce Newman has been my close student for almost thirty years. Having resided in both India and Nepal for a long time, Bruce spent many years seriously studying and practicing Tibetan Buddhism with a number of well-known, highly qualified Buddhist meditation masters.

Being a diligent practitioner, Bruce successfully completed the traditional four-year retreat at Samye Ling in Scotland and thus qualifies for the designation of "lama." Presently, he resides at Tashi Choling Retreat Center, founded by H. H. Dudjom Rinpoche, in Ashland, Oregon, where Bruce has been teaching meditation and guiding others in general Buddhist practices for almost a decade.

Given Bruce's exceptionally kind nature, stable disposition, and innate intelligence, I am confident that he will be able to share his insights with others and help them on the Buddhist path. I am pleased that his new book will soon be published and wish him all the best.

Chökyi Nyima Rinpoche

Preface to the 2022 Edition

Welcome to the second edition of my book, *A Beginner's Guide to Tibetan Buddhism*. I wrote the original version more than twenty years ago after returning from living in South Asia and being on retreat in Scotland. It is now the very end of 2020, and I'm sure I don't have to remind the reader how times have changed.

But there are some wonderful changes too. Tibetan Buddhism has grown and thrived in the West. It no longer seems an alien subject; through the efforts of many great lamas, practitioners, and translators, it seems to be much more a map of who we are and who we can be rather than an exotic place we might visit.

I have changed too. I'm almost seventy and have spent the intervening years teaching and practicing. Of course, I have learned a few things in the process, so when approached by the good folks at Shambhala Publications for an updated edition, I was very happy to share what I have learned with a new audience. So thank you very much to Shambhala, its president Nikko Odiseos, and especially my editor, Tucker Foley.

I am no enlightened master, just an older student. My greatest aspiration in life is to share what I have been so lucky to learn from my teachers with people who are perhaps just getting started in Tibetan Buddhism. If you learn something useful reading this, then the difficulties I have encountered will have been well worth it.

So all my best to you, dear reader. May all your aspirations be effortlessly fulfilled!

Acknowledgments

This book would not be possible without the help and inspiration of a great number of people. Foremost are my teachers. I've been very fortunate to have many, but my two primary teachers are Venerable Chökyi Nyima Rinpoche and Venerable Gyatrul Rinpoche.

Many people suggested that I write a book. Most importantly, my wife, Susan Bosworth, and my root teacher, Chökyi Nyima Rinpoche, who basically ordered me to write it and wouldn't let me quit!

Also, many people read the various drafts of the manuscript and offered suggestions. The two most helpful have been my dear friends Gaea Yudron and Barbara Caselli.

I also extend my heartfelt appreciation to the patrons and sponsors, both past and present, whose generosity and trust have made it possible for me to devote my time fully to the Dharma. I won't mention any names, but you know who you are. Thanks again.

Thanks also go to my agent, Jimmie Young, who showed up seemingly out of nowhere, and to all the good folks at Snow Lion who have made so much of the precious Dharma available to us over the years.

Lastly, to all my friends and students along the way. Through our connection, I have learned a great deal about the manifold ways that buddha-nature unfolds in different practitioners; the lessons have been invaluable.

A Beginner's Guide to Tibetan Buddhism

Introduction

I wanted to call this book *Tantra for Dummies*. Unfortunately, the…
for Dummies name is trademarked. Nevertheless, this is going to
be that kind of book.

When you buy a computer, it comes with an instruction manual.
It is usually too brief and obtuse, and it never talks about the stuff
you're really interested in. So you go buy a book like *Windows for
Dummies* or *Macs for Dummies*, and it leads you through everything
you have to do, step by step. It doesn't assume you know anything,
and it leaves nothing out.

When you study Tibetan Buddhism, either by reading books,
listening to teachings, or participating in a center, a lot goes unsaid.
A great deal of background knowledge is assumed by the author,
the speaker, the older students running the center. It takes a while
for the neophyte to gather this background and learn the ropes, and
by then, who knows? You may have become discouraged and quit.

I don't want you to quit. Tibetan Buddhists have a system of wisdom and technique that is just amazing. The more I learn about it,
the more impressed I am. Also, I'm sure your interest is sincere—you
really want to better yourself and perhaps attain a level of realization. So in this book, we'll try to make the pieces match.

Perhaps it will make things clearer if I begin by talking about
myself and how I got involved in Tibetan Buddhism and how I've
struggled and persevered, zigged and zagged, over the years. I feel
some reservations about talking too much about myself, that as a
Buddhist I should be more anonymous and self-effacing and make

| 1

the presentation more traditional and less personal. However, when I was struggling at the beginning of the task of writing this book, my primary teacher, Chökyi Nyima Rinpoche, advised me to make the book more personal and autobiographical. When I took his advice, the material seemed to just pour out of me. With time I've come to believe that, as much as anything else, what we older students have to offer is our own personal story of practicing the path. Tibetans have been enthralled by the stories and songs of Milarepa for centuries; they've served as models and guides for countless followers. I'm no Milarepa, but perhaps the reader will be able to learn and benefit from reading about my limitations and the errors I've made along the way. I strongly feel that by sharing experiences that are unique to Westerners in our modern age, we are offering support to all Western practitioners.

With that said, here's my story.

I was never a very good sixties person. In many ways, my heart wasn't in it. In some ways, I didn't believe the jargon. And I was just too shy and withdrawn to truly participate. But in any case, that's where my story starts.

I went to the University of California in beautiful Santa Barbara from 1968 to 1972. My major field of study was theoretical chemistry; that is, applying quantum mechanics to explain chemical phenomena. I truly fell in love with quantum mechanics with its paradoxes and seeming parallels to Asian thought.

I also began a major love affair with drugs, especially smoking marijuana, but whatever positive or consciousness-expanding effects drugs may have had on me were soon overshadowed by the increasing numbness, depression, dullness, and withdrawal that smoking caused me.

My first exposure to Buddhism was through my best friend's older brother, who began an involvement with Buddhism that led him to a center in Scotland (where twenty years later I did a four-year retreat) and a monastery in Thailand. I developed both an interest in Buddhism and a fear of it. It just didn't seem like something you could do in your spare time. If one truly believed its premises, that we are suffering in illusion, then it seemed that one would abandon everything and commence intensive practice immediately, which is, of course, what many have done over the centuries. Buddhism seemed to demand a little more than going to church on Sundays and being a nice person. Nonetheless, its analysis of phenomena in terms of emptiness seemed to agree with the insights of quantum mechanics with one major difference: Buddhism offered a path to experience these truths rather than just speculation about them. No matter how profound the insights of scientists, science doesn't claim to offer a path of personal transformation.

By the time I graduated in 1972, I was really torn. My involvement with drugs made continuing my education problematic and rendered my social life disastrous. Also, my interest in Asian spirituality made Western science seem irrelevant to a life bent on understanding reality.

Since I had some money from my family, I decided to follow in the footsteps of a couple of friends and travel in the Third World. I was hoping that a change of environment would give me the opportunity to change my personality and break my drug habit; I was also sincerely interested in exploring Buddhism and Hinduism in their countries of origin. I traveled for about a year and a half and unfortunately only deepened my dependence on cannabis. I did, however, make a connection with the Tibetans in India and Nepal.

In order to meet a traveling companion, I went to Dharamsala, India, the residence of His Holiness the Dalai Lama and home to many Tibetan refugees. As soon as I got off the bus, I immediately felt a kind of inner bliss, a unique experience for me at the time. I began attending classes at the Library of Tibetan Works and Archives at a school for Westerners established by His Holiness. I was deeply impressed by the rigor with which the lama, Geshe Ngawang Dhargyey, taught the class. The material was all systematized into outline form. I reasoned that with a structure like this, any errors in their system would be revealed quickly. One must be very confident of one's system to organize it like this.

My father, Samuel, was an extremely brilliant man. He excelled in any intellectual pursuit to which he applied himself. I grew up having to debate with him about everything. Along with my scientific background, this made it impossible for me to trust anything that could possibly contain any loopholes, articles of blind faith, or items that simply contradicted logic or common sense. I had approached my earlier studies of Asian religion deeply afraid that I would eventually turn up some discrepancy or contradiction that would completely unravel my faith and force me to abandon my commitment. When I heard Geshe-la speak so authoritatively, clearly, systematically, and logically, it was more miraculous to me than a human flying, and I knew that I had found my path.

Unfortunately, I still had a lot of ordinary things to work out. I had my drug problem and all the unresolved emotions behind the problem. Suffice it to say, it took me another year and a half of tortured soul-searching before I returned to Dharamsala in early 1975 at the age of twenty-four to begin my spiritual path in earnest.

The training in Dharamsala emphasized philosophical studies as a preliminary to meditation. As someone who had already studied scientific views of reality and was used to getting into altered states through drugs, I never felt completely at home with that approach. While there, I did, however, learn the basics of the path very well, and I'm very grateful; it's provided a very firm foundation for all my subsequent study and practice. At the same time, I was able to immerse myself in a Western community that was completely committed to the path; many were ordained, and many were doing long, solitary retreats. There was a real sense of adventure for me and a feeling of escape from all that I had been involved in up to that point.

At the same time, I began studying in short retreats with two Theravadan masters, a Burmese master named Goenka-ji and an English monk called Longpe. They taught meditations that are now popularly known in America as *vipassana*. Their instruction gave me my first taste of meditative experience, an awareness of the body's energetic processes, and simple techniques that I could and would fall back on for decades. I still teach mindfulness to my students; I don't feel its value can be overemphasized.

After ten months of study at the library, I began craving a more meditative approach within the Tibetan tradition. A couple of Americans recommended that I visit Kalu Rinpoche in Darjeeling, in northeastern India. I did and was immediately impressed by his powerful presence and obvious meditative qualities. He seemed to hold the whole valley in his meditative absorption. From Kalu Rinpoche I received authorization to begin the *ngondro*, the preliminary practices of the Vajrayana.

As I began my prostrations, the first of the ngondro practices, my health collapsed. So began a pattern of weakness, lethargy, and dullness that persisted right through to 1995, when the brilliant doctor Shandor Weiss diagnosed me as having cannabis toxicity and was successful in detoxifying me. In the twenty years in between, I had wonderful opportunities to practice but was always hampered by my physical condition.

After leaving Kalu Rinpoche, I could no longer stay in India because of visa problems, so I went to neighboring Nepal. I settled near the famous Great Stupa of Bouddhanath outside Kathmandu. There are many monasteries there, now more than twenty, and I introduced myself to the abbots of a large white monastery called Ka-Nying Shedrup Ling, where His Holiness Karmapa was about to begin a series of empowerments to consecrate the new monastery.

Since then, that monastery has proved to be my spiritual home. The abbot of the time was Tulku Urgyen Rinpoche, one of my most important teachers; his son Tulku Chökyi Nyima Rinpoche has become my principal teacher and root lama.

Under Chökyi Nyima Rinpoche's guidance, I completed most of my ngondro in Nepal in 1976. I returned to Dharamsala in 1977 and did about five months of retreat. Because of family problems, I returned to California later that year.

In California, I worked some odd jobs; tried to get healthy; watched my father die; and began studying under Gyatrul Rinpoche, His Holiness Dudjom Rinpoche's West Coast representative.

Along with Chökyi Nyima Rinpoche, Gyatrul Rinpoche is a lama to whom I owe more than I can ever conceivably repay, and I've maintained my connection with him to the present.

I returned to Nepal in 1980 and spent the next eight years either practicing near my teacher or in Manali, a very lovely spot in the Himalayas in northwest India. I also worked in Kathmandu as an English teacher.

At my teacher's order, I went to Scotland in 1988 to do a four-year retreat at Kagyu Samye Ling, where my friend's older brother had studied in the sixties and where I had visited during my hippie travels in 1969. We first had to build the retreat center, and then we actually began practicing in 1989. I will be mentioning this retreat frequently; it's a constant source of stories and examples.

At the conclusion of the retreat, I made a brief visit to Nepal and then returned to America with a little money from my generous retreat sponsor to get me started. I was very lucky to be able to settle first at Gyatrul Rinpoche's retreat center south of Ashland, Oregon, and then close by. After about a year, Rinpoche asked me to begin teaching, which I had wanted to do, both to earn a little money and to experiment with some ideas I had about teaching, and I started my teaching at his center in San Francisco. Not long afterward, I began teaching in Ashland and fell in love with my first serious student, Susan Bosworth, whom I have since married. We're now living in town where I am teaching, practicing, and writing this book.

So why am I writing this book? The short answer is my lama told me to. Also, several friends felt it would be a good idea to put some of the things I say while teaching into book form. The longer answer is that I perceive a problem with how Tibetan Buddhism is being transmitted to and in this country, and I want this book—along with my classes—to do as much as possible to ameliorate that problem.

Whenever Buddhism has come to a new country, there has been a transition period from when the old traditional form is accepted and practiced to when it is transformed into a form more accessible to the new host. For instance, Buddhism was introduced into China by Bodhidharma, who is called the First Patriarch of Chan or Chinese Zen. But it wasn't until Hui Neng, the Sixth Patriarch, that Buddhism evolved into a form that was accessible to more Chinese and had truly become a Chinese rather than a foreign religion.

Often, when Buddhism travels from one country to another, it comes as part of a "package deal" with many other aspects of the original country's culture. For example, when Buddhism spread from China to Korea, it brought with it the arts, literature, and so on of a larger, more civilized country. This perceived superiority of one culture over another made it easier for the new hosts to accept the new religion.

This is hardly the case with the spread of Tibetan Buddhism to America and the rest of the West. We have very little interest in other aspects of Tibetan culture. Besides, our scientific background makes it difficult for us to accept anything new without a lot of investigation.

Tibetan Buddhism is a truly astonishing system. The more I study it, the more overwhelmed I am by its depth and profundity. But Tibetan Buddhism obviously evolved within the Tibetan situation. Its system of practice is perfectly designed to bring ordinary Tibetan lay and ordained people from their present state to complete enlightenment, almost like a car on an assembly line in Detroit. So how does their situation differ from ours? In almost every way imaginable.

Let us look at some of these differences to try to understand how they may influence both the presentation of Buddhism and our understanding of it.

First, in Tibet most Dharma material was presented for ordained monks and nuns—in other words, people who were full-time Dharma practitioners. For the most part, they were the only ones who could read and were interested in the more advanced topics of tantric Buddhism. We Westerners, on the other hand, generally come to the Dharma at an older age and often with too many commitments to spend a great deal of time studying and practicing;

however, we are literate and intellectually sophisticated. We often find the teachings that are intended for the Tibetan laity too simple and unsatisfying, but the teachings that are presented for the ordained are too time-consuming to practice.

Second, Tibetans grow up with a deep sense of reverence and respect for the Dharma and for the lamas who teach and represent it. Although the teachings always advise one to question the Dharma with an attitude of sincere investigation, the very success of Buddhism in Tibet made most of that questioning seem irrelevant and often disrespectful. We, on the other hand, haven't grown up within a Buddhist culture. On top of that, we are taught always to question and demand proof. Some teachings are presented in the West without a question-and-answer period. A Tibetan may feel that since the lama is a buddha, the presentation must have been perfect, so how could one even begin to question? However, we Westerners might feel alienated or confused by the lack of questions and might sense that the teaching was more a ritualized affair than an exchange of information.

Third, Buddhist practitioners in Tibet were supported both emotionally and materially. Here in the West, they generally are not.

Fourth, because of the harshness of Tibetan life, people were accustomed to hardships and were more willing to take them on for the sake of their practice. Here, we just buy more stuff. We're also definitely willing to take on some hardships, but what we consider to be hardships would be seen as luxuries in Tibet. One lama living in America has said that if he were to teach about the correct posture for meditation and insist that his students use it, he would be opening himself up to lawsuits.

Fifth, also because of the simplicity of Tibetan life, their minds were also much simpler. They had fewer distractions, less to think about. Among the Tibetans I have known, I have observed that even when encountering difficulties, they deal with them and then move on without looking back. Therefore, when they meditate, they are able to remain undistracted and progress through the practices. We, however, are almost never able truly to quiet our minds, and the very profound techniques of Tibetan Buddhism never seem to work as advertised. It can make us feel let down, like failures.

Sixth, and perhaps most important, most of us come to the Dharma with a kind of psychological woundedness that would be almost unheard of in Tibet. Tibetan lamas were just stunned when they first heard that many Westerners hate their mothers. This woundedness results in two major problems for us: first, we have to go through a long process of healing before we are stable enough to meditate properly, and second, we have many hidden agendas that can make our practice go astray. (This will be discussed in later chapters.)

So, on the one hand, we have this wonderfully pure and profound Dharma with these incredibly high and realized lamas, and on the other, we have us, possibly confused but genuinely sincere, intelligent, and interested. But because of the newness, the language and cultural problems, and the aforementioned differences, there's still a gap. We're not quite getting it. Western yogis give up on retreat; Western monks and nuns often abandon their ordinations. Dharma centers are rife with politics, and many people get very hurt in these places. New students wonder why the older students don't seem more together.

This book is my attempt to fill this gap—to make a bridge between the traditional teachings and the person you really are. I find most teachings and books idealize the listener or reader. They seem to assume that readers have lots of leisure and will easily be able to practice the techniques that are taught, and that once they practice these techniques, results will come quickly.

If you're one of the lucky few for whom progress has been rapid and smooth, this book isn't for you. It's for those of you who are new to Tibetan Buddhism and feel overwhelmed by its complexity, as well as for those of you who have been practicing for a while but whose experience hasn't lived up to your earlier expectations.

This book is not a substitute for more traditional teachings. There are many great lamas who are teaching and incredible books available in your bookstore. You will need to have some previous exposure to these teachings in order to follow my discussion here. This book is to help you make sense of and apply those already perfect traditional teachings, rather like the...*for Dummies* books I mentioned at the beginning of the introduction.

The first text I received teachings on and studied extensively was Je Gampopa's *Jewel Ornament of Liberation*. It was written in the twelfth century in Tibet, just as Buddhism was beginning to spread and flourish there. In this text, Gampopa gives a complete overview of the Buddhist path from the very beginning to the attainment of complete buddhahood. Although I am not claiming in any way to have any of his qualities, I am taking his book as guidance and inspiration for this, especially in the progression of material from chapter to chapter.

There are four major orders of Tibetan Buddhism—the Gelug, Sakya, Kagyu, and Nyingma. Although I've received instruction in all four, my primary focus has been with the Kagyupas and Nyingmapas. Therefore, my presentation will reflect the perspective of those two traditions. I don't feel the differences between the four are very major; most of what will follow will be applicable to any student of Tibetan Buddhism. However, you should note that if your interest happens to be in the Gelug or Sakya traditions, you may notice some minor differences or change in emphasis.

I use the first and second person a lot in this book. I hope you don't mind. I talk about myself because I feel that since I've spent forty-five years practicing, I've made forty-five years' worth of mistakes. Where I've erred, so might you. By sharing these mistakes with you, it is my hope that some of you will be able to avoid them. I was lucky and lived in Asia with much leisure; when I erred, I had the opportunity to correct myself. If you—with your busy lifestyle, multiple distractions, and competing spiritual paths—err, you might very well abandon Tibetan Buddhism for something more initially rewarding. Also, with my use of the second person, it might seem I feel readers must be fools who will make every possible mistake. That's not my intention at all; it's simply the most natural way of writing for me.

Mentioning all the pitfalls might also make the book and the material it represents seem bleak and foreboding; that again is not my intention. I sincerely hope that by applying the advice, warnings, and hints in this book, you will find that your exposure to the wealth of Tibetan Buddhism will be as rewarding as you would wish.

CHAPTER 1

Buddha-Nature: The Ground

I am at present working on updating this book after twenty years. I am writing during the COVID-19 pandemic, with a monumental election approaching, just after half our small town burned to the ground. With all this chaos, confusion, and misery, one thing has really struck me: the deep and profound kindness of others.

In our shattered community, across the country, and around the world, there are people who are so filled with love and compassion that they are willing to step up and sacrifice to benefit others.

To me, this compassion is an expression of something both deep and innate that dwells within each of us. In some, it lies dormant and unacknowledged forever. In others, it can shine forth at unexpected times. What is it that does dwell within us?

Often there is one experience that suggests that things are not what they seem and points to a deeper truth within us. Anything could trigger this sense of something deeper. One of my dearest friends met the monk Matthieu Ricard on a train ride in India. The monk's composure intrigued my friend to the degree that he changed his travel plans, sought out Buddhist teachers, and has been diligently and sincerely practicing since then.

I met a fellow who was a diver in college. During a competition, he had an experience while diving where time stopped, and he felt he was floating forever in space. When the dive ended, he walked away, never dove again, and became interested in Buddhism.

Recently I visited the Boston Museum of Art. In the Japanese section, they had a lovely collection of Buddhist art. I sat down and quietly gazed at the beautiful statues. I recalled my difficult adolescence and the solace and peace I found in oriental Buddhist art and the inspiration and direction those wonderful images provided for me.

My teacher, Venerable Chökyi Nyima Rinpoche, is the abbot of a large monastery in Nepal. He tells me that many Westerners come to him to learn something about Buddhism after trekking in the Himalayas. He says that the vastness of the mountain panoramas gives these trekkers some sense of the basic vastness of their own minds. This experience inspires them to take the next step.

Others have found their initial inspiration through the religious upbringing they had as children. They experienced their religion of birth as something powerful and meaningful but found that they lost connection with it as they grew up. However, they always longed for that inspiration and meaning.

Because I was a child of the "sixties," many of the people I knew got their initial inspiration from taking psychedelic drugs. These drugs gave us a new perspective—or at least some sense that there was a different, more profound way of perceiving the world. And although I am in no way advocating their use, probably much of the initial interest in Asian spirituality came from people's involvement with drugs.

A different example is the Buddha himself. As a pampered prince, he was sheltered from the suffering of the world. But upon escaping his palace, he discovered the all-pervasiveness of suffering and determined to understand its origins and find a solution.

So, whatever the cause, we have had some experience, some glimpse, some understanding that reveals new vistas of human potential and forever changes how we see the world. One problem though: these experiences do not last. Eventually, we return to being the same people we were, with the same thoughts and perspective.

One thing has changed, however; now we know better. It is as if we have seen through someone's disguise and can no longer believe their façade, even though they still appear the same. Actually, that is exactly what has happened. We have penetrated the disguise of our ego.

We now have some sense that there's a better, vaster, more profound way to deal with life. Our old habitual patterns, which we have taken for granted for so long, now seem constricting. It's like returning to a prison after a brief but glorious trip outside. It can be painful and depressing; we might even want to run away and hide from our new insight.

It was like that for me. As I mentioned in the introduction, I was incredibly inspired by my initial contact with Tibetan Buddhism. However, upon my return to my family in America, I felt a return of all my deep emotional problems. I feared returning to India because of the risk of more serious drug addiction, and I feared studying Buddhism because I thought it might simply be an escape. I was completely torn—it was as if two armies were doing battle inside my head. I was hardly aware of the outside world during this period, though I was somehow able to hold down a job as a research chemist. However, my yearning for a life in harmony with my initial insights eventually prevailed.

Before I returned to India and began practicing, I used to follow my thoughts and feelings blindly, completely believing in my self-images and in the socially constructed reality around me. When there were gaps—anything that could possibly threaten this fabricated world—I would lose myself in distraction. Unfortunately, this is a common experience for most of us, since we have no system for understanding those glimpses and no societal support for following up on them.

A friend of mine, when she was in college, was sitting on a knoll looking up at the sky with two of her girlfriends. They all saw the most wonderful sight, a group of female deities frolicking in the sky. For my friend, it was transformative and instrumental to her beginning a search that eventually led her to become a committed Buddhist practitioner. Years later, she happened to meet the other two girls. They denied any memory of the experience.

In a very real way, our society is structured around denying these experiences and feelings. Spiritual seekers do not make good consumers. We live in a culture of addictions, from substance abuse to workaholic patterns. It's always sad for me to see how busy some of my old friends are; I frequently speculate that they too are trying to escape the logical conclusions of their own insights.

Some of us will spend our lives compulsively ignoring that gnawing feeling, that deep yearning. But for some, this is no longer possible. We are no longer able to fool ourselves completely and are no longer completely satisfied with who we are. *This is the discovery of buddha-nature as the ground.*

But all these stories have one thing in common: *something* changed an ordinary situation into a profound spiritual opening. After all, anyone can surf, dive, meet a monk, see some statues, or confront the sufferings of others without an accompanying spiritual awakening. In fact, the overwhelming majority of people experience these things all the time with hardly a ripple in their awareness. What makes us different?

To summarize, although all beings possess buddha-nature, for it to begin to awaken us, we must have prayed and aspired, and purified our karma. Then we begin to get the message.

We have all had a yearning for meaning in our lives. We might give it other names—truth, value, love, cosmic consciousness, ecstasy. But it is inevitable that when our stomachs are full and there's a roof over our heads, we begin to question and long for something deeper.

In Buddhism that yearning is, in itself, proof of the existence of something deeper within us. If there weren't something there, how could we be aware of its absence? Do we have any desires for completely nonexistent things? Some of us will dismiss that yearning; others will be consumed by it.

What is buddha-nature? It is the potential for all beings to become enlightened, to be buddhas. It is not as if only the Buddha and a select few have it, and they teach us through their pity. Nor is it that some of us have buddha-nature while others don't. Nor is it that humans have it while animals don't. As long as there is sentience, there is buddha-nature.

We may feel like the most miserable people in the world. We might feel we have neuroses and depravities that others can barely imagine. We might think of ourselves as the lowest of the low, completely unworthy and totally unlovable. Believe me, I've spent a considerable part of my life feeling these very same things. No matter how you feel right now or what you think about yourself, you still possess this buddha-nature. No matter how rotten the house is, it's still built on the ground of enlightenment.

At the present moment, this buddha-nature is concealed from our awareness, like the sun being completely concealed behind clouds. Yet just as we can sense the presence of the sun even on the cloudiest day, we sometimes have some sense of our buddha-nature; some sense that there's something more to life; some capacity beyond our normal way of thinking, feeling, and perceiving. Please remember what I just said: This yearning is proof of the existence of this ground. Don't be too harsh with yourself; listen and respect this great need within yourself.

Sometimes this newfound commitment will accompany, not something wonderful, but an experience of death—that of a friend, a parent, or possibly the discovery of a terminal illness within ourselves. It may also come with a lesser kind of death—the loss of a job, a divorce—experiences that help us pierce through the bubble of our self-satisfaction. In all these experiences, we discover that the ego is not doing an especially good job of managing our lives.

When we acknowledge the importance of our new or renewed insight, when we feel inspired by our discovery, we start to take some steps, however tentative, to learn how to return to the ground, how to experience it more and more often and with greater intensity, duration, and clarity. We probably begin by reading and sharing our insights with our more sympathetic friends. If we are fortunate, we find a teacher, receive their instructions and blessings, and begin and sustain a meditation practice. *This is taking the buddha-nature as the path.*

When, through our diligence, our experience becomes stable, and we reside effortlessly in our own ground, *this is the buddha-nature of fruition, complete buddhahood.*

Tibetan lamas like to explain subjects like this in terms of these three: ground, path, and fruit. *Ground* is the basis, the foundation.

Path is what you do with that foundation. You might have a seed, but you still have to plant and water it. Finally, the plant grows into maturity. That is the *fruit*. This book will be discussing all three—ground, path, and fruit—in terms of buddha-nature. As in the example, we all have the seed, our buddha-nature, but we also must plant it and nurture it to fruition.

Tibetan Buddhism is called Vajrayana. A *vajra* is an indestructible weapon, something like a diamond scepter. It also refers to buddha-nature, which is indestructible; always residing within; and able to destroy the enemy, consisting of obscurations, discursive thoughts, and disturbing emotions. *Yana* means "vehicle." Vajrayana is the vehicle, the spiritual path, where the whole approach is centered on the concept of this buddha-nature.

What is this buddha-nature then? It is defined as "the disposition to buddhahood" in the *Uttaratantra*, the primary Buddhist text on buddha-nature. Tulku Urgyen Rinpoche says, "[Buddha-nature] is like a wish-fulfilling jewel. It is present in all sentient beings just like oil is present in any sesame seed."[1] He adds, "Buddha nature is all-encompassing: this means that it is present or basic to all states, regardless of whether they belong to *samsara* or nirvana....The buddha-nature is present just as the shining sun is present in the sky. It is indivisible from the [enlightened body, speech, and mind] of the awakened state, which does not perish or change."[2]

Khenchen Thrangu Rinpoche says, "Each of us possesses buddha-nature. We each have the seed of enlightenment within ourselves, and because the potential can be actualized, we possess an enlightened essence."[3]

Let's explore buddha-nature as ground or basis a little more. In the Tibetan tradition, the main teaching on buddha-nature is the *Mahayana Uttara Tantra Shastra*, which has been translated into English as *The Changeless Nature*. This teaching was given by the future Buddha Maitreya to the great Indian yogi and scholar Asanga almost two thousand years ago and is still studied in Tibetan monasteries and Buddhist centers around the world. The discussion that follows comes from that text and Jamgon Kongtrul Rinpoche's commentary:

> If the Buddha element were not present,
> There would be no remorse over suffering.
> There would be no longing for nirvana,
> Nor striving and devotion toward this aim.[4]

If the Buddha element were definitely not present, not a single person would grow to feel sorrow and remorse over the suffering of samsara. No one would long to attain nirvana. No one would strive for this aim, exerting themself to apply the means to attain it, nor would anyone have devotion in terms of this wish: "If only I attained it." Contrary to this, the generation of sorrow, remorse, and so on is present. Since these are the function of the disposition, the disposition to buddhahood is established as being present.[5]

Maitreya presents more reasoning to demonstrate the buddha-nature's existence:

> The buddha-essence is ever present in everyone because
> the *dharmakaya* of perfect buddhahood pervades all,
> the suchness is undifferentiated, and they all have the
>   potential.[6]

In this oft-quoted but difficult to understand passage, Maitreya gives three reasons why all sentient beings possess the enlightened essence. I will rely on Khenchen Thrangu Rinpoche's explanations to clarify this passage.

In relation to "the dharmakaya of perfect buddhahood pervades all," he writes,

> In the future beings are capable of giving rise to Buddhahood.
> In other words, Buddhahood can manifest in all beings because
> they are completely pervaded by the dharmakaya [the mind of
> the Buddha] already.[7]

About "the suchness is undifferentiated," he says,

> Within the ultimate nature of everything, [suchness], there is
> no separation between a good nature and a bad nature. There
> isn't the bad nature of ordinary beings and the good nature of
> enlightened beings in the ultimate nature of phenomena. It is
> completely undifferentiated. Because the bodhisattvas of the
> past accomplished the state of realization, we also can accom-
> plish the same if we practice properly.[8]

Finally, he explains the phrase "they all have the potential":

> The third reason all beings possess the Buddha potential in them
> is that it is evident in different degrees [categorized into five
> types of potential]; but in having the potential within them they
> can accomplish Buddhahood.[9]

Maitreya classifies all beings into five different families based
on their present capacity to follow the path. Because all beings fall
into one of these five families, they have some relationship with
buddhahood and therefore have the potential.

The terms *dharmakaya* and *suchness* refer to the ultimate truth,
the truth of emptiness. Emptiness can be clearly established
through logic; indeed, this is the main task of philosophical studies
in Tibetan monastic colleges. Thus, simply put, we possess buddha-
nature because it is true; it is our personal experience of emptiness.
It is just the way things are.

If suchness is true, then our own ego-centered perspective can
logically and experientially be shown to be defective or false, and
as the preceding anecdotes demonstrate, we ourselves can see the
faults and limitations of our present point of view and have some
trust in a higher reality. Since suchness or emptiness is the truth of
our world in general ("suchness is undifferentiated" and "the dharmakaya...pervades all"), it is not the possession of a limited, select
few. We don't have to worry whether we're among the select. We

are. We're sentient. Discovering our buddha-nature means understanding the absolute truth of the entire world in which we live, not
merely a soul within our being. We speak of our buddha-nature as
our essence, something that can be discovered within us, but it's
not like finding a pit in an apricot. We may find it by looking within,
but what we find is all-pervasive. This is probably something most
of us have sensed—that a deeper truth pervades the world in which
we find ourselves.

The quotation from Maitreya may not seem to be rigorous, logical proof. The bottom line is that our fundamental potential for
enlightenment, along with one or two other premises in Buddhism
such as in the law of karma, cannot be proved logically but can be
explained so that they seem reasonable. We can accept these beliefs
because they are reasonable as a basic starting assumption. All
systems of thought begin with a few essential axioms and then go
on to build a logical system based on them. If a system is logically
self-consistent and leads to no contradictions with experience, then
we can trust the validity of that system. For example, in geometry
we start with *point*, *line*, and *plane*. These elements are undefined;
nevertheless, we intuitively grasp their meaning. Based on these
three basics, a wonderful system was built that has remained valid
for thousands of years.

Likewise, the Buddhist system starts with a few fundamental
core elements that are then developed into a complex system. The
validity of this system is demonstrated by its logical consistency
and, most importantly, by the confirmation given by countless practitioners over the last twenty-five hundred years. Thus, although
the concept of buddha-nature cannot be strictly proven, it can at
least be demonstrated to be reasonable, sensible, and worthy of
further consideration and investigation.

I'm also trying to demonstrate how the formal study of Buddhism
corresponds to our initial insight and inspiration. Remember your
own experience, ponder what you've heard and read, and try to
reach some firm conclusion. It's very important to work gradually
and systematically to resolve all doubts regarding buddha-nature.

In a sense, it's a lifetime project—our doubts slowly become more and more subtle.

I remember some of my own process. I studied the theory of quantum mechanics and tried to understand the deeper philosophical issues it revealed. My experience with drugs convinced me of the existence of a deeper reality. I read some of the books that were available then, such as the *Diamond Sutra* and the *Sutra of Hui Neng*; I thought deeply and tried hard to reconcile these different perspectives. I spent a great deal of time and effort on this task, and I feel much of my later diligence was based on this effort. Practice is always more productive when not hampered by doubt and the hesitation it creates.

What is this buddha-nature? Once we have cleared up most of our doubts regarding its existence, we must still be convinced of its value. Is it really worth pursuing? Maybe we'll be disappointed when we become enlightened: "Hey, that wasn't worth it. I want my money back!" Lord Maitreya says,

> Like the purity of a jewel, space, and water,
> It is always undefiled in essence.
> Its qualities resemble those
> of a valued gem because it is powerful,
> of space because it is unalterable
> and of water because it moistens.[10]

Maitreya explains the qualities of our essence. It is undefiled by the usual garbage of our minds—our incessant thinking, our turbulent emotions, and our erroneous self-centeredness. No matter how neurotic or upset we may be, no matter how debauched or evil we may become, our buddha-nature remains our buddha-nature. It never loses its purity. No matter how dark and stormy the clouds may become, they never affect the sun. They might decrease our ability to perceive it, but the sun doesn't lose its luster. If buddha-nature is simply the true nature of things, how could it possibly become defiled?

The positive qualities of our nature are indicated by the metaphors of a jewel, space, and water. The gem refers to the mythological wish-fulfilling jewel that can confer any boon on its possessor. Likewise, our nature is beyond any suffering. Suffering comes from not knowing the truth, from abiding and acting in error or misapprehension. However, realization of our nature will satisfy our deepest needs and aspirations because we will no longer be separated and alienated from our world with all the ensuing attachment and aversion. Therefore, it is likened to a jewel. Realization of our buddha-nature is more precious than any jewel or any imaginable wealth.

Not only will its realization be completely satisfying, but once perfected, it will be unalterable like space. Space can never be changed. You may fill your room with clutter, but the space itself is unaffected. Our buddha-nature may be obscured by our negativities, but it is not polluted by them. And because buddha-nature is unalterable like space, when we do attain realization, the realization is permanent. It will not be a glimpse that fades, a "high" from which we come down. When stabilized, it's forever.

The metaphor of water has always been more difficult for me to understand. I have requested clarification, and what I have learned is this: when a cloth is wet, the moisture permeates the cloth; in the same way, buddha-nature pervades all phenomena. Every aspect of our own experience will be pervaded by it.

Lord Maitreya shows through metaphors how buddha-nature manifests in ordinary beings like us. Here's one:

> If an inexhaustable treasure were buried
> In the ground beneath a poor man's house,
> The man would not know of it, and the treasure
> Would not speak and tell him "I am here!"
>
> Likewise a precious treasure is contained within each being's mind.
> This is its true state, which is free from defilement.
> Nothing to be added and nothing to be removed.

> Nevertheless, since they do not realize this, sentient beings
> Continuously undergo the manifold sufferings of
> deprivation.[11]

As discussed earlier, some people can be fairly successful in propping themselves up and satisfying their desires. Some are miserable, with all kinds of gaps and holes in their self-image. But who is completely happy? Who doesn't feel at least some discontent, some mild paranoia, some ill-defined malaise? This discomfort is the sun of our nature patiently burning through the thick clouds of our habitual patterns. My own metaphor is a slumbering animal awakening in its cage—our discontent is the animal's yearning to be free. Sometimes we're lucky, like those trekkers and surfers, and our nature shines fairly clearly, if only for a short while. We're forever transformed, and we aspire to strive to integrate this experience until it becomes our reality—the realization of nirvana.

CHAPTER 2

The Teacher

Having glimpsed or intuited the ground, we desire to repeat the experience. We might try to recreate the original circumstances, but even if we are successful, it becomes clear that we can't spend our whole lives trekking in the Himalayas or surfing in Hawaii. If our initial glimpses were chemically aided, we might find ourselves descending into pretty dangerous territory as we strive to repeat or hold on to the original experience. I know this from my own experience—the more I tried, the lower I descended. We may reach the conclusion that although we have stumbled onto something of paramount importance, we have no idea how to proceed.

Sooner or later, however, we discover that our glimpse has been described by all the major contemplative traditions of the world. It dawns on us that we are far from alone; rather, we have joined an old and dignified club. From the beginnings of history, men and women have asked the same questions and have felt the same deep stirrings and longings. Beyond that, many have ventured further and discovered a path and, finally, a fruition that has brought them complete satisfaction. Some of them have gone on to found traditions that are still with us. Furthermore, these traditions have mapped out the path from our present state of consciousness to the goal, provided techniques for following that path, and continue to have living teachers who can guide us along that path.

At this point, we may try to read as much as we can, talk to our friends and acquaintances with similar interests or experiences, and perhaps visit some centers or listen to talks by various teachers. We are searching. Either we find a tradition that we feel inspired by, that seems sensible and true, or we meet a teacher who embodies everything we have been searching for. For example, we could meet a great Sufi teacher who really blows our minds and so decide to become Sufis. Or we could, say, believe Zen Buddhism is the tradition that makes the most sense and start to check out various Zen masters.

I was initially exposed to both Hinduism and Zen, but I was won over by the Tibetan Buddhists, by both the earthy warmth and joy they manifest and the rigorous intellectual system they maintain. In this book I will not discuss the relative pros and cons of various traditions, try to convince you of the superiority of Vajrayana Buddhism, or gloss over the very real differences between different religions. I will simply assume at this point that, for whatever reason, you have decided that Tibetan Buddhism warrants a closer look and will continue based on that assumption.

I am assuming that serious aspirants at this time have conducted some kind of investigation into the various paths available. Through reason or intuition, logic or feeling, they have come to the conclusion that the Buddhist path is the right one for them. And when the search is refined, they feel most drawn to the Tibetan tradition.

What's the next step?

Start with reading. When I started practicing Tibetan Buddhism, there were very few books available, and most of them were a little off, often remnants from the British empire. The availability of a new book was like Christmas. Now the opposite is true: there are so many books that one person couldn't possibly read or even keep track of them. Where do we start?

I just googled "Tibetan Buddhist reading lists." I got 965,000 hits. I checked a few of them out, and they all seemed very helpful. Here are some of the different kinds of books you should know about.

Sutras are the recorded teachings of the Buddha himself. His more advanced students had photographic memory. They got together and wrote everything down. They are preserved to the present day in many Asian languages.

Without a guide, you will probably find it difficult to discover sutras that are useful for you. Also, the translator may be more of an academic and less of a practicing Buddhist. In older translations, the translator may not have consulted with a master who could have explained the deeper meaning. Nonetheless, these are still the words of the Buddha and will give you a strong sense of the origins of our tradition.

These caveats hold true for translations from both Sanskrit and Tibetan. Especially with Tibetan, look for books where the translator worked with a living lama.

A note on translation: Modern translators are often more accurate than those of previous generations. Many of the senior ones have done years of retreat besides their study of languages. And they often work closely with a lama who speaks English and knows the West. I'm very happy with this continuous improvement in the quality of translations. For example, the Sanskrit *abisheka* or Tibetan *wangkur* used to be translated as "initiation." Now "empowerment" is most often used (*wang* means "power"). Even among modern translators, the same word may have different translations. *Yeshe* can be "basic wakefulness" or just "wisdom." The reader will not know that these different translations actually refer to the same thing!

The converse can be true also. Different Sanskrit or Tibetan terms can have the same English translation; for example, *prajna* and *jnana* can be translated as "wisdom," *sheszhin* and *rigpa* as "awareness."

I recommend that serious newcomers take a little effort to create a small glossary with the various translations for themselves.

There are also books by modern Western authors like the one you are now reading. The advantages and disadvantages should be clear: we are generally not very realized or accomplished, but we know the language and culture and are sharing the same journey as you.

My favorite books are the ones written by modern Tibetan lamas who have Western educations, speak and write in English, and have immersed themselves in our culture. Their writings have been revelatory for me! There is such a greater depth of meaning—it is like comparing a color photo with a grainy old black and white. The lamas whose books have been most useful for my students and me are Dzogchen Ponlop Rinpoche, Tulku Thondrup Rinpoche, Kyabgon Traleg Rinpoche, Dzigar Kongtrul Rinpoche, and Dzongsar Khyentse Rinpoche.

It is likely that your reading and other preliminary research will convince you of the necessity of finding an appropriate teacher. If that is the case, in the next chapter I will offer some guidelines to simplify and expedite that search. However, you might feel that a teacher is unnecessary or perhaps even detrimental to the path; in that case, I will try to demonstrate the necessity of having one.

When I first became interested in Eastern spirituality in the sixties, we were all quite naive. Also, many teachers or gurus were making the most extravagant claims. Everyone seemed to be the avatar or messiah for our age. It seemed that if only we could meet this person, find our guru, all our problems would be over. We would be given a simple practice that we could effortlessly accomplish, giving rise to cosmic consciousness. I remember having a feeling that finding a guru was the culmination of the path rather than the beginning of it.

We're all a little older now. We've lived through fourteen-year-old avatars, messiahs with fleets of Rolls-Royces, and gurus who have given their students AIDS. We certainly have a right to be hesitant and skeptical.

So why are gurus necessary? I will give you my personal reasons, what I've learned from experience, and hope that I haven't left out anything important.

First, lamas give meditation instructions. Not only do they know the myriad of techniques, but also through their clairvoyance, they know the ones that are most appropriate for us. We might have spent the last nine lifetimes practicing the deity Vajrayogini. A truly qualified lama will know this and will guide us correctly. Our own choice of practice would most likely not be as accurate and could be based on fantasies and wishful thinking. As a teacher myself,

I really appreciate this; I feel that I am able to help students with their practice but that I have no real guidelines regarding which kind of practice to recommend to them. I don't have the slightest idea with which practices they are karmically connected, and most students are usually either uninformed or overwhelmed by the various choices available. So the guru will know what kind of practice is right for you and will be able to instruct you in its techniques and meaning. They'll also know when you're ready to move on to something new.

Also, when we have difficulties or obstacles in our practice, our teacher will know the techniques for removing them. Believe me, some really strange things can happen when you begin to meditate diligently. It is not always obvious what to do about these experiences—or even whether they're good or bad. I've talked to a couple of people recently who get hot when they meditate. Is this good or bad? Typically, we take anything that's different as a positive sign. It's easy to understand that rationale: if we hadn't been meditating, it wouldn't have happened; therefore, it must be a sign of progress. But it takes a certain degree of experience and perhaps study to put these experiences in their correct context.

When unusual experiences happen, if we are without guidance, we may become discouraged and quit if we feel that the experiences are negative. Even more likely is that we become puffed up and arrogant if we believe our experiences to be extraordinary. Someone I know once had a series of the most amazing experiences I've ever heard—the kind of visions and realizations for which I've been secretly longing for decades. The problem was that in the absence of a close relationship with a qualified teacher, he sincerely believed that he was realized and able to begin teaching. He occasionally got himself into some jams. Luckily, he straightened himself out through meeting real teachers.

The same thing happened to me. Forty-five years ago, I attended a short retreat after only a few months of practice and had the most extraordinary experience of my life. I really thought I had made it! I was seriously pondering how I was going to teach my disciples.

Either the leader of the retreat was not all that qualified, or more likely, I didn't communicate with him thoroughly enough. Imagine my chagrin when the experience faded, and I returned to my normal, neurotic self.

Experiences like this are one thing; recognizing buddha-nature is another. By its very nature, it's ineffable. We can easily fool ourselves into believing we understand when, in fact, we don't. Only a deeply realized master can clarify these points for you. We would consider someone foolish if they tried to teach themself medicine or a foreign language. How much more difficult is the stabilization of buddha-nature!

The second reason gurus are important is that they act as role models. They embody everything we strive for. If they did it, so can we! Whenever I'm feeling really sorry for myself, I remember that there once was a time when my teacher was as confused as I am. This thought always gives me encouragement. Also, since Buddhism is centered around the concept of egolessness, it is daunting, paradoxical, or outright absurd to dedicate oneself to a life of seeming psychological suicide. Meditation often feels like a process of dissolution and can feel confusing, chaotic, and threatening. The teacher acts as an example of someone who has actually given up their ego, their self-centeredness, and has proceeded through the dissolution process without becoming a martyr or a vegetable. In fact, they are highly functioning human beings who seem to be having a lot more fun than I am.

Many of my students fear that if they stop identifying with their thoughts, they will become somewhat dysfunctional. They feel that they need to indulge in their usual discursiveness and that it is necessary to have an ego or self-image around which to structure their lives. The presence of the lama is living proof that this is simply not the case.

Third, the lama is a source of blessings. Although it is impossible to demonstrate in a laboratory the nature and existence of these blessings, I'm sure any sincere practitioner feels from the bottom of their heart that they are indeed being blessed. I feel that this blessing takes three broad forms. First, things may go more smoothly in the outside world. Money may be there when you need it. You may get the last room in a hotel at two in the morning. Situations that maximize your growth and learning spontaneously happen (unfortunately, such situations may seem quite painful and confusing at the time). None of these things can be counted on or predicted, but we recognize them intuitively as signs of grace. Then there is the transmission of energy that is also the blessing of the teacher. We feels currents of energy awakening in the body, releasing blockages and becoming the basis of deeper meditative experience. We may experience this as something like an electric shock when being touched by a lama, or we may feel it more continuously when we practice. However we experience it, it is a great aid in our unfolding. Lastly, the teacher transmits the experience of buddha-nature, either in their presence through a formal empowerment ceremony or in the solitude of the student's own practice. This transmission is, of course, the most profound meaning of blessing and in and of itself makes a lama indispensable. Since this point is of crucial importance, I will speak more of it later.

Fourth, the lama is a source of unconditional love. It's truly amazing and deeply touching to be loved in that way. No matter how poorly I follow their instructions, they are there. No matter how much doubt or negativity I have toward them, they are there. If I'm seething with arrogance or hatred or shame that I've just masturbated, they still love me. As meditation can and will reveal the most negative, despicable things about oneself, it's easy to fall into a pattern of self-condemnation. The unconditionality of the lama's love can be a lifesaver, pulling us out of that kind of swamp. Being accepted on such a deep level by another human being gives me the strength to accept myself and gently let go of these shortcomings rather than continue to condemn myself without having the strength or courage to change. As we all know from our ordinary relationships, being loved threatens and ultimately heals the most negative of self-images. How much more so when one is loved by an enlightened being! It gives you a firm, healing ground to stand on.

When I talk about devotion in a later chapter, I will mention how that love also creates a sense of strength and independence within us.

Fifth, the lama is a source of authenticity. Buddhism, and in particular Tibetan Buddhism, is a system where teachers are rigorously trained before being authorized to teach. Once they become teachers, they regularly report back to the lamas who are their superiors or who authorized them in the first place. Students can have some sense that their own training is being monitored, not only by their teacher, but by the tradition as a whole, the same tradition that has been cultivating highly realized beings for centuries. I myself check back regularly with my own teachers; explain what I'm doing as a teacher; share my problems, difficulties, or insights about my students; and petition for feedback, guidance, and support. After a conference like this, I return to my students confident that what I am teaching is of benefit to them.

Sixth, the lama is an object of surrender. Having such an external referent, one can begin to let go of one's ego. It may seem paradoxical or contradictory to speak of both surrender and independence coming from relating to the teacher, but later I'll try to demonstrate how that can be so.

Without a teacher, one has no choice but to rely on one's ego as the mediator of one's spiritual life. This is something like putting the prisoners in charge of the prison. We may tend to give ourselves advice that protects rather than dismantles the self. We may feel we are listening to our hearts when we're simply listening to our desires. Perhaps even more dangerously, one may rely on visions or inner voices. While such visions may be valid, one might also be cultivating schizophrenia—schizophrenics often get guidance from inner voices. I've seen it happen even to the point where the external teacher was rejected in favor of the voices in the head. If you feel you have a disembodied teacher of some sort, check with an embodied one. If your spirit is a valid guide, the master will confirm it. If not, they can save you from major problems.

On a deeper level, the guru is the manifestation of our own enlightened nature. Without a guru, this process of projecting our enlightened nature and later integrating it could not happen. The practices of devotion and guru yoga, so crucial in the Vajrayana, would have no basis.

I'm suspicious of people who say they don't need a teacher. Is there anything of value we've learned without one? Is there anything we've ever attempted that has been more difficult than attaining enlightenment? So why are we resisting? Perhaps it's better to look at and understand the resistance than to find fault with a teacher.

Longchenpa, the great Nyingma master of the fourteenth century, poetically summarizes the need for a teacher:

> Just as a patient is in need of a physician,
> People of a ruler, a lonely traveler of an escort,
> A merchant of a guild-master, a boatman of a boat,
> So in order to calm the emotions, to make evil harmless,
> To overcome birth and death...and
> To cross the ocean of fictitious being, you must rely on a
>   teacher.[1]

Longchenpa goes on to praise teachers:

> If someone were to praise only partially such a person who is
>   a helper of living beings
>
> And whose qualities are so vast he would have to say:
> As he makes them cross safely over the ocean of fictitious
>   being he is a steersman,
>
> An incomparable leader of those who have started their
>   journey...
> He is the bright lamp dispelling the darkness of the loss of
>   pure awareness.
>
> He is the wish-granting tree from which comes the happiness
>   of all who are alive.

He is the auspicious jewel by which all desires are
    spontaneously fulfilled.

He is the countless rays of the sun of great kindness.
He is the moon with its white light of prosperity and
    happiness, removing afflictions.[2]

As the great Indian yogi Naropa quoted to his Tibetan disciple,
Marpa the translator,

Before any guru existed
Even the name of Buddha was not heard.
All the buddhas of a thousand eons
Only come about because of the guru.[3]

CHAPTER 3

Finding a Teacher

Through reading the previous chapter, or perhaps through investigating your local spiritual scene, you have probably started to entertain the notion that it may be important to find a teacher. You might have already met a few by now. Some may be Tibetan, some Western; some may be monks or nuns, others laypeople. Some might live near you, while others were just travelling through. It could be difficult to know how to proceed.

When I was in college, I heard a former Harvard professor speak of his teacher, the Indian saint Meher Baba. I formed the impression that the spiritual journey was one of finding the "right" guru, and after that it would be "happily ever after." He would read my mind, give me the right practice, and that would be that. Very Hollywood.

Later I felt the spiritual path could be broken down into three stages: find a guru, do what they tell you to do, and become enlightened. I have pretty much followed that approach and still believe it is valid for the most part. The trouble is that finding a teacher isn't what it used to be.

When I first went to Asia in the seventies, high Tibetan lamas were very accessible. His Holiness Dudjom Rinpoche, then the patriarch of the Nyima lineage, held an open house every day, and anyone could just drop in. What an extraordinary opportunity! Younger lamas were fascinated by the modern world and eager to learn English. Incarnate lamas wanted to know about boom boxes and motorcycles. It was almost like they were your most interesting or fascinating friends. They would even drop by our house for a cup of tea.

In the West, it was different, although many lamas were still accessible—most started out small, perhaps a few students meeting in someone's living room. And they had no responsibilities other than to teach Westerners. If they settled in one place, they were easy to get to know. I will talk about relating to a teacher in a later chapter, but for now let us use the following as a model: we are looking for a teacher who has some special qualities and abilities, with whom we can communicate smoothly, and who can guide us step-by-step regularly over a period of many years. But that isn't so easy anymore. It is difficult to find someone who can meet all three of those criteria.

What has changed? Tibetan Buddhism has grown immensely. I first met the great Tibetan lama H. E. Tai Situ Rinpoche in northern India in 1976. He invited me to visit him at his monastery. I did, and I spent three days "hanging out" with him, chatting and asking questions, teaching him English, and helping him with his English correspondence. Later, over the years, I would see him in Nepal at public events, and occasionally I would get a short interview with him. Lastly, I saw him where I did my group retreat in Scotland. I was one of eight hundred in the audience.

My own teacher, Chökyi Nyima Rinpoche, used to be very accessible at his monastery in Kathmandu. Now I see him once a year at a seminar in northern California. I get an interview between five and ten minutes long. I spend months trying to figure out what to say: all my ups and downs, joys and sorrows, and what he wants me to do: meditations to practice, subjects to teach, how to deal with health and money problems, and so on. All in ten minutes! Then I spend months trying to figure out exactly what he said and what he meant and really regretting that there was no time for a follow-up question.

So the situation has changed greatly over the years. Because of the growth of Tibetan Buddhism in the West, the lamas are getting busier, more remote, and more difficult to see and form a meaningful personal relationship with. However, there are more Western teachers filling the gaps now, and it is quite likely that the new student will learn many of the important points of Dharma from a Westerner much like themselves.

So how do we find a teacher? Some people are lucky: they find their teacher almost by magic, like something out of a spiritual storybook. Others aren't so fortunate: they flounder from teacher to teacher, never really connecting, sometimes getting burned out, sometimes getting hurt or becoming bitter and angry. Or perhaps they always dwell on the periphery of a Dharma scene, vaguely knowing that they're missing out.

A friend of mine was living in a small refugee community in northern India when she heard a certain famous lama was passing through. She immediately knew he was going to be her teacher and wept excitedly in joyful anticipation. She became his student and spent many years in strict solitary retreat. She is a most amazing person.

I was lucky too. I met my teacher after I had been practicing for about a year. Chökyi Nyima Rinpoche was the opposite of any images I had of the archetypal guru. He's a little younger than I am and about a foot shorter. Hardly the old wise man with the white beard. When I met him, I didn't know anything about him, his credentials, or his lineage. He hardly spoke a word of English. What I did find, however, was that the advice he gave, in the most basic, broken English, seemed to have a deep and most profound effect on me. He would say something simple, and after a month I would discover that his words had reverberated inside me and changed me on some fundamental level. I was very moved, and after several months of this, I clearly felt he was my teacher. As soon as I determined this, I was filled with a deep joy and have not had a moment of doubt since.

I sincerely hope that you have this great good fortune. Some would say that such an occurrence is due to karmic connections from past lives. Perhaps there's not much we can do about it. But until this kind of connection ripens for you, I will offer some advice about finding a teacher. I don't believe we can be too naive or fatalistic about this. Perhaps you are destined to meet your guru, but there are a lot of teachers you can learn from in the meantime, and this learning can only hasten your eventual reunion.

Many, many Tibetan lamas are coming to the West these days. They represent a bewildering number of lineages and bear an equally bewildering number of titles. Since it seems valid to examine their credentials before going further, let us review these lineages and titles as a first step in establishing the bona fides of any particular teacher. Traditionally, we are supposed to examine a teacher carefully before taking Vajrayana teachings and empowerments from them; in the modern world that may not be possible, and we may have to judge more quickly based on credentials and reputation.

As I mentioned in the introduction, Tibetan Buddhism is divided into four main orders, or lineages. They are sometimes called sects, but that word has a negative connotation that doesn't apply here. The four are Gelug, Sakya, Kagyu, and Nyingma. They are *very* similar, and their primary difference is historical. From about 800 to 1200 C.E., there was a strong flow of ideas from Buddhist India to Tibet, which had just started to develop its own Buddhism. Indians went to Tibet to teach; Tibetans went to India to study. The four major lineages arose from this spiritual commerce. For instance, the oldest lineage, the Nyingma, was founded by Padmasambhava, who brought Buddhism to Tibet around 800 C.E. The Kagyu order was founded by Marpa the Translator, who went to India in the eleventh century and studied under the Indian yogis Naropa and Maitripa.

All four lineages hold to an identical set of Buddhist beliefs and principles. They all teach Buddhism in the form of the three yanas while emphasizing the Vajrayana. They all teach renunciation, the enlightened motivation of *bodhichitta*, and the correct view of emptiness. The only real distinction I have discovered is in how the traditions balance meditation and study. Gelugpas emphasize study somewhat more, Kagyupas and Nyingmapas focus on practice, while Sakyapas seem to fall in the middle. I would like to add here that it is far too simplistic to say, for example, that Gelugpas are scholars while Kagyupas are solitary yogis. Monks and nuns of all four lineages engage in study for many years and then gradually shift to a more contemplative lifestyle. All of these orders have produced centuries of highly realized beings. It is quite a serious fault to belittle one tradition at the expense of another. You should follow the tradition to which you feel closest while retaining respect for them all. Some people will feel comfortable studying more than one of these traditions; others will find this confusing and prefer studying only one.

Within the four main orders, there are many subdivisions. These divisions are based on both the traditions of different monastic centers (called monastic lineages) and the mastery of various techniques of meditation (called practice lineages). In addition, there are some smaller lineages outside these four, such as the Jonangpa, who specialize in the practice of Kalachakra. You can find out more about these different lineages through reading or by talking to older students. Since I've studied mostly within the Kagyu and Nyingma traditions, this book will represent my feeble attempt to transmit a little of their wisdom. If you find any contradiction with what you've studied in other traditions, I may be wrong, or you may have discovered an interesting fork in the road.

With respect to titles, we must start with the most ubiquitous, that of *lama* itself. *Lama* is the Tibetan translation of the Sanskrit term *guru*. To me, it has come to mean someone who is completely qualified to guide me on the path, who can lead me to recognize buddha-nature, and who knows all the techniques to help stabilize that recognition. This person should have all the qualities and capabilities that I mentioned in the last chapter.

However, the term *lama* has come to acquire a bewildering number of different uses. Some of them are as follows:

· Any Tibetan monk. This usage is common in many of the older books produced in the West—hence, the archaic term *lama-ism* for Tibetan Buddhism. The word *lama* is rarely applied to Tibetan or Western nuns or Western monks.
· A term of respect for an older Tibetan monk. We would like to think that he has made it by now.

· Someone, Western or Tibetan, lay or ordained, who has completed a traditional three-year retreat. During that retreat, one
should in theory have developed the qualities of a real lama.
My teacher refers to me as a lama because I have completed
such a retreat.
· A Dharma teacher, whether highly realized or not. This could
be someone who runs a small center.
· A Nepalese family name used by many Tibetan refugees. A Euro-
pean friend of mine married a Tibetan in Nepal; she is now Mrs.
Lama.
· A real, legitimate, fully qualified spiritual teacher.

You can see that the title *lama* can mean almost anything. Therefore,
the title should have very little weight in your search.

The next most often used title is *tulku*, which is Tibetan for *nir-*
manakaya, one of the three "bodies," or aspects, of a buddha. In
English, it means something like "emanation being" and refers to
a buddha or bodhisattva who consciously emanates or takes birth
in our world in order to benefit us. The Dalai Lama is, of course,
the most famous example of this, being the fourteenth consecutive
emanation of Chenrezig, the buddha of compassion.

There now are literally hundreds of tulkus. On one trip to Tibet,
H. E. Tai Situ Rinpoche recognized 160 of them. They come in all
shapes and sizes. Some are dignified and powerful abbots of huge
monasteries; some are dashing young playboys. Some live their
lives anonymously; after their deaths, one may hear rumors that
perhaps they too were incarnations. We see how we took their hum-
ble goodness and gentleness for granted. Many are being reborn in
the West, which gives me great hope for the future of our culture
and the role of Buddhism in it. Unfortunately, very few are being
reborn as women, or if they are being reborn as women, they are
not being recognized. Perhaps this will change with time.

Some tulkus are quite amazing. I recently met the four-year-old
incarnation of His Holiness Dilgo Khyentse Rinpoche and had no
doubt regarding his recognition and no difficulty in seeing his pre-

decessor in him. It was as if the older lama were superimposed on the child and somehow still accessible to his followers.

I once read a very profound meditation manual by the Third Khamtrul Rinpoche. In the conclusion, he wrote, "If you wonder about my qualifications for writing this book, I first recognized my buddha-nature at the age of two and had completely stabilized that recognition by four." One can also read accounts of the amazing qualities and miraculous abilities of the various Karmapas. There are two books about his various incarnations translated into English. There is now even a website that shares the various miracles performed by the young Karmapa Urgyen Thinley in Tibet!

Most tulkus, once recognized, get an early and thorough education and training. Some seem almost effortlessly and spontaneously enlightened; some develop through their training. One of my teachers told me that perhaps 30 percent of tulkus are not real; their recognition is politically motivated, perhaps to gain the support of a rich and powerful family.

As I mentioned earlier, Westerners are also now being recognized as tulkus; two of those that I've met, Lamas Wyn Fischel (Lama Drime) and Tsering Everest, appear to have exceptional qualities. More and more tulkus from all four traditions are being recognized in the West. I both pray and anticipate that they will have a profound effect on our culture.

Although I'm unable to judge the realization of others, tulku or not, I've been impressed with the tulkus I've met, young and old, whether traditionally or more contemporarily trained. It seems like a wonderful system and an excellent way to ensure the continuation of the teachings, since these children are able to begin their training at such a young age and without becoming too corrupted by modern culture.

If, however, you have doubts about a tulku, try to find out who recognized them. Was it an unequivocal recognition by one of the great lamas, or something a little more dubious? What was their training like? What do other lamas have to say about this person? (Beware of subtle nuances here; no lama is ever going to trash another.) How do the tulku's older students respond to your doubts? A little caution or hesitation on your part is good; in fact, the traditional Vajrayana texts all recommend it. With time the enlightened qualities (or lack of them) will speak for themselves.

Other titles include *geshe* and *khenpo*. These are academic degrees, like a Ph.D. Whether or not a geshe or khenpo is realized is hard to say. They are generally strict monks who teach in a very thorough, methodical style.

Druppon means retreat master, someone with great meditative experience who oversees a long group retreat. Expect this person to be very ascetic, to emphasize retreat, and to teach that if you simply practice more diligently, everything will be all right. (And that is most likely correct!)

All monasteries have "throne-holders," the most revered lamas of their monasteries. The larger the monastery or monastic system, the greater the fame and esteem of the lama. Most throne-holders are tulkus; for instance, the throne-holder of Palpung is always the Tai Situ Rinpoche. Some are based on merit, such as at Ganden Monastery, where the head is simply the most accomplished disciple of the previous throne-holder.

Kyabje is becoming more widely used these days. It means something like "source of refuge" or "noble refuge" and is almost always used for the most respected and revered lamas. The Western titles "His Holiness" or "His Eminence" roughly correspond, but these are certainly not literal translations. Also, there doesn't seem to be any standard in applying them. Who exactly determines who is or is not a kyabje, holiness, or eminence? When I started practicing Tibetan Buddhism, only the Dalai Lama was "His Holiness." The title then spread to the heads of the various lineages, such as His Holiness Karmapa and His Holiness Dudjom Rinpoche. "His Eminence" seemed to be reserved for throne-holders. But slowly we've experienced title inflation, and a little standardization would be useful. It's only normal to want to venerate and promote your teacher; however, most of us find it somewhat confusing and off-putting.

Guru Rinpoche, or Padmasambhava, the most important founder of Tibetan Buddhism, had twenty-five major, fully realized Tibetan disciples. Before he left Tibet, he entrusted them to reveal, in their future lives, teachings that he had concealed. The teachings are called "treasures," or *terma*, and the lamas who discover them are *tertons*. Some do not accept the validity of termas in general, and there are claims that certain tertons are bogus. However, a genuine terton is a most amazing lama, someone whose teachings have been formulated exactly for our times. Many centers in the West practice termas. His Holiness Dudjom Rinpoche was the most famous traditional terton to bless the West with his presence; Chögyam Trungpa Rinpoche, who did so much to plant the teachings firmly in America, revealed a very comprehensive and relevant set of teachings, known as *Shambhala: The Sacred Path of the Warrior*.

Many lamas are called *rinpoche*, or "precious one." It is a title of respect used for tulkus and other highly regarded lamas. Many newcomers think it is a family name and then mix all the lamas up. It is often used as a form of address; you might say to your teacher, "Rinpoche, please answer this question."

Titled or not, you might find a truly qualified lama and still not connect with them. It is often a matter of style.

You may find many of the older teachers quite traditional. They teach Westerners the same way they taught in Tibet. Kalu Rinpoche summarized this approach when he said, "Westerners have defilements, Tibetans have defilements." In other words, the teachings, as they are, are pure and perfect. There is no need to reformulate them for a different audience; in fact, it might very well corrupt the teachings and dissipate the blessings of the lineage. Younger teachers, exposed to Western concepts from an earlier age and perhaps even educated in the West, may try to make the teachings more relevant or accessible to the average Westerner. They recognize that Westerners have different backgrounds, needs, and attitudes than Tibetans, that a traditional approach might alienate them or at least play upon their fascination with the foreign and exotic. They may use scientific, psychological, or Christian concepts, or they may talk about the teachings in the context of work or relationships. It is very important to realize that there really is no fundamental difference between these two approaches: these teachers are simply taking the same pure teachings of Lord Buddha and making them accessible, comprehensible, and relevant for different groups of people. As time goes on, this Westernizing trend will only increase; Buddhism has always adapted to the culture of its new hosts.

Another stylistic distinction is in the lifestyle lived or espoused by the teacher. Broadly speaking, there are three main lifestyles: those of laypersons, of ordained monks and nuns, and of yogis. A layperson is one who practices while having a family and career; an ordained monk or nun practices in a monastic environment; and a yogi or yogini practices retreat in solitude. Gyatrul Rinpoche, our lama here at Tashi Choling in Oregon, meditated in hermitages in Tibet for twenty years. He definitely encourages the yogic approach, and most of his more committed students aspire to a life of retreat. Some lamas encourage their students to become ordained, perhaps facilitating their finding of sponsors. In some centers, monks and nuns have a much easier time getting interviews with their teacher than do their lay counterparts. Trungpa Rinpoche always encouraged his students to develop realistic careers and to function and be successful in the world.

Some teachers emphasize study, including the study of Tibetan, saying that if one meditates without sufficient study, one can only go astray—a blind man roaming in the desert. Others emphasize practice, saying that life is too short to spend a considerable amount of time studying. Different teachers are masters of different systems of meditation and will encourage their students to do these practices. Many teachers have various projects, such as building or publishing, that demand much volunteer labor. Students of these teachers must be willing to delay or postpone their own aspirations or practice to participate in these activities.

There should be a good fit, therefore, between your aspirations and what the teacher has to offer. If you like to offer your services as a carpenter, find a teacher who has building projects. If you want to learn *dzogchen*, make sure the lama knows it well before committing yourself. When I met my teacher, I was interested in learning the yogic practices called the Six Doctrines of Naropa, and I wanted to meditate diligently in solitude. My teacher was a master of these practices and always sincerely encouraged me to practice, discouraging me from study or any other kind of nonmeditative spiritual activity. It was a good match.

Also, you should consider the logistics. Many years ago, an incredible terton visited the United States from Tibet; since that time, however, he hasn't been able to return. I imagine that his Western students are finding it difficult to clarify their doubts and confusions and receive further instruction since he hasn't been back. So consider a teacher's accessibility: Do they live in your town, or do they visit once a year? If they're not around very much, have they left a representative? And if so, is that representative someone you can trust and with whom you can communicate? When your prospective teacher is around, how easy is it to get interviews? Do they speak good English, or do they have a competent translator?

Everything I have said boils down to this: Can you really communicate with this teacher? Can you really open your heart and trust them? Do their replies really touch you deeply—that is, do they understand the real question behind your question, and do their answers feel like someone has just illuminated a darkened room?

One of my closest teachers, Dzigar Kongtrul Rinpoche, will always answer my questions by addressing the real issues behind them. If I ask him about retreats, for instance, he will read me like an open book and speak to my doubts about traditional methods of practice and their relevance for Westerners.

If your prospective teacher is unqualified, they won't be able to answer you skillfully. If you and they are not compatible, you will feel their answers or teachings miss the mark and are not really what you need to hear. If they are unavailable, your relationship will not develop any depth; you will feel they don't know or understand you, and you might make mistakes or waste time in their absence. But when you find the right one, the magic begins.

Now that we have some idea of what we are looking for, how do we actually go about finding it? It's a bit like finding a mate; there are no magic formulas guaranteed to work, but if you do nothing, it's guaranteed not to. So please put some effort into it.

The higher lamas often travel about. Check to see if there are events such as teachings and empowerments (more on those later) that you can attend and make that initial connection. If there's a workshop or retreat, you'll have much more exposure while also receiving teachings and instruction. If you live in a small town, you probably will have to travel to attend these events.

Forty or fifty years ago, many of us went to South Asia to seek out the lamas among the Tibetan refugees. It was both challenging and rewarding. We often formed very close relationships with our teachers. Now so many teachers are coming to the West, it isn't as necessary as it used to be. Unless you are going to Asia to participate in a program offered to Westerners, you might find it overwhelming to deal with all the difficulties of being in a foreign environment without knowing Tibetan or how to get around. Lamas will be busy dealing with their monasteries and the local laity. When lamas come here, they have no responsibility other than teaching us, either in our language or through a translator.

It would also be wise to attend any centers that are near you. You will familiarize yourself with the lama's activities, and they will eventually show up, as will other lamas who are invited. This is an excellent way to find a teacher. Again, if you live in a small town, you might have to travel.

Google or any online search engine can be a valuable friend. You will find out who is where and also learn something about the prospective teachers, courses, and events.

Due to the growing popularity of Tibetan Buddhism these days, it will probably be more challenging forming a close personal relationship with a great master. I hope you are able to, but don't have high expectations that may be difficult to fulfill. Your best chance of having that kind of relationship would happen if you were to throw yourself into the activity of the center; your presence would be noticed.

Often the high lamas who travel around will establish other teachers at their centers. They could be either Tibetans from their Asian monasteries or their more advanced Western students. These teachers will most likely be much more accessible but perhaps not able or willing to give you instruction or advice on the more profound topics of Vajrayana.

When I go to the dentist, most of my time is spent with the hygienist; the dentist might only just pop in for a short visit. Likewise, the local teacher might be able to provide 90 percent of the guidance you need; you might be able to have only an annual interview with your main teacher. If that is the case, use your time wisely; inquire about subjects only they can address, and leave the rest to someone else.

I feel I would be remiss if I didn't mention some of the scandals that have occurred involving lamas teaching in the West. They always involve abuse of power and often money or sexual issues. It's really a topic for a whole book, but the aspiring student needs to have some qualifications in mind before committing to a teacher. One should check carefully, talk to older students, and perhaps google the teacher's name to see if they are abiding by standards of behavior you are comfortable with. Some students will say, "How can you judge an enlightened being's behavior? Perhaps it is skillful means or crazy wisdom." But I would say, "How can an enlightened being engage in behavior that creates suffering for others?"

People abandon the Dharma when they are victimized by their teacher. Others go through long periods of therapy to get back on track. So be careful; investigate thoroughly; and be clear with yourself on what you want, what you need, and what you are willing to keep an open mind about.

We can read stories of the great practitioners of the past and their stuggles to find and be with their masters. This is still going on in the present day. Studying in South Asia may sound romantic, but I was constantly ill. In the end, I left because I developed asthma in the area surrounding my teacher's monastery. I put up with illness for many years because I appreciated the preciousness of being able to be close to my teacher and to practice. I hope your interest in the Dharma inspires you to take on some hardship if necessary, because no other relationship is as important. And I hope you will find a teacher who will lead you to enlightenment.

CHAPTER 4

Events and Empowerment

Most of your exposure and education in Tibetan Buddhism will be through the various events that are available. I'll discuss the different kinds that occur and conclude with a more detailed account of empowerments.

First, there are lectures and classes. We usually use the term *teaching*. These can be from either a touring lama or a local lama or teacher. They are often commentaries on traditional texts and, when necessary, are presented through a translator. They can range from the most beginning topics to the most advanced and may emphasize philosophy or meditation.

This can present a problem to new students. They can attend many of these classes or lectures but be confused about how to integrate the material with previous teachings or internally within themselves. These teachings can become like random collections within themselves and, without proper context, are open to misinterpretation. One day, for example, you learn Middle Way philosophy; the next month, calm-abiding meditation. How do these two relate? Are they connected, are they sequential, or do they have nothing in common at all? Trying to figure these things out can often be daunting for the new student.

Also, the topics can be quite advanced. There is the danger that new students will feel either frustrated or discouraged at their lack of understanding—or worse—misinterpret the teaching, think they understand, and practice incorrectly. Frequently, there is no question-and-answer session.

As the Dharma grows in the West, centers have established more organized teaching programs that resemble more traditional Western or Tibetan academic programs. Students are trained systematically, and there is ample opportunity for questions and discussion. The programs are devised with the modern, busy Westerner in mind so that the material is both comprehensible and relevant.

As an example of this, I have devised a program called Marig Munsel, Pacific Yeshe Nyingpo's four-year program. Here in Ashland, it meets in two four-hour sessions one weekend a month. We focus on both traditional and modern texts while always being aware that, as Western laypeople, we have distinct spiritual needs and capacities.

As the teacher, I have been deeply moved and pleased by the growth and transformation among my students, as well as the deepening commitment to practice and involvement in the sponsoring centers. I feel that Westerners can really flourish in the Dharma when they are instructed in a manner that is familiar and meaningful to them.

There are now many online programs, which present the opportunity to learn almost any topic of the Dharma from qualified teachers in the comfort of your home. The positive aspects of this are clear. The Dharma is now available to anyone with an internet connection, especially those of us who live far away from the urban centers where most lamas and centers are. You can learn what you want, from whom you want, at your own pace wherever you live. I have heard that one center is even offering an online three-year retreat—you stay at home and get all your empowerments and instructions on the Web!

The limitations are also clear. In most cases, the student will not have the personal support and friendship of a cohort and will be limited in forming a deep, personal relationship with a spiritual master. I used to be a little reluctant to depend on a computer for meditation instruction—as a teacher, I felt there was great benefit in the instructor knowing the student and dealing intimately and intuitively face-to-face. Now, having taught Zoom classes during the pandemic, I feel much more positive about the experience and hope to continue even after the pandemic is over.

Chökyi Nyima Rinpoche has a program called Tara's Triple Excellence (TTE) Online Meditation Program. It is based on a terma (a revealed treasure teaching) of Chokgyur Lingpa and teaches the Buddha's path from beginning to end. Although I haven't participated, I have gotten extremely positive feedback from those who have.

The next kind of event we'll discuss is retreats. Retreats can range from a single weekend to three years. They are generally held somewhere in the country, often at a rural center or a retreat center that rents out its space to various groups.

There are many advantages to an organized retreat. You can be taught a particular meditation in a systematic, experiential way. The environment can be prepared to make it sacred, blessed, and supportive to meditation. Your food and housing will be taken care of for you. There is an external discipline to keep you on track, and you will be far away from your smartphone and laptop, your job, and your family. The instructor will probably be either a lama or a senior student who will hold a space or field that you can drop into. Most people will have significantly deeper meditation in a retreat like this than they would on their own.

A variation on this would be what the Tibetans call a *drupchen*. A drupchen is an intensive version of the group rituals called *pujas*—a day-long puja, either three or four sessions a day, for seven to ten days. There are hours of chanting liturgies, almost always in Tibetan, and very elaborate rituals. A high lama is often the officiating *dorje loppon* (Vajra Master). Until you become familiar with the liturgy, you will probably get lost frequently and generally find the whole thing confusing, incomprehensible, but somehow incredibly powerful.

Then there's pilgrimage. Pilgrimage is an important part of many religions, including Buddhism. Many are now well organized and led by notable scholars and teachers. They offer the opportunity to travel to distant destinations in relative comfort with most of the hardships removed and to get important and interesting information on the sites visited. The four sites associated with the life of the Buddha in India and Nepal are most important—Buddha himself said that visiting these four was how he wanted future students to remember him. There is Lumbini in Nepal, where Lord Buddha was born, and three in northern India: Bodh Gaya where he became enlightened; Sarnath, where he first taught; and Kushinagar, where he entered nirvana. Other places may include the Kathmandu valley in Nepal; Sikkim, Ladakh, and Bhutan in the Himalayas; Burma and Sri Lanka; and many places in the Far East.

Finally, there is empowerment. Empowerments are central to Tibetan Buddhism, so I would like to speak at greater length about them.

The gateway to the Vajrayana is the ceremony known as "empowerment." This is generally a very elaborate ceremony where a highly respected lama confers the blessings of a particular Buddhist deity, such as Chenrezig, the buddha of compassion. It plants a seed in the student's mind which will ripen eventually, through practice and devotion, to manifest the enlightened qualities of that deity. An empowerment marks the formal entrance of the student to the tantric path.

Most empowerments take only an hour or two, while some can take a few days. However, many empowerments can be strung together in ceremonies lasting many months. The most famous of these is the Rinchen Terdzod, a collection of empowerments of the terma tradition of the Nyingmapa school.

We might hear that such a ceremony is going to take place in our community and desire to go in order to learn a little more about Tibetan Buddhism. Or we might wish to meet a famous lama who we hear is bestowing the empowerment. We might even travel great distances. A friend of mine recently traveled from Oregon to Australia to receive the Kalachakra empowerment from the Dalai Lama.

As we approach Vajrayana Buddhism, we become aware of these ceremonies taking place, and they may afford us our first opportunity to connect with Tibetan Buddhism in general or a particular lama. Or, once committed, we might attend to deepen our connection, to receive the blessings of a great or famous master, or because we are interested in the associated practice.

When Tibetan Buddhism first came to the West, empowerments were called *initiations*, a word we inherited from our Theosophist predecessors. The word is still used today and is completely interchangeable with *empowerment*; they are simply two different translations of the same Tibetan word.

What is an empowerment? In this section, I will discuss the empowerment ceremony. I will not consider the spontaneous transmission of insight from teacher to student—that will come in a later chapter. In terms of the ceremony, an empowerment is almost always associated with a particular deity, or *yidam*. There are thousands of yidams in Tibetan Buddhism, and each one has its own initiation ceremony.

Each empowerment is also associated with a particular lineage. So a Gelugpa Manjushri empowerment will be different than a Sakyapa one. Each of the different lineages of Tibetan Buddhism has its own set of empowerments and specializes in the yidams it practices the most. For instance, the Kagyupas practice Chakrasamvara a lot. Most people would feel it to be especially auspicious to receive the Chakrasamvara empowerment from a high Kagyu lama. Gelugpas also practice Chakrasamvara, but they are particularly famous for their practice of Yamantaka, the wrathful form of Manjushri. The Nyingmapas specialize a lot these days in Vajrakilaya.

A lama, who is called the Vajra Master in the ceremony, always bestows an empowerment. They will have received it from another lama, who received it from another lama, and so on, backward in time. The lama should be qualified, basically according to the guidelines already discussed, but as the teacher may only briefly be passing through our community, we might have to decide whether or not to attend based on reputation. Our teacher here in Ashland, Gyatrul Rinpoche, has brought many great lamas here to give empowerments. Some I have not heard of, but I do not hesitate to attend because I trust Gyatrul Rinpoche's integrity and judgment.

An empowerment is a ceremony. I will discuss empowerments in a general way from the point of view of purpose and structure. My words are based in part on Tsele Natsok Rangdrol's *Empowerment*, perhaps the most definitive account available in English.

An empowerment is an authorization to do the various stages of meditation associated with a particular deity. Taking an Amitabha empowerment authorizes you to practice the meditation and mantra recitation for Amitabha Buddha. Also it authorizes one to do any other practices associated with that deity. So along with the main practice of Amitabha, you can do the long-life practice and the consciousness transference to the Pure Land of Great Bliss. Tsele Rinpoche says,

> Unless you first obtain the ripening empowerments, you are not authorized to hear even a single verse of the tantras, statements, and instructions. Unauthorized people who engage in expounding on and listening to the tantras will not only fail to receive blessings; they will create immense demerit from divulging the secrecy of these teachings.[1]

So we need the empowerment for our subsequent Vajrayana practice to be successful. If we aspire to do a certain practice, we should exert some energy into obtaining its empowerment. Sometimes we aspire to do practices that seem to have nothing to do with deities—for instance, the yoga of the inner heat (*tummo*) or dzogchen. Nonetheless, their teachings are generally contained within a particular deity's practice, for which it is necessary to attain empowerment.

The empowerments have a ripening or purifying effect on the practitioner; in fact, they are often called "ripening empowerments." If our buddha-nature is likened to a seed, the empowerment ripens this seed and purifies the obscurations that prevent the seed from growing. Every section of the empowerment purifies a particular obscuration of our being. For instance, the vase empowerment purifies our obscurations of body and ripens our physical constituents into the body of a deity.

At the most profound level, the empowerment is a direct transmission of the ultimate truth of Buddhism. As we previously discussed, we all possess the buddha-nature, but it is obscured. Furthermore, we don't know how to recognize it. If we are ready and have a pure connection with the Vajra Master, the recognition can be transmitted through the ceremony. As Tsele Rinpoche explains,

> Free from platitudes and mere lip service and exactly in accordance with the master's words, the disciple should understand how the world and beings, everything animate and inanimate and comprised of the aggregates, elements, and sense factors, has, since the very onset, never been anything but the mandala of the deity. Right then, through the master's kindness and instructions, the disciple's obscuration of momentary delusion is cleared away. He is able to understand how the external world is in fact a celestial palace and its inhabitants are indeed a mandala of deities.[2]

Like this, each section of the empowerment introduces us to a different aspect of our true nature, purifying on the spot the various habitual tendencies that prevent our recognition. Perhaps this recognition sticks and we are realized from this point on. Or the recognition is only temporary, but having seen, we are able to access this awareness in subsequent practice. Either way, we are truly fortunate!

Although every empowerment is different, they generally follow the same basic structure. More elaborate ones begin a day early with a preliminary ceremony (*tagon*) preparing the students. Otherwise the students prepare themselves by washing and putting on nice, clean clothes. This is not a hippie event, and an overly laid-back hippie mentality has no place here—this is the kind of attitude we are trying to let go of. Preparing ourselves like this purifies the body. Meanwhile, the initiating lama begins his preparation early also, and when we enter the shrine room or auditorium, they will have already been there a couple of hours, doing the preliminary rituals and generating themself as the deity.

As we enter the shrine room, we are given saffron water to purify our speech and recite a mantra to purify our minds. It is appropriate to prostrate to the lama before sitting down; if that doesn't feel right

for you, you may not be ready for Vajrayana. In some empowerments, the master speaks English, or most of the proceedings are
translated and the students can follow step-by-step and attempt
to do the visualizations associated with each stage. In others, very
little explanation is given, and just a general overview or brief introduction to each section is explained. Remember, they didn't have
any public address systems in Tibet; in public ceremonies, people
received the empowerment through the strength of their faith and
devotion. You will probably find, as a sophisticated Westerner, that
the more you know about the ceremony, the richer your experience
will be. By trying your best to follow with the visualizations, you
are more open to receiving the blessings and transmission of the
ceremony. If you can't follow, I've heard it's best to relax the mind
into a state of trusting openness.

The ceremony itself starts with the offering of a *gektor*. *Tor* is
short for *torma* and means the sculptured ritual cakes seen in all
Tibetan shrine rooms. In this case, it is small and painted red. It is
being offered to the *geks,* negative or obstructing forces that can be
seen as either external beings or one's own negativities and dualistic thoughts. Here is a good chance to let go of all that internal
dialogue we always carry around and most likely brought into the
ceremony with us. We are in essence saying, "Dear geks, please take
this wonderful offering and leave us alone. Don't disturb or hinder
our ceremony." For those that refuse the torma and still remain,
wrathful techniques are used: *gugal*, a tree-resin like frankincense,
is burned in a censor, and mustard seed is scattered while the master
recites wrathful mantras. The gugal and mustard seed appear to the
geks as weapons. Now that the environment has been sanitized,
a protective canopy called a vajra tent is imagined, encapsulating
the proceedings.

The lama will probably give a short talk recounting the history
of the empowerment and its corresponding practice. He might, for
instance, mention how it originated in India, spread to Tibet, the
vast number of practitioners who attained realization from doing
the practice, the ease and simplicity of the practice, and the power
and profundity of its blessings. All of this is to engender faith in

the disciples. They should feel that this is really something special, they are very lucky to be participating, and they are committed to what lies ahead.

At every empowerment you will hear how unique and special it is. Don't think, "But they said the same thing at the last one!" The praise is to engender the proper faith and openness, not to be the basis of comparison.

Next refuge and bodhichitta prayers are repeated after the lama. If you don't know what this means, I will be explaining them in a later chapter. They correspond to the Hinayana and Mahayana levels of practice and commitment. The *samaya* vows (explained at the end of this chapter) are given with some saffron water or alcohol to seal the commitment, along with a stern warning about what may happen to those who break these commitments. At this point, we have reached the point of no return and have committed ourselves to being tantric practitioners. The next section, "the descent of blessings," invokes the blessings of all the buddhas, bodhisattvas, and deities while music is played and the students meditate on a visualization that the master has just described, usually imagining countless buddhas in the form of the deity melting into them.

What is the purpose behind all this? Tsele Rinpoche explains it quite clearly:

> In fact, it is necessary to purify our karmic perception of everything outer and inner, the world and beings, as being ordinary and solid. Consider the methods and auspicious coincidences necessary for this to occur. During any empowerment ritual, at the time of the descent of the wisdom beings, a blindfold is tied on the recipient in order to interrupt the thoughts that cling to visible forms as ordinary. Music is played to stop the thoughts that cling to sound as ordinary. Smoke prepared from substances such as incense and resin causing the wisdom to descend is spread to halt the thoughts of smell as ordinary. Consecrated nectar [the saffron water or liquor] is given to interrupt thoughts that fixate on taste as ordinary. The physical position of the sevenfold posture of Vairocana or the vajra posture is taken to

stops thoughts that cling to touch as ordinary. Finally, the steps of visualization, emanating and absorbing are taken to interrupt the deluded clinging to our mind as ordinary.[3]

So, through these preliminary rituals, the student should feel more open and responsive, ready for the main part of the empowerment that follows.

Although empowerments follow many forms, they almost always have either three or four main sections, which I will describe briefly. The bestowing of the empowerment consists of the master reciting the text, possibly translated so the recipients can also participate by visualizing the various stages taking place, touching the disciples with various blessed symbolic objects, and giving consecrated substances for the disciples to eat or drink. Since most empowerments involve many participants, and it would be too time-consuming for the master to do this for each student, they often personally bestow the empowerment on a few people close to them who then bring these articles through the audience. Or possibly the various articles are left in front of the hall, and the students file through and make contact at the end.

If there are three main sections, the first is the body empowerment. This purifies the defilements of body such as illness and authorizes the disciple to visualize themself as a deity. The speech empowerment purifies defilements of speech and breath and allows the student to recite the deity's mantra. And the empowerment of mind purifies the mind and permits the student to dissolve the visualization and rest their mind in the buddha-nature.

The empowerments for the higher levels of tantra have four main sections. They empower us to practice the systems of meditation toward which we as Westerners usually aspire, and their sequence and structure should be studied and understood over the course of our involvement with the Vajrayana. This same pattern of four will keep arising in different formats. When you understand it, it will help tie together seemingly unconnected aspects of the Vajrayana.

The first empowerment in this system is the vase empowerment, sometimes subdivided into five for the five buddha families. This initiation purifies the body and allows us to practice the development stage, the visualization of a deity and the recitation of its mantra. As a result, we attain the nirmanakaya, the emanation body of a buddha.

The second is the secret empowerment, purifying our speech. We are authorized to practice the completion stage, the practices using the inner energies of the *tsa*, *lung*, and *tigle*. We attain the *sambhogakaya* as a result.

Next is the wisdom empowerment, purifying the mind. We are permitted to practice the meditations of union, resulting in the dharmakaya.

Last is the fourth, or word, empowerment. It purifies the body, speech, and mind and the tendency to see them as separate. It authorizes us to practice the profound practices of mahamudra and dzogchen and results in the *svabhavikaya*. This empowerment can directly introduce us to our rigpa, our self-cognizing awareness that is our buddha-nature. It quite often takes the form of the lama holding up a crystal while saying a few words about the ultimate nature of the mind. This is a profound pointing-out instruction, and we should be especially attentive to it: with faith and interest, we may be able to experience something of great importance.

At the end of the empowerment, the disciples approach the master and offer a *kata*, the traditional Tibetan scarf, and a cash donation.

What are the signs that one has genuinely received the empowerment? Tsele Rinpoche explains it this way:

> The foremost disciple experiences the dawning of self-existing, coemergent wakefulness. The next best experiences pure perception with overwhelming and intense devotion while the manifestation of experience blazes forth, while the disciple of lesser caliber should at least feel slightly exhilarated.[4]

I think it's safe to say we're all probably the last, so we can at least hope for some kind of energetic experience, perhaps feeling "blissed out" or the kinds of experience Hindus call *shaktipat*. As the ritual is usually powerful and awe-inspiring, we may feel great devotion and reverence. And if we follow directions carefully and with trust and faith during the fourth empowerment, we might glimpse our buddha-nature, the coemergent wakefulness.

At the end of the empowerment, the master may give us a commitment practice, that is, tell us to do a certain meditation every day. It might be nothing or something very general, such as continuing to practice virtue or the Dharma; it might be a short recitation, such as one rosary of OM MANI PADME HUM; or it could be rather long, such as a one- or two-hour daily practice. A dear friend of mine once had five hours of such practices to do every day. On busy days, she was unable to sleep.

Since the recipients have already drunk from the samaya water at the beginning of the ceremony, they have no choice but to follow the lama's command. To ignore the commitment is said to have the direst consequence. Empowerments given to large groups in public, especially here in the West, generally have light commitments; however, it is the student's responsibility to determine beforehand if they are really ready for this. If you do not feel you will be able to keep the commitment, do not take the empowerment. Also, if you do not feel you can maintain some trust and respect in the Vajra Master and pure perception and loving-kindness toward the other participants, it is probably better not to take it.

Also, other samaya vows are implicit in the empowerment even though they will probably not be mentioned during the ceremony. Nonetheless, it is your responsibility to find out what they are and to try to keep them as well as possible. There are thousands and thousands of these vows, some clearly more important than others, and many nearly impossible to keep. I will mention a few of the most important ones, but try to study them from your teacher. Find out which ones they feel are the crucial ones, how to keep them, and what to do if they are broken.

In Vajrayana, we believe our buddha-nature is obscured by our ordinary thoughts. So to maintain a continuous sense of our underlying true nature, we vow to maintain pure perception or sacred outlook. We vow to always view our surroundings as a mandala with all beings as deities, all sound as mantras, and all thoughts as the expression of enlightened awareness. Not so easy! I at least try to cut out strong indulgences in negative judgments and to see the pure and positive side of things. My teacher said that although people are always messing up, careening here and there as they go through life, they all have good hearts. I try to perceive or acknowledge this good heart and not get too caught up in reacting to the minor irritants of their quirks. I try to apply this to the other points as well. Not getting too irritated by my environment, but trying to see the beauty and vastness in all places. Not getting stressed by grating noise, but using it to open my mind. I can't claim to be very successful, but I'm trying, and at least I can use these approximations as a starting point. So pure perception is both the starting point and the central concept in both Vajrayana practice and keeping the samayas.

There is also a set of fourteen vows that accompany any empowerment. A description can be found in many books, but especially in Dudjom Rinpoche's *Perfect Conduct*. Three of these I feel are most important. First is to respect the officiating master. One should view this person as the deity itself and not let doubts and negativities pervert one's view of them. Especially don't lose your temper and fight with them!

Second, maintain pure view toward all the Buddhist teachings. Don't think some teachings or teachers are better than others. What possible benefit can come from thinking like this? Just consider that the wide variety of teachers, teachings, and techniques are available to suit the various needs of diverse beings—no hierarchy is implied. They are like different medicines for different illnesses. Especially maintain pure perception and respect toward the Vajrayana. Some people think that it is an aberration of the Buddha's teaching or at best a merging of Buddhism with Hinduism or Bon, the original religion of Tibet; abandon this attitude.

Third, maintain pure perception toward the other students, your vajra brothers and sisters. No matter how irritating and neurotic they may seem, they possess buddha-nature and are trying their best. Besides they probably think the same of you. So don't fight, don't argue, and don't gossip about them behind their backs. If there's someone you really can't bear, simply avoid them.

In addition to these three vows, maintaining some kind of regular practice is essential.

Taking empowerment propels you into a whole new world and, as you've probably gathered from this chapter, assumes a willingness to let go of the old one. There's no doubt that something powerful, awesome, and vast is taking place. No matter how thick-skinned we are, there's an undeniable grandeur to the ceremony. Beyond that is the very real possibility of a glimpse or an intuition of a mode of being well beyond our small world. We have reached the point of no return on our journey, and in a sense our searching phase has come to an end; there's no turning back now.

CHAPTER 5

Centers

Tibetan Buddhist centers are all over the place now. Even small towns have them—Ashland, Oregon, where I live has twenty thousand people and three Tibetan centers.

Part of your beginning steps on the path is to find a center near you. If you are new to the area or have no Buddhist friends, Google is once again your best friend. Google "Buddhist centers in [name of town or city]." You'll probably turn up something; if not, your options are an online program or community (which we'll discuss later), moving, or going it alone.

I wouldn't recommend going it alone. I will be speaking of online programs and community in a later chapter, but for now I'll say that support is essential at all stages of the path. It is even more so at the beginning.

Your search may have turned up centers that are Buddhist but not Tibetan. Don't hesitate to give them a visit. However, most of my discussion will focus on Tibetan Buddhist centers.

What happens at these centers? First, there will be teachings. If a high lama is in residence or has sent a representative, these should take place on a regular basis. Otherwise, your center might have "events," where teachers are invited for limited periods to teach, give empowerments, or lead short retreats.

If the lama is not in residence but has sent a representative, you may assume that this person may not be a completely enlightened buddha or as completely realized as the lama who sent them. These residential lamas or teachers, whether Tibetan or Western, are there to help you and are doing the best they can. Since they probably aren't at the same level as their superior, you can't expect them to display the same qualities. As a beginning teacher myself, it's a constant challenge to set aside my own attitudes and needs to teach as purely as I can. I'm sure I make lots of mistakes. Luckily, I've been given no administrative responsibilities, which is where a lot of the problems can arise. The American invention of the separation of church and state was a brilliant idea. Someone can be a good teacher and genuinely care for their students; that doesn't mean they'll be skillful at running an organization. So learn what you can from these people but never completely surrender your critical facilities. You'll be able to learn a lot. Teachers like myself know the territory, speak your language, and have the availability and time to work with you over a long period of time, to really listen to you and hear you out. Then when the high lama is there, they can give you more of an overview and direction. Answers to many questions and high teachings may come only from the high lama; lots of the basics can easily be dealt with by people like myself.

Remember that teachers are people too. We need money, assistance, appreciation, and companionship.

Centers have a regular program of rituals. This program generally follows the Tibetan lunar calendar (it's worth picking one up) and usually comprises what are called *tsoks* (Tibetan) or pujas (Sanskrit), rituals centered around offering and sharing food. Some centers are moving away from the Tibetan calendar and adopting a weekend system. But if they are sticking to the tradition, the most likely days will be as follows:

· Tibetan eighth: always a peaceful deity such as Tara or the Medicine Buddha.
· Tibetan tenth: Guru Rinpoche Day. Guru Rinpoche, the founder of Tibetan Buddhism, promised he would visit anyone who did his practice on this day. All Kagyu and Nyingma centers will do his puja on this day.
· Tibetan fifteenth: Full moon. Another peaceful deity such as Amitabha or the Medicine Buddha.

· Tibetan twenty-fifth: Dakini day. *Dakinis* are female emanations of the buddhas, either wrathful or semiwrathful.

· Tibetan twenty-ninth: Protector day. Protectors are the very wrathful guardians of the teachings. You probably will not be allowed to attend unless you've had the empowerment for this one.

· Tibetan thirtieth: New moon. Another peaceful day.

Many Westerners, myself included, have a problem with Tibetan rituals. They just seem alien and strange. Also, when lamas teach, they rarely speak about rituals, even though they are the main events at the centers. Furthermore, the rituals are almost always done in Tibetan, although with time, more are being conducted in English. Very few Westerners I've met have a really good sense or understanding of what these rituals are about. I'll speak more about this in a later chapter.

Nevertheless, rituals are very important. If you go to monasteries in the East, they're doing long, elaborate pujas all the time. They obviously serve a purpose. In a later chapter I'll talk a little about the theory or meaning behind pujas; for now, see them as your entry into the center. In my retreat, I told our retreat master that I didn't like all the pujas. He told me to think of them as social events. I thought that was glib and superficial at the time; however, I've learned that there's a lot of truth and benefit to what he said. These rituals present a good opportunity to meet the other students at the center. By sharing the offering with them, you are participating in a bonding and healing ceremony with people who share your deepest aspirations in a pretty alienated world. It's hard to stay angry at someone after you've done puja and shared food with them. You'll also learn skills, such as making and offering torma, that will come in handy if you ever do solitary retreat. So suspend your disbelief a little and make an effort to participate.

The other main activity of your center is work. Lots of things need to be done, and all centers depend on volunteer work to get them done. That means you. This presents quite a challenge to us—we're already busy, and we didn't get involved in Buddhism to be, say, bricklayers. We will be constantly tested regarding our commitment and priorities around this issue—how much to contribute, how much to pull back, how much to practice, and so on.

There are also real personal benefits to these projects. Not all of us are ready for intensive meditation, no matter what our aspirations are. Work gives us a chance to surrender our concepts about spirituality, accumulate merit, and please our teacher. We get to know the other students and form close friendships with them. A lot of our most painful emotional issues come up in these interactions; people push our buttons, revealing many of our hidden faults. We have a chance to heal and grow. If we're committed enough, we will be pushed to our limits, which is where some of the juiciest stuff is found.

If we read the stories of great meditators of the past, we rarely hear of any that started right away as yogis or yoginis. They almost all spent an apprenticeship serving their gurus. Milarepa spent many years building one useless tower after another for his guru, Marpa. Only then was he considered ready for meditation. If you recall from the story, he escaped and received instructions from another lama. He practiced diligently in retreat but with absolutely no benefit. He was forced to return to Marpa and continue building.

Milarepa is an extreme example, of course—he killed thirty-five people with black magic. However, the period of apprenticeship seems universal. Zen always talks about "chopping wood, carrying water." In monasteries, monks spend many years absorbed with their duties before they begin retreat.

Before I started my retreat at Samye Ling in Scotland, they had just finished building their temple. It had been an eight-year project, but they had to hurry for it to be ready in time for the consecration. The abbot, Akong Rinpoche, put them on a schedule of working from 7:00 A.M. until 10:00 P.M., seven days a week for three months. Can you imagine what this kind of routine would do to you? How it would constantly test your commitment and trust? How through your exhaustion, your defenses would break down and all kinds of negativity would come streaming to the surface of your awareness? I have great admiration for those dedicated students.

I personally feel I missed out on something by starting out right away with intensive meditation. I'm sure I would have benefited from a period of work. Perhaps many of the difficulties I later encountered in my practice might not have arisen so strongly if I had had a chance to work them out through virtuous Dharma activity and service. However, I probably would have rebelled against any teacher who suggested it.

One of the main benefits of work comes from the physicality, focus, and exhaustion involved. We often come to the Dharma with a variety of mental sufferings. Some people are wounded, some are very cerebral, others are somewhat self-absorbed. Hard physical work cuts through a lot of that. Through hard work, you no longer have the energy to think or to indulge so much in habitual or negative patterns. As time goes by, you find that you have changed for the better.

Another benefit of work is that there is no benefit for the ego. You can use study to build up the ego: "I am the smartest." You can use meditation to build up the ego: "I am the best meditator. I had the most amazing experience." But work—"I am the best trench digger"—I don't know. Workers drop their own personal spiritual ambitions to align themselves with their teacher's activity. This can be very transformative. More on this in the next chapter.

What kinds of jobs will you be asked to do at your center? First, there's the day-to-day organization of the center and the extra organization needed whenever your center is putting on an event. The latter will push you to your limits—don't expect to get much sleep at those times. Then there's secretarial and publishing work. Most centers transcribe and publish many of the teachings given there. They also might publish the texts used in their rituals. There's always a need for transcribers, editors, and so forth.

Many important jobs are associated with community outreach. Centers need to extend themselves into the broader community for many reasons. They might need more students offering assistance simply to survive. Also it is necessary to interrelate with the larger community in order to accomplish different objectives like getting building permits, nonprofit status, bank loans, and grants.

Here the center must present itself as professional, competent, and mainstream, and successful professional students are often best at accomplishing these tasks.

Country centers need construction workers. The need is generally unending: temples, lama's residences, retreat centers, monasteries, and just ordinary maintenance. If you have those skills and show up, you will be very welcome! You may have a difficult time leaving, however. Some country centers may have a work-study program—if you work so many hours a week, you may get room, board, and some retreat time.

The job people typically like the most is serving the lamas, whether resident or visiting. You may be cooking, cleaning, or driving. This usually presents a wonderful opportunity to get to know the lama better.

There is also maintaining the shrine. This is a good way to learn about rituals and make friends with some of the more serious older students, the experts who can teach you what to do. You may learn how to make the ritual offerings called tormas or play some of the traditional instruments.

Another activity that your center may have is studying the Tibetan language, and I suppose this is as good a place as any to discuss the various pros and cons of learning it. I've spent thousands of hours and have gotten almost nowhere with it. So you might want to call what I'm about to say sour grapes.

Tibetan is completely different than English—it's not like learning German or French. As you know, it uses a different alphabet. The word order and grammar are also very different. There's nothing that exactly corresponds to our ideas of clauses, sentences, and paragraphs. It uses words where we would use punctuation marks.

Also, there's quite a difference between written classical Tibetan and spoken colloquial Tibetan. There are dialectic differences in spoken Tibetan—imagine learning English from an American for a short time and then trying to practice with a Scot or Australian. Since many of the texts are written in verse, key words are left out for the sake of meter—words that Tibetans would understand are missing, but that leave us floundering for the meaning. All in all, it's a daunting task.

And look what we're trying to learn. Buddhist philosophical, psychological, and meditational texts—not exactly "Dick and Jane." So unless you're prepared to study until you attain a high degree of fluency, how will you use your knowledge?

With time, more and more of the younger lamas are learning English—many of them are already wonderfully fluent. And, sadly, the great older ones who never learned it are passing on. So once again, unless you develop a high degree of fluency, what are you going to talk about?

Nonetheless, the reasons for learning Tibetan are also very strong. I'm sorry I never learned it—it would have made things a lot simpler. You can recite your liturgies, prayers, and pujas and know what you're doing. The words of all our prayers are believed to be blessed—they were written by enlightened beings, and there's a power and transmission contained within the words. If we do our practice in English, we lose a lot of that blessing. If we do it in Tibetan, we don't understand what we're saying, and we're flying on blind faith. Group practice especially is almost always done in Tibetan. It's difficult to struggle to pronounce the Tibetan words, remember their English meaning, and visualize all at the same time. Knowing Tibetan is extremely helpful here. Gyatrul Rinpoche said doing one's practice in English is like being deaf, while doing it in Tibetan and not understanding it is like being blind. Not much of a choice!

Few of the deeper texts and meditation instruction manuals have been translated yet, and it could be ages before many of the lesser-known practices are addressed. When you learn the practice of, say, Amitabha, there are commentaries on the practice that teach you everything you have to know—how to do it, the signs of success, and remedies for obstacles. They're a wealth of precious information. Learning Tibetan would be like discovering buried treasure.

Since we often don't have frequent contact with our teachers, being able to open a commentary on the practices we are doing could prove to be helpful. And they will mostly be in Tibetan.

There are also many words that simply cannot be translated into English. They describe experiences that few people in our culture have had, so we haven't invented the vocabulary to discuss them. Even if you never learn fluent Tibetan, it is good to learn what a few of these words mean because the English translation will always be misleading. A good example is *rigpa*. It is defined as the self-reflexive awareness that cognizes the buddha-nature. Recognizing and stabilizing rigpa is the whole point of Buddhism. But how do you translate such a term? Often it is translated simply as "awareness," but if you heard that word, would you know what it was really referring to?

As I mentioned earlier, there is not yet a consistency of translation. The same Tibetan term can be and is translated with more than one English word; an English word like "awareness" can have more than one Tibetan term. Unless you are familiar with the Tibetan, it is possible to completely misunderstand something you read in English because of the ambiguity.

So to summarize this discussion of learning Tibetan, I recommend that if you're good at languages, enjoy studying them, have the time, and are committed to attaining a certain level of proficiency, then by all means go ahead, especially if you are young; it will expand your horizons and options. If you're unable to, rest assured there's plenty of material already translated with more being published every day. And many teachers can now speak English with you.

With every passing year, the need to know Tibetan becomes less essential. I'm constantly discovering amazing teachings that are now taught directly in English. For example, Dzongsar Khyentse Rinpoche has made available his commentaries on some of the most important texts in Buddhist philosophy. Also, as we age, our ability to learn a language diminishes and the amount of time we have to apply those language skills also shortens.

No discussion of centers would be complete without discussing center politics. Unfortunately for this discussion but luckily for me, since I usually keep a low profile, I haven't had much experience with the worst of it. What usually seems to happen is this: we want access to the lama or to certain activities of the center, but that access is denied by certain of the older students. We might feel hurt and annoyed. We might also start doubting the wisdom of the lama who gave these people authority in the first place. Try to be cool. Be diplomatic. Examine your own unacknowledged needs for power, recognition, or mothering. These people usually become indispensable by doing the lion's share of the work, so they've earned their position. Consider it all "grist for the mill," and integrate it into your practice. So many of these problems come from people projecting their unacknowledged needs and aggression onto others. Try to understand what is going on, especially your own behavior.

Don't forget when you go to a new center that everybody there is just like you—sincere in aspiration but still a little neurotic. So everybody's stuff gets played out in public view. It's like living a soap opera. I haven't heard of any center that isn't like that, and every one I have been associated with has had its difficulties. We're all getting pushed from all sides—by our worldly commitments, by our teacher, by our practice, and by the other students in the center. Flare-ups are inevitable, and sooner or later you will be in the center of one. It just seems to be the nature of the path. A famous Korean Zen master said, "I put all my students in a big bag like potatoes and shake them until they rub each other's skin off!"

Center difficulties can appear like small civil wars. People's tempers flare, people's egos are on the line and getting crushed, and unfortunately people leave feeling completely burned out or terribly hurt. It's good to remember that your actions can have a profound positive or negative effect on others, so think twice before speaking or acting, and remember to consider the welfare of others.

You may also find your new center cliquish, with older students hanging out together and not being very friendly to newcomers. It's usually not conscious behavior on the old-timers' part; they're simply happy to see old friends. If you're friendly and willing to work, you'll probably make friends and be accepted in no time. I've noticed it here at Tashi Choling. People come with a positive, friendly attitude and a willingness to share in the chores, and all of a sudden there are no cliques, no old-timers, and all the doors are open.

Perhaps what we really get from centers is support. We're living in an extremely nonspiritual environment. Everything about our culture can be seen as a conspiracy against meditative awareness. It's so important to have friends we can share our struggles and aspirations with.

I often wonder about my students—people from the larger community take my classes because they sincerely want to learn something about meditation. But when the course is over, what happens to them? Many even have unsympathetic spouses. Meditation is difficult enough in the most supportive of circumstances; it's really worth putting up with some of the problems of a spiritual community to reap the very real benefits. Without the support of a community, it is difficult to maintain one's practice; it's always like swimming upstream.

I often run into former students who may have taken many classes from me. If they haven't joined a Buddhist community, they are almost never still practicing. The ones that have joined are practicing regularly. It may seem counterintuitive because center activities would decrease the amount of time one would have for personal practice, but that almost never seems to be the case. Participating in a center seems to be a time-efficient way of getting the support one needs to maintain a practice in an extremely materialistic culture.

One of the many things I really admire about my teacher Chökyi Nyima Rinpoche is his ability to make people feel like part of a family. During the first retreat at his new center in northern California, he married Susan and me, and he used the occasion to create a loving environment and melt everyone's heart. At the end of the retreat, we had a little talent show with retreatants putting on skits or singing songs. Rinpoche was present, howling with laughter. These warm feelings make people feel connected and that they belong. These feelings later fuel devotion and the discipline necessary to persevere in practice.

Sometimes, there's an "outer circle," a group of disgruntled older students, who get together to bend or break the rules and complain about others, confusing cynicism and negativity with sophistication and insight. I would avoid them if possible; it seems like a good way to break your samaya vows. There might be another outer circle of more serious students who are more interested in practice than center activities and therefore keep a low profile. You may find what they have to say insightful and useful.

An interesting situation that I've noticed over the years is that sanghas develop certain styles of ignorance. A group of students has a particular view of the teaching or the teacher that newer students assume is valid, and the sangha grows with that view at its core. I've seen sanghas with a "wild yogi" ideal, where drinking and promiscuity were an accepted part of the practice. Other sanghas believe backbreaking work prepares one for intensive meditation. Another believes that the lama intentionally tries to keep their students confused and in conflict. While there may be some trace of truth in any of these views, I didn't hear the lamas themselves propagating these ideas; it generally seemed to be assumed on the part of the students. Once a few people start propagating those views, it catches on and others join in. New students think it is the correct view or feel subtle social pressure to conform, so be aware and careful.

You may find a seeming disconnect at your center. The lama might give mostly advanced teachings and empowerments. There might not be much instruction on ritual or work, even though that is what is going on. This is probably because the lama focuses on the subjects only they are qualified to teach. As centers mature, lamas understand the other activities also must be given a context, or there are senior students who will give the needed explanations.

With the advances in technology, the growth of the Dharma, and the isolation caused by COVID-19 restrictions, much of what would have been happening in centers has now moved online. At first this seemed strange, off-putting, and impersonal. But I have gotten used to it. I have no idea about the Dharma centers of the future, but online classes and programs have filled the void, and if you give them a chance, you may find them very meaningful.

Since the pandemic started, I've taught several Zoom classes. I was hesitant at first, but I've come to see their value and place in the bigger picture. It's wonderful to have participants from all over; one was from Bolivia, another from Austria. I have taught a class to my teacher's sangha in Mexico City. And in small classes with time for discussions, there is an intimacy, caring, and support that is desparately needed right now. People who would be completely isolated have a place to go where they can share the most important aspects of their lives.

We were able to take a Chenrezig empowerment from His Holiness the Dalai Lama on Zoom. Does it have the same blessing as being there in person? Perhaps not. But it was the Dalai Lama in my living room!

My wife recently completed on online retreat with her teacher. She felt the power and blessing were profound. So perhaps we are seeing a major shift in the meaning of community and how the Dharma is transmitted that will continue as life returns to prepandemic conditions.

So welcome to your new center. Don't think that becoming a Buddhist is like going to the movies, where you pay your ten bucks for a seat and at the end you just walk out. There's no "just walking out" in Vajrayana Buddhism. Your commitment demands that you give more of yourself than that. From your involvement in your center, you can learn a lot that's extremely precious even if it's sometimes painful, you can make lifelong friends, and you can deepen your connection with your teacher.

CHAPTER 6

Getting Ready

When I first started getting interested in Eastern spirituality, I noticed a common theme: beginning aspirants generally had a long period of apprenticeship, usually around twelve years, to complete before they received meditation instructions. Although Milarepa is the most famous example, I noticed it in the Hindu and Zen traditions also. And of course, in Tibetan monasteries, young people have a long period of training before embarking on a more contemplative path.

Obviously, this apprenticeship serves a function; people "just off the street" are not often ready to begin meditating seriously. Some preparation is needed. We are most likely not willing or able to commit to building stone houses like Milarepa or another traditional preparation. So I am going to describe some of the ways we can change and grow so that when we have an opportunity to practice, it will be more effective.

Before I start, however, I want to make an important point. I feel that in today's society, Buddhism is often equated with meditation. Some traditions are actually named after the meditation done—Vipassana, Zen, and Rigpa. Mindfulness meditation is being taught everywhere these days and has even made the cover of *Time* magazine.

It would be easy to conclude that meditating is the sole practice of Buddhism. I think that is misleading and a disservice. It's nice to get together and meditate in the temple, but never forget the people who labored to build the temple and the generous donors who paid for the construction. That was their practice, their expression of faith and commitment. Without them, we might be sitting in a rocky, muddy field. So, who is most important—the sponsor, the builder, or the meditator? I think a moment's reflection would reveal that all three need each other; if one were missing, there would be no use for the other two. They are equally important in the way the various organs in the body are equally important.

I'll start with sponsors. Tibetan Buddhism is expensive! We all pay for events, and some of us pay dues at a center, but great fundraising efforts are needed to pay for land and construction, statues, *thankhas* (embroidered paintings of dieties) and brocade, travelling expenses for lamas, livable "salaries" for translators and ritual masters, and so on. This money comes from somewhere.

The sponsor may have inherited or earned their wealth. Their main practice will be to donate that money in a way that maximizes its benefit. Also, because of their familiarity with the world of money, they will often be the center's board members or officers, dealing with government officials over nonprofit status and building permits, budgeting the center's expenses, and overseeing fundraising efforts.

These jobs are time-consuming and thankless. The sponsors may wish that they were meditating rather than meeting yet again with an officious county bureaucrat, but they know that they are the best at their job, and if they don't do it, no one else will.

Next is service. I'm going to break it down into devotion-based service and compassion-based service.

Devotion-based service means that one's main practice is doing the jobs that the lama feels need doing. This can be as personal as attending the lama by cooking and cleaning or as distant as building and publishing. Attending a lama sounds like fun, but especially when travelling, it is exhausting work. You need to be up before the lama, and you go to sleep after the lama does.

Likewise for more ordinary work. If you're working in, say, building or publishing, you might be sacrificing everything about a normal life to get the job done. You let go of thoughts of career or retirement, and you might also let go of aspirations to meditate. However, you share the lama's vision for spreading the Dharma and benefiting sentient beings, and nothing is more important to you than helping in any way you can. Letting go of your personal preferences and agendas is necessary to get the job done.

I've noticed over the years that those who choose this path (or have it chosen for them) often become exceptional beings whether they are great meditators or not. Letting go of their ego and its small world and allowing the lama to act through them invokes great blessing.

I have an old friend who was the main attendant of one of my teachers. He labored tirelessly, organizing construction and dealing with obfuscating Asian bureaucrats. He worked upward of sixteen hours a day, seven days a week. Unfortunately, he died relatively young. However, his dying displayed all the signs of complete accomplishment. Such is the power of devotional service.

Compassion-based service is different. There's a lot of suffering in the world. Many people who hear Lord Buddha's teachings feel inspired to do something that alleviates the obvious suffering we see all around us. This can take many forms, from caring for their old grandmother to devising more energy-efficient technology to protect the environment. One's personal (and hence the ego's) needs are put aside for the welfare of others.

Scholars and translators also serve. We wouldn't know a word of the Buddha's teachings if someone hadn't translated them. The amount of material that has been translated is small compared to the total amount in print. There is still a lot to do. Besides simple translating, there is the digital preservation of texts. I met a man who put the whole Tibetan canon on flash drives and distributed them around the world.

Scholars who become professors make alien and difficult concepts clear and accessible to other academics. They can articulately defend Buddhism from Western fundamentalists who believe we're worshipping demons or Western intellectuals who think we're a cult. We've made great progress in these areas over the last few decades, mostly because of the tireless outreach of His Holiness the Dalai Lama, but also thanks to the men and women who join panels, interfaith discussions, radio talk shows, and so forth. As my teacher says, "Buddhism is not a religion, it is common sense." Thanks to these scholars, more of the general public is coming to understand this.

Buddhist academics also provide a point of entry for college students who might have a budding interest in the Dharma. It seems less threatening and rebellious to attend a college class than to visit a center.

Another valuable function of scholars is in the research of the role of meditation on the mind and body. This is extremely valuable. We live in a scientifically oriented culture, and if Buddhists can demonstrate the positive effects of meditation on the brain, we have a valuable platform from which to share the Dharma.

We wouldn't know what our teachers were saying if there weren't interpreters. When they travel with lamas, not only must they prepare their translations for the teachings, they often have to translate interviews and even oversee the personal needs of the lama if that person is unable to communicate in a Western language.

The next component of Buddhism is rituals. Some people find a path in the immensity of Tibetan rituals. If you are a member of a large center that does a variety of monthly and yearly rituals, you have probably noticed the team of assistants called *choppons* who make the elaborate tormas and prepare the food offerings (tsoks). During the puja itself, they run around, basically enacting what the liturgy is saying. During empowerments, they labor tirelessly to have everything ready before the empowerment and to assist the Vajra Master during it. Being a choppon is a great way to have a real internalized sense of what tantric practice is all about. You are actually enacting the ritual with your body rather than simply chanting or trying to visualize. It is also a necessary and important service to the community.

Buddhism's most famous path is, of course, meditation. This is the most straightforward path to actually attain liberation. Unfortunately, that takes a lot of meditation. For the meditator to make any significant progress, they must radically simplify their life, reducing activities, external stimulation, emotional involvements, and financial expenditures. This simplification allows them to spend more time meditating and have less external and internal distractions while practicing. This is perhaps the most familiar of the Buddhist paths I'm delineating and probably needs no more elucidation. I'll be speaking of meditation a lot in future chapters.

There is also the path of ordinary laypeople, those who don't change their lifestyle but attempt to integrate the Dharma into all the activites of their daily lives while maintaining a regular daily meditation practice. I will be speaking more on that when I discuss the four thoughts.

Hopefully by now you have more information and more of a sense of the opportunities open to you. What these paths all have in common is that they present opportunities to step beyond your limitations, boundaries, and ego into a vaster and more open and meaningful world. You are by no means limited by these paths; you could find yourself practicing a combination of them or alternating between one and another. Your interests and situation will determine which of these paths is most appropriate for you, but I can guarantee that if you practice any of them sincerely, faithfully, and intelligently, you will grow and progress along the path to buddhahood.

Now that we have a sense of how we want our path to unfold, we can attend to another aspect of getting ready we can call "unlearning." Meditation, especially mindfulness meditation, is all over the media. Also, many self-proclaimed gurus are offering speedy and hardship-free adventures to expanded consciousness. And due to the power of the media, the louder one proclaims one's beliefs, the more others listen and those concepts enter the mainstream.

Buddhist concepts and meditation get mixed up with many other systems. People equate Buddhism with quantum mechanics; scientists take MRIs of advanced meditators to see how their brains are different from those of ordinary folks; others write about how Jesus went to Ladakh in northern India to study Buddhism. Tantra, which traditionally refers to a vast system of esoteric teachings within Mahayana Buddhism, now most often refers to using meditation to have better, longer-lasting, and more intense sex.

When I first got interested in Tibetan Buddhism, some of the earlier books that were available had been written or translated by British explorers from Victorian times. These authors often had a background in theosophy, which, at least at that time, believed that acolytes went through a series of initiations in subtler realms of existence on their path to awakening. Hence our use of the term *initiation* for what we now call *empowerment*. They also believed they were preparing themselves and the world for the imminent coming of Maitreya Buddha as a messiah. So Buddhism was seen through a theosophic lens.

Our interest in Dharma comes from somewhere. We didn't spontaneously decide to seek it out. We live in this society—with its books, media, educational system, and other people—and absorb lots of various ideas about Buddhism and meditation. If we hadn't, we never would have heard about Buddhism or meditation.

There's nothing wrong with this—it's an inevitable outcome of living during these times. Unfortunately, a great deal of what newcomers think they know about Buddhism is wrong, confused, or misunderstood. For example, if there were a tantric initiation in your community, a newcomer might think they were going to be transported to astral planes for higher teachings or learn secret lovemaking techniques. Needless to say, both of these ideas would limit the efficacy of the empowerment.

So the beginning part of our practice of Buddhism is, in large part, a practice of unlearning. We must be willing to examine all we think we know about the Dharma and the process of meditation. The teacher must be willing to provoke and challenge us to go through this process. It can be difficult if we have developed some degree of intellectual understanding or had some meditative experiences we think are important, profound, or indicative of our specialness.

If we are not willing to be blank slates, all we learn will be colored by this previous understanding, which in most cases will render the instructions almost useless. Chögyam Trungpa Rinpoche likened the process to placing a variety of vegetables in a giant pot and cooking them. The onion wants to maintain its smell; the carrot, its color. But the cook knows these vegetables must be cooked until they make a delicious stew.

It might be painful to unlearn a lifetime of possible misinformation; more difficult is to understand that your previous meditative experiences do not impress your Buddhist instructor in the least.

One of the greatest Tibetan yogis of our time, Chatrul Rinpoche, resided in India. One day he was visited by a famous non-Buddhist guru. The guru turned up the palms of his hands; deities were dancing on both of them. Chatrul Rinpoche said, "So what?" and walked away.

The point is that even if you can make deities appear on the palms of your hands, your previous experience and accomplishments will probably not be acknowledged. You must be prepared and willing to unlearn what you know and become an odorless, colorless vegetable.

Perhaps the most important thing we have to unlearn is our alligience to a scientific perspective. When I was at college, I was completely fascinated by quantum mechanics. I aspired to be a theoretical chemist, someone who applied quantum mechanics to explain chemical phenomena. I remember my physics textbook had a section on the philosophical implications of quantum mechanics and noted that there seemed to be some correlation between these implications and Asian thought. I read these sections over and over.

Later, books like *The Tao of Physics* and *The Dancing Wu Li Masters* came out. Although I drank them up, I sensed the parallels they were drawing were not quite right. Of course I became more interested in Buddhism, but I never forgot my scientific roots.

So I've been following this dance between science and Buddhism for fifty years. To examine the philosophical parallels between Buddhism and science is beyond both the scope of this book and my abilities, but I will try to explain how a scientific perspective can color, distort, and impede our understanding of Buddhism.

One example is using scientific research on meditators to somehow prove that what we are doing has some validity. Although I see some truth in that and am heartened by meditation's acceptance in mainstream Western culture, I think there is a serious danger here. If Buddhist practitioners accept scientific beliefs uncritically, it can be an obstacle to their acceptance of the deeper truths and insights of Buddhism, especially Vajrayana. What would happen if there were no correlation between meditation and laboratory tests—would we stop meditating?

Science has provided many amazing benefits for us humans. I would never have met my teacher if there hadn't been airplanes. I probably wouldn't be able to write this book if there weren't computers and prescription drugs to keep me going. But when science veers into "scientism," difficulty may arise.

According to Wikipedia, scientism is belief in the "universal applicability of the *scientific method* and approach, and the view that empirical science constitutes the most authoritative worldview or the most valuable part of human learning—sometimes to the complete exclusion of other viewpoints." The philosopher Tom Sorell provides this definition of scientism: "Scientism is a matter of putting too high a value on natural science in comparison with other branches of learning or culture."

It has also been defined as "the view that the characteristic inductive methods of the natural sciences are the only source of genuine factual knowledge and, in particular, that they alone can yield true knowledge about man and society":

1. It is used to criticize a totalizing view of science as if it were capable of describing *all* reality and knowledge, or as if it were the *only* true way to acquire knowledge about reality and the nature of things;

2. It is used, often pejoratively, to denote a border-crossing violation in which the theories and methods of one (scientific)

discipline are inappropriately applied to another (scientific or nonscientific) discipline and its domain. An example of this second usage is to label as scientism any attempt to claim science as the only or primary source of human values (a traditional domain of ethics) or as the source of meaning and purpose (a traditional domain of religion and related worldviews).[1]

A simple example would be karma. Because there is no scientific proof for karma, many people dismiss it as part of a more primitive belief system.

After much thought, reading, and conversation, I've come to believe that there is a fundemantal difference between the Buddhist and scientific description of reality. Science is interested in objective truth—meaning that it is true for people of all cultures, times, and so on, even if they do not know it or recognize it to be true. So for a scientist, an apple is the apple that is free from any personal or cultural overlays.

For a Buddhist, the apple we talk about is the *experience of an apple*. From the start, the Buddha and Buddhism have emphasized the primacy of the mind. The objective truth of the scientists, while of value, just doesn't concern us that much. When we talk about karma, for instance, we are talking about the causal relationships that happen as our experience unfolds. When we talk about rebirth, we are referring to the continuity of experience.

When we understand that basic difference between the scientific objective truth and the Buddhist subjective truth, we can let go of the need to either prove or disprove Buddhist tenets by scientific analysis. We can accept and try to understand these tenets on their own terms.

A good example would be learning to speak a foreign language. The best way is to move to a country where that language is spoken and not use your native tongue at all. If we are always trying to translate the new language back to our native one, it will greatly impede the process. Likewise, if we try to "translate" Buddhism into scientific concepts, we will always harbor doubts about the teachings that seem to contradict science, such as rebirth, and fail to really immerse ourselves in the teachings.

Next, I would like to discuss preparing yourself physically and emotionally. Tibetan Buddhism has two main physical practices: prostrations and *trulkor*. Prostrations are often done daily but can be quite hard on the body, especially the knees. Trulkor is usually taught in retreat as part of the *tsalung* or tummo practice, the meditations where one generates heat and bliss in order to enhance realization. Even if one were to learn these exercises, it would be difficult to find the circumstances to practice them outside of retreat.

As of now, there are no widely taught practices that would be the equivalent of hatha yoga or tai chi. If we were to commence practice of Tibetan Buddhism, we would have to address the needs of the body. We could rely exclusively on Buddhist practice, but eventually most practitioners introduce non-Buddhist disciplines into their routine.

First, and most obvious, we have to stay healthy in the ordinary sense of the word. It's a lot easier to meditate when the illness of the body is not distracting you from your practice. It's also easier to stay healthy than to turn around a chronic illness and become healthy once your health has deteriorated. Of course, if you do have physical limitations, there are practices for integrating them into your practice, but if that isn't the case, don't let a sense of aestheticism become an obstacle.

Stay limber. Stretch, do yoga, get massages. If your body isn't limber or relatively stress-free, your mind will drift toward the pain and tension when you meditate. We have so many therapies in our culture for dealing with tension and tightness; avail yourself of them.

Your body also contains the subtle channels that control the flow and movement of vital force in your body. As your meditation deepens, you will become more aware of this movement and sense how it either helps or hinders your practice. Consider this and what you can do to lessen the hindrances and increase the positive effects.

Once again, this may involve movement or bodywork as an adjunct to your meditation.

When there is either injury or physical abuse, the body tends to seal off these areas as an unconscious protection from their immediate effects. As a simple example, after getting a dental filling, my mouth will feel somewhat traumatized, and I have to use my meditation to bring healing attention back into that area. Unfortunately, over time traumatized areas in the body harden and have profoundly limiting repercussions for one's emotional and spiritual well-being.

On the emotional side, dealing with abuse is one of the most important issues I would like to address in this book. It is also something that I have not heard explicitly addressed by my teachers. As I mentioned earlier, there is something profoundly different about the early childhood experiences of Tibetans when compared to us.

I know there are countless people who are experts in dealing with abuse and I'm sure there are countless techniques for it as well. I am in no way an expert. I also should apologize for whatever errors or overgeneralizations I make in my presentation, but I feel the matter is of such importance that I would be remiss not to mention it. What I strongly emphasize here is that if issues of abuse and trauma are not explicitly addressed, this could have many unfortunate repercussions for your practice. Hopefully, persistent meditation can overcome their effects, but it might be wise to be more focused on a direct cure.

Let me give an example. Suppose someone is sexually abused as a child. As a coping mechanism, they blocked sensation to the lower part of their body. With that blockage there, they were able to get on with their life. However, one effect of that blockage is that their breathing is constricted. They cannot breathe deeply into their lower body, and their breath is shallow. The effect of their shallow breathing is that they always feel some anxiety, which they probably don't acknowledge since it has such a long-buried cause and is a fairly constant sensation. When they begin to meditate, they do so anxiously. Of course, this isn't correct, but it is just the way they do things. If they are instructed to breathe deeper into their belly, the feeling of anxiety can be overwhelming; in fact, they could have panic attacks.

They may have the habit of dissociating from their body during meditation; it's so much nicer to not be in the body! They then develop a view and understanding that supports their dissociation; they might even appear very spiritual to others. However, anything that makes them return to their body brings them great distress. This misdirected kind of meditation can proceed indefinitely; it is not self-correcting.

Rather than just continuing to meditate and hoping for the best, they need a teacher who can say, "I understand your situation. We need to name it and deal with it." Dealing with it may not necessarily involve abandoning meditation or going to a therapist instead; their teacher may be able to guide them through this painful and difficult process.

You might think, "What about me? I was never sexually abused." But something as innocent as your birth can have a profound effect on your later growth and subsequent spiritual development.

Let me use myself as an example. I've often wondered why I've had so much difficulty meditating; I've also wondered about some of the origins of the worst of my neuroses. I have no memories of abuse. My parents weren't the most loving, but they also were far from the least. Then I read something recently that triggered something my parents told me: my birth was very difficult for my mother. She was rushed straight to surgery after giving birth. So with no ill intention on anyone's part, I was abandoned and failed to make that initial crucial bond with her. I can't prove it, but I have come to believe deeply that much of my neurosis is due to this initial failure.

When the personality coalesces around this kind of experience, all of our subsequent perceptions and relationships are tinged and corrupted. It's like the Tibetan teaching that listening to the Dharma incorrectly is like putting tea in a bowl that has poison in it. One's practice, if not poisoned, is at least to some degree heading off in the wrong direction.

Although a great number of us have been abused in some way,

most of us haven't. But what most of us have experienced is something called "childhood emotional neglect." We weren't hugged or snuggled enough. We were pressured to excel and not appreciated for who we are, or our parents were themselves too wounded to show or express love toward us.

Signs of childhood emotional neglect are these familiar patterns:

· You have difficulty asking for help.
· You often feel disappointed with, or angry at, yourself.
· You judge yourself more harshly than you judge others.
· You compare yourself to others and often find yourself sadly lacking.

Sound familiar? There are long lists of these patterns online, but most people will recognize themselves in just these few examples. These patterns are difficult to recognize and extremely difficult to eradicate, in large part because we really believe we are as bad as we think. In fact, we may have spent a lifetime building up a case. For myself and others I know, the root cause is being insuffiently loved as a child. It completely contaminates our self-image, and that contaminated self-image makes it very difficult to meditate wholeheartedly and joyfully.

There are many therapeutic methods in the West, but I suggest two Buddhist techniques that can be very helpful. The first is *tonglen*, giving and sending, a technique we will explore in the chapter on refuge and bodhichitta.

The second can be adapted to any Buddhist practice that involves the visualization of the Buddha, gurus, or deities. When doing these visualizations as part of your practice, stop and reflect on two truths. Taking the Buddha as an example, trust and believe he is really in front of you and not just a product of your mind. The Buddha has said that he will appear to those who imagine him with faith. I don't think he was lying.

Remember this quality of the Buddha: he has unconditional love for all beings. I talked about unconditional love in my discussion of gurus, but here we're actually putting it into practice. No matter what you think about yourself, do you doubt the Buddha loves you unconditionally? We see ourselves as intrinsically unlovable; the Buddha sees us as pure, enlightened beings who are momentarily distracted. Who do you think is right? Allow yourself to bask in that love. Feel soaked in that love. All your negative thoughts and self-loathing are washed away by that love. If you allow yourself to surrender to this process, you can truly blossom.

The next topic is mindfulness. Cultivating mindfulness is very important. I'm sure you know how mindfulness has pervaded modern life. It is emphasized in non-Tibetan Buddhist traditions, but in our tradition, it is generally not taught as a separate practice. It is considered an important aspect of any meditation. Since you may not get specific instruction on mindfulness, I will talk about it at length.

Often, when chatting with my friends, we would discuss what the most important principle in Buddhism is. I would usually say mindfulness, since without mindfulness, the practitioner is not aware of their mental landscape. Without that awareness, one has no idea what to abandon and what to cultivate. And without that knowledge, there is no path.

So no matter what I was teaching, I would always emphasize mindfulness. Then one day, a student asked me to define mindfulness. I was irritated—I felt everyone knew what mindfulness was and that the student was just splitting hairs. I repeated a stock answer that I always gave. But that question stuck in my head. I read up on it, but it seemed like different authors had different approaches and answers.

In the general public, mindfulness is usually associated with attentiveness or being in the present. But if mindfulness were the same as attentiveness, then night watchmen, race car drivers, and seamstresses should all be spiritually advanced by now. Likewise with being in the present—aren't animals and infants always in the present—and with what results?

My inquiries led me to conclude that there is a spectrum of

mindfulness—states that vary from simple attentiveness up to nondual awareness. But the key point is to notice the difference between mindfulness and attention—the benefits of mindfulness will not arise with simply being attentive.

With attention, the mind is placed on an object, but it is generally accompanied by one of the five negative emotions. A tennis player will watch their opponent serve with complete attention, but that attention is mixed with the desire to win and the fear of losing. Obviously, that is not a transcendent approach.

Mindfulness, however, must be free of desire and aversion to be a true spiritual state. Freedom from attachment and aversion is equanimity. So when we have both attention and equanimity, we have mindfulness and this mindfulness is extremely beneficial to our meditation and to daily life.

Most of the use of the term *mindfulness* today is really talking about attention. In a lot of situations, attention is enough. If you have a tendency to get angry or to overeat, simply being aware of the emerging thoughts is enough to change your behavior. If you are always self-critical, attention will make you aware of that and give you a chance to change those thoughts.

However, if you are noticing a lack of progress or a sense of being stuck in some negative mental state, you should check if there is some attachment or aversion there. If you can let go of the attachment and aversion and be equanimous, the mind will become unstuck and the meditation can progress.

To use a mathematical example: imagine an x- and a y-axis. The x-axis is attention. Say we are watching TV. We don't want to be overly absorbed in the show to the point we believe it is real and we are shouting at the actors to be careful. But if we were to view the show as simply dots on the screen, we would be too distant. We want to be in the middle. The y-axis is feeling. On one extreme is attachment; on the other, aversion. Equanimity is in the middle of these two.

Where these two meet is true mindfulness. The closer we are to this point in our meditation, the better and more effective our meditation would be. We do have to put some awareness into checking where on these two axes our attention is and learn to gently bring it back to the right point.

A great explanation of the correct way to maintain mindfulness is in Dzogchen Ponlop Rinpoche's wonderful book *Emotional Rescue*:

> In the UK there is an underground transit system, nicknamed the Tube, that serves London and the neighboring areas. When the train pulls up and the doors open, a recorded voice comes over the sound system saying: "Mind the gap." It's a reminder to passengers to watch for the open space between the station platform and the train as they board, to prevent accidents...
>
> If you're stepping onto the Tube in London, you have to mind the gap because you don't want to fall in and get injured. When you're working with your emotions, though, you "mind the gap" a little differently. In the moment when you're having strong feelings, it's every bit as dangerous not to be mindful of the gap between yourself and your emotions.[2]

To use myself as an example, I've often been depressed. When applying mindfulness, I just experience being mindful of depression. For a long time, I'm stuck. It's because there is some subtle identification with the depression. I feel like I'm doing it right, but I'm subtly sucked into it, not really minding the gap. I've fallen in, I can't extricate myself, and nothing changes.

I think this is a very important point. Mindfulness has so successfully permeated our culture, but there are some limitations if the teachers have not been thoroughly trained. What I just said about depression could be equally true regarding physical pain. If you have a back problem, you can spend a long time being mindful of how much pain you feel. I don't see much benefit in that.

Another example is when dealing with people suffering from trauma or abuse. I've seen people in that situation meditate and just get stuck in a panic attack. Despite their best efforts to apply the teaching, the meditation simply becomes torture. If this applies to you, be very careful. If you have a negative chronic condition and are having difficulty with mindfulness practices, make sure you discuss your situation with your teacher. It may be more efficacious for you to do a different kind of meditation, one that focuses on positive, healing images such as the ones Tulku Thondup teaches or the thought-transformation practices of *lojong*, which will be discussed soon.

The most benefit will come from activities that give rise to the strongest negative emotions. These could be dealing with conflict or anxiety-provoking experiences such as flying. Be gentle with yourself, but slowly try to bring awareness into these situations. It will be difficult at first, but with persistence you will be able to do it. And you will find it incredibly freeing, so please give it a try. Once again, don't do anything foolish—you don't need to walk in a dangerous neighborhood at night just to let go of your fear. In that case, your fear is an appropriate reaction to the situation.

To conclude this section on mindfulness, I'd like to summarize the reasons why it's so important. First, it's a crucial foundation for any meditation. There aren't any meditations, Tibetan or otherwise, where it's okay to be mindless or distracted. Through learning mindfulness as a separate practice, one learns a crucial component of any practice.

Second, mindfulness is extremely useful in daily life. If, say, our main practice is a complex deity meditation, it might be difficult to do those visualizations while working or driving. However, mindfulness is always applicable. And it is always beneficial.

Third, as I have mentioned, emotional healing is an important factor for the success of one's practice. Without sufficient foundation in mindfulness, it is highly possible that visualization practice could accentuate an already dissociative state of mind. The practitioner could actually be cultivating mental illness to some degree. A firm foundation in mindfulness prevents that from happening, reverses the dissociation, and allows the meditator to continue in the Dharma from a healthy, wholesome perspective.

I have discussed several processes in this chapter that are helpful for beginners to keep in mind as they begin their journey. Of course, I am not advocating perfection in, say, emotional healing *before* one begins practice. But there is great value in identifying and naming processes that are already happening. By doing so, subsequent practice will be efficient and rapid.

CHAPTER 7

Path Buddha-Nature: Instruction and Practice

In the last chapter, I delineated some ways in which your involvement in Buddhism might evolve. Of these paths, the one I am most familiar with is the path of meditation. Much of the remainder of this book will focus on that since it is my area of relative expertise. Even if your path is different, say service, meditation will give you the presence of mind to follow that path with clarity and intelligence.

If I have any skill as a meditation instructor, it's for one main reason: I'm an awful meditator. I've meditated from several to many hours a day for forty-five years, and nothing amazing has happened, and it has almost always been a struggle.

It is rare that someone comes to me with a difficulty that I haven't struggled through myself. For a variety of reasons, a lot of this struggle took place without clear or sufficient guidance. Luckily I had decades to work some of these issues out. You probably don't. That is why it is so important to have a teacher.

Many people come to me after trying to meditate based on instructions in books. I have never met anyone who has done well that way. They always have a collection of strange theories and expectations regarding meditation and no way of knowing how well or poorly they are doing.

Some people feel exceptional—that they are better or worse than everyone else. It's a strange aspect of American culture that people want to feel special. Parents try to make their children feel special;

if they are not successful, that person as an adult will go from relationship to relationship looking for someone who makes them feel special. What can be worse for meditation is if you have actually succeeded in feeling special.

Feeling special is a big obstacle to meditation and putting instructions into practice. You will feel that the harder aspects of practice are just for ordinary people and not for someone like you. I've noticed this a lot in people who have had some kind of psychic experience—powerful dreams, visions, seeing auras, and so on. They feel these experiences make them exceptional and that they are on a fast track to enlightenment. In reality, this attitude will completely undermine their efforts. People who are used to failure and disappointment often do better—they can accept instruction and criticism, are not afraid of making mistakes, and are content with doing the best they can.

Just as harmful is feeling that others are better than you, that the instruction you hear in a teaching may be applicable to them but not to someone who is as wretched and pathetic as you. Not helpful. Get over it.

Some people want to meditate but don't want to be Buddhists. They are either interested in the worldly benefits of meditation (for example, relaxation, lower blood pressure) or believe in a generic spirituality. One of my teachers instructed me never to separate my teaching from the path to liberation. Indeed, meditation is always a means to an end. The point is, your goal determines what the meditation should be and what constitutes a proper or improper practice.

Some people believe there is a generic meditation that exists free from religious dogma or beliefs. But what is the goal of such meditation? If it is relaxation, then you have a belief in the value of relaxation. If it is awareness, then you have a belief in the value of awareness. You then have a dogma of the value of relaxation or awareness. So some belief is inescapable. Whatever criteria one uses to determine a good from a bad meditation is the beginning of a belief system. And it is naive to think that all these belief systems are the same.

We believe that the enlightenment of Lord Buddha is the pinnacle of human experience and replicating it for both ourselves and all other sentient beings is of supreme value. Therefore, all Buddhist meditation will be seen through the perspective of whether or not we are moving toward that goal.

Even within Tibetan Buddhism, different meditations have different goals and techniques. For example, if I am practicing calm-abiding, when thoughts arise, I do not distinguish between good thoughts or bad thoughts. I just let them go and return to the object of meditation. If I am meditating on loving-kindness, I am cultivating loving thoughts and feelings and abandoning thoughts of aversion and indifference.

Therefore, if someone asks what they should do when thoughts arise, the answer is another question: "What meditation are you practicing, and what is your goal?" We must always practice meditation within the framework of a conceptual understanding of the meditation technique and its place in aiding us on the Buddhist path.

The new practitioner cannot be stupid. It is not enough to do what you want, call it meditation, and do it for a certain period of time and expect any real benefit. Discernment is crucial. Part of that discernment is learning to follow instructions clearly.

I've led classes in which I've taught a particular technique. Later I solicit questions. Someone might ask something that doesn't make any sense to me, and I ask them to repeat the instruction. They'll talk about a meditation they were doing about visualizing light through their chakras or something along those lines.

I reply that I can only guide them if they follow my instructions as best they can. There might be nothing wrong with what they are doing, but it is beside the point. They are playing a tuba in a piano class.

So the student needs to determine the importance of having a meditation instructor, the importance of viewing the meditation in the context of the Buddhist path to enlightenment, and the importance of following instructions precisely and intelligently. With those conditions, the student will definitely benefit and progress.

Many people teach meditation these days. I'm assuming your instructor is or will be a qualified teacher from an authentic center. Don't be afraid to inquire into the credentials of any teacher—I myself have letters authorizing me as a teacher from my two main teachers.

Traditionally, teachers are supposed to be clairvoyant. Since meditative experiences are difficult to articulate, and we often misinterpret these experiences, history has shown the importance of directly knowing the mind of the student. However, these days, it will be hard to find a teacher with those qualities. Thus, it is best to assume that you will need to articulate your positive and negative experiences rather than expect the teacher to automatically know and be able to guide you without you saying anything.

Study is invaluable here—although I wouldn't recommend getting instruction from books, reading authentic texts and learning the traditional terminology will give you a shared vocabulary with your teacher. If your teacher is Tibetan with imperfect English, try to learn a few of the Tibetan words for meditative experiences that I mentioned earlier—for example, *namtog* for discursive thoughts, *mugpa* for dullness, *dewa* for bliss. But be wary of using jargon or foreign terms that you have just picked up like *chakras* or *rigpa*. If you haven't properly studied the relevant topics, you will mean one thing and your teacher will understand another.

You may be fortunate enough to study under a great master who is indeed clairvoyant. In that case, they will know exactly what your experience is, exactly how to guide you, and exactly which of the myriad kinds of meditation will be best for you.

Most likely you will learn the various techniques in a group setting with little or no opportunity for questions. To learn details like whether to repeat a prayer three or seven times, a senior student will suffice. But for anything deeper than that, a more intimate relationship with a more qualified teacher is necessary.

In many centers new students are assigned teachers from among the senior students. Or you may ask the head lama on whom you should rely for day-to-day guidance and questions. If no one like that is available, ask the lama for guidelines for finding someone who can help.

You may need to go online, using e-mail or Skype to connect with an instructor. Or you may have to occasionally visit a different town or city where a teacher will be available. But I feel it is necessary to have someone with whom to communicate the ups and downs of your practice.

Often when I am teaching meditation, I try to solicit questions regarding how the students are doing. It may be my unskillful way of trying to get people to open up, but I'm often met with a roomful of blank stares. This is very frustrating for me and sad for the students.

When you practice, *something* must be happening. You might have a constant, unbroken stream of negative thoughts. You might be falling asleep all the time. But this is what is happening. There is no benefit in pretending it isn't happening or feeling ashamed that it is.

Don't assume the teacher has nothing to say that can help; they probably do. Remember what I said at the beginning—anything bad that can happen in your meditation has probably already happened in mine, and I figured out a way to deal with. It's probably the same with your teacher.

If you are in a group, don't be ashamed. Everyone has similar problems. If it is too embarrassing to talk about, speak in more abstract terms—"wanting to have sex with a coworker" could be expressed as "lustful thoughts."

When you are in a group, everyone learns from the students who open up. The teacher's response will often be useful for most students, and the original questioner will be doing a great service for everyone there. As an instructor, I will answer questions in much greater length if I feel the answer is applicable to everyone.

Try to have regular one-on-one meetings with your instructor. Don't be afraid of discussing your real-life problems and how they interact with your meditation. Try to describe your positive and negative experiences clearly, without jargon whose meaning you are not sure of. As a matter of fact, asking questions about technical

Buddhist terms regarding meditation and how they apply to your practice can be very valuable. If you are reading something about meditation and you feel that it is applicable, bring it in and show a passage to your teacher.

Don't expect praise if you are having good experiences. Your teacher will not want to stoke the fires of your pride. And don't forget that those experiences arose simply because you were following the instructions of Lord Buddha; if anyone deserves praise, it is him.

It is not necessary to talk about your past. In the West, we have this notion that our difficulties arose from experiences when we were young. Therefore, we need to tell our teacher about our youth so they can understand the root of our present problems and advise us accordingly. But I've never heard a lama solicit early memories to benefit a student. Rather, lamas are concerned with your present-moment fixation on what's arising in the mind.

Remember that if your teacher is an ordinary person, they might be wrong or simply not get the main point of your inquiry. One problem I have as a teacher is that whatever I am dealing with in my own practice, say using less effort in my meditation, I tend to see that as the universal remedy for whoever I happen to be talking to. It's hard not to get excited by my own latest discovery, sometimes to the point of missing what the student is trying to say. So feel free to repeat your question, ask for clarification, or even argue a bit with the teacher. We all are trying to do the best we can, and we would much rather help you than have some miscommunication swept under the rug because of too much respect or decorum.

In this day and age, it is amazing to come across Lord Buddha's teachings. It is likewise amazing to have teachers available who speak your language and are willing to guide you along the path. If you don't take advantage of this wonderful situation, it might be a long time before it arises again. So rejoice in your good fortune, and more importantly, take advantage of it!

Hopefully, you will have the opportunity to meet great masters and receive profound instructions from them. You must be prepared to take advantage of this tremendous opportunity.

A most extraordinary event took place at the Orgyen Dorje Den center in San Francisco in the summer of 1994. Venerable Gyatrul Rinpoche, a most accomplished meditation master, was teaching an amazingly deep and detailed meditation manual on how to recognize and stabilize buddha-nature. He was assisted by the translator B. Alan Wallace, a brilliant scholar and serious practitioner. Rinpoche taught throughout the weekends, giving profound instructions. On Wednesdays, we had a question-and-answer session, sometimes with a short sitting. Rinpoche eventually canceled the Wednesday session. Very few people had been asking genuine, meaningful questions based on their own experience. It was a terribly sad missed opportunity.

I began teaching at the center soon after. Most of my students were people who had attended Rinpoche's teaching. I was appalled to learn how little my friends understood of the context of that summer's teachings or of the correct protocol for questioning and learning from a master.

The greatest advantage to living in Asia is, of course, the proximity and accessibility of so many great teachers. While living there, it is quite easy to form a close, ongoing relationship with a high lama and to learn from them how to go about understanding buddha-nature. Since I had that wonderful opportunity, and since it became apparent that many Western Buddhists did not have a similar experience with their teachers here in America, one of my highest priorities as a teacher and Dharma friend has been to explain to students how buddha-nature is apprehended through the close guidance of a master.

In the first chapter, I talked about buddha-nature as ground, the basis of our being and the force that propels us into a spiritual life. In chapter 4, I talked about empowerments as a way to gain further or deeper insight into our true nature. By now you may be saying, "I never really glimpsed the ground before I started. Nothing much happened to me during the empowerment. What's he talking about anyway?" Or, "Isn't understanding buddha-nature too advanced for me? Don't I need many years of strict practice, many years of philosophical studies, even to approach this subject?"

Actually, no. In fact, there are several traditions or styles for introducing students to the nature of the mind. In one tradition, yes, lots of study is necessary. In another, deep meditative absorption is considered necessary. But there is a third tradition where the introduction can be made early in the practitioner's career, and this one may be the most appropriate for the propagation of Tibetan Buddhism in the West. This tradition seems to be in accord with prophecies made centuries ago about the spread of the dzogchen teachings. It is in this tradition that I've been trained, and it's from that perspective that I'm writing this book.

I'm not going to describe the nature of the mind to you. It's beyond my ability as a teacher. There are many excellent books in English on mahamudra and dzogchen. Great lamas are freely spreading these teachings. What I am trying to do is to help you relate correctly to your teacher. I hope to help you avoid a missed opportunity like the one I just described. Although I'll be writing in the context of receiving the pointing-out instruction, the teaching that reveals buddha-nature, what I say will be of general use in getting instructions from your teacher on any topic. So read the following with both purposes in mind.

How does this pointing-out take place? Sometimes a teacher will give you the introduction directly. That is, you'll be with them either alone or in a group, and they will do something to make you experience your buddha-nature on the spot. It could happen while taking an empowerment, especially during the fourth empowerment.

There are more spontaneous, less ritualized ways for this transmission to happen. We've all read Zen stories of the disciple who attained satori when struck by his master. This has also happened frequently in the Vajrayana tradition. Naropa became enlightened when Tilopa beat him with his sandal. When this happens to an advanced practitioner, the experience could be permanent; the disciple is enlightened from that moment on. For the beginner, the experience is most likely fleeting. After it fades, it is the student's lifelong job to learn how to access and recreate that experience. As beginners, we are granted these glimpses so we can access them later in our practice, and so we know what we are looking for.

We can't sit around waiting for the introduction to happen. The most common way for one to be introduced to the nature of the mind—that is, buddha-nature, or rigpa—is simply through instruction, hearing teachings from your master on how the mind really is. It's up to you to clear away doubts and arrive at genuine experience.

For example, your teacher may say, "The nature of the mind is empty." Figure out what that means. Does it mean free from thoughts, blank? Does it mean nonexistent? Look carefully at your own mind. What does emptiness really mean? Try to experience it. Is it like space? Is it completely calm? Remember all the other teachings you've had on the nature of the mind, emptiness, or buddha-nature. What kind of experience are they pointing to? Do you have only an intellectual understanding? Even on that level, is your understanding consistent with all the teachings you've heard? If you've had some experience, is it consistent with all that you've previously been taught?

At this point in the process, we begin to form a mental image of what the experience might be like. Then, we try to actualize that experience. If we are able to do that, then we can see how it compares with what's been described. We have to continue checking and inquiring.

Are you starting to understand what's involved here? We have to assume that the lama didn't give this teaching just because they love to talk or show off their own deep understanding. And you are no more stupid or less developed than anyone else in the audience.

At this point, one of two things may have happened: you've had some experience that you think or hope is *the* experience, or you haven't. If you haven't, you can report, "Rinpoche, I've been trying to meditate on what you said when you said, 'Mind is empty.' But nothing has happened. I don't understand—I have no idea what you're talking about! Can you give me one word of advice on how to proceed?" Then you take that advice and start all over. A word of caution: they may not answer you straightaway. They might say that you have to do some other practice, such as the preliminary practices, to clear away obstacles to your understanding. Complete these practices to their satisfaction, then report back for further clarification and instruction for however long it takes. At this point, you'll know that your practice is proceeding in the right direction.

If you had some experience, report back for confirmation. Don't assume you've understood. There are countless ways to get it wrong, and if you do, it will make the rest of your practice wobbly, since it will based on a wrong view. It would be like building a house on a rotten foundation.

When you report back, you can say, "Rinpoche, in your teaching you said that mind was empty. Since then I've been trying to meditate on your words, and I've had the following experience…" It's very difficult to put these kinds of experiences into words, but try; it's really worth the effort. Study helps here—it provides you with the vocabulary to explain yourself. You might ask, "Is this really it?" They may ask you several questions, often to discern whether you're talking about a real experience or mostly mixing it up with what you've read or heard. If they say "no," "not quite," and so on, then you go back to the beginning. If it's a definite "yes," then ask for further clarification, some instruction on how to proceed. Even if you have recognized and your teacher has unequivocally confirmed your recognition, there's still much more to learn. First are the techniques for repeating and stabilizing the recognition. (This is, of course, many lifetimes of work!) Second, there will be doubts, and you'll have experiences you're not sure how to categorize. "Was that last experience really rigpa? Perhaps it wasn't empty enough." This can go on for a long time. The doubting and questioning can start to become problematic after a while, but it's necessary in the beginning to make sure you have it right.

There's a more elaborate and systematic form of introduction wherein the teacher asks the student questions, and the student is expected to meditate until they reach a definite conclusion. The teachings I mentioned at the beginning of this chapter were of this form.

The lama might ask, "What color is your mind?" You are expected to come up with an answer. You might say, "Blue," or that you were unable to find any color whatever. The lama will then give you the next instruction in the form of another question such as, "Where in the body does the mind abide?" If you are diligent, eventually you'll begin to have experiences. This is the point. You can reply, "I was trying to ascertain the shape of my mind, when I had the following experience..." and then it's as I've already described. The questions are simply to get you to look deeply into yourself in a way that you probably never have; consequently, the questions, which were relatively straightforward at the beginning (I know that my mind has no color), become deeper and more difficult as you proceed.

Don't lie to your teacher or try to impress them. What's the point? The worst thing that can happen is that they'd believe you. Try to forget what you've read. When looking at your own experience, formulate it using your own words; try not to use Buddhist jargon. Don't say, for example, "I've experienced emptiness," but rather something like, "I've had an experience in which my mind became vast and spacious." Don't assume anything. Don't assume you've understood. Don't assume the lama can read your mind and knows for sure what you've experienced. It is not that the lama doesn't understand or know what you are really experiencing; rather, it is that your assumptions make it difficult for you to be open and receptive.

This dialogue can go on with more than one lama, especially among those who have a similar approach to introducing you to your nature. This can happen in the West, where you are receiving guidance from various lamas as they pass through. Remember the three approaches to introducing buddha-nature that I mentioned at the beginning of this chapter? If you can, stick with teachers who share the same approach or you can become confused. If one lama says, "Mind is empty," and you meditate on those words and then later ask a lama who favors the philosophical approach, they might say, "You can't possibly understand the empty nature of the mind! You haven't studied enough yet. Learn Tibetan, study these texts, and this will lay the ideal foundation for you. Otherwise, you can't possible understand, and you'll go astray."

The opposite can also happen. You can be developing deep concentrative absorption under one teacher who has said, "You can't possibly understand rigpa while you have a monkey mind. Your chaotic thoughts obscure your true nature, and if you try to understand, you will waste your time." When you report to another lama, perhaps a simple yogi, they might say, "Concentrative states are still dualistic and conceptual. They will only keep you in samsara. Go straight for the main point!" Very confusing, eh?

If you remember that there are three main styles for introducing the mind's nature, you won't get confused. If you recall, the approaches were introduction through philosophical study, introduction through progressing through the stages of meditation, and the more direct style of introduction. When receiving teachings from a lama, ask yourself into which of these approaches their teaching mainly fits. Of course, this is a general guideline, and lamas are also capable of being flexible; they can often accommodate more than one style. In the beginning, however, it's probably better to discuss the mind's nature with lamas who have similar approaches.

If you are receiving instruction from more than one lama, you can ask, "Rinpoche, when Lama A was teaching here last spring, they said that the mind was empty, and since then, I've been trying to understand, with little success. Can you help me?" or "I had such-and-such an experience during the empowerment last fall. What does it mean?"

As a matter of fact, this is what my teacher has recommended to me. "When you meet a great teacher, ask their help clarifying your experience of rigpa." Believe me, lamas really appreciate it when you ask sincere questions about buddha-nature that come directly from your own experience. You'll make their day. They much prefer those kinds of questions to any other query. Sometimes my friends tell me that they feel shy presenting their understanding or experience to the lamas. While I respect their humility, there is really nothing better to discuss with them.

Of course, not all your interactions with lamas will be about the nature of mind. But the same protocol should apply. I've seen so much flakiness pass for real communication with a teacher. I'm not saying we need hours and hours to unburden ourselves completely in front of them. Perhaps a fifteen-minute interview will suffice. It should, however, be authentic. Use your time wisely; ask questions that come straight from the heart. Also, never confuse your fantasies and projections with what your teacher really said. As this is an important point and a mistake we all seem to make, I will give a few examples.

I first started studying Buddhism in Dharamsala in India. There was a class for Westerners at the Library of Tibetan Works and Archives founded by His Holiness the Dalai Lama. At the conclusion of each class, we would file out the door while bowing to the geshe who taught us. Sometimes he would smile at someone; often he would merely continue to prepare to leave. Among the students, this was taken as a form of divination. If you were thinking of, say, going to New Delhi for a break and he smiled at you while you were exiting, that smile would be interpreted as an approval of what you were daydreaming about—you could safely proceed on your trip. If he didn't acknowledge you as you were leaving, it was considered a "no"—sorry, no trip. I know it sounds silly (well, it does to me), but many people believed in this. "The lama is omniscient; he knows what I'm thinking. Everything he does is meaningful; everything is a teaching." Hard to argue against.

Recently, I heard a discussion between two long-time students of a certain lama. One student said that it's taken him twenty years to put together the pieces he's received from his teacher. He concluded that the lama intentionally only gives bits and pieces, leaving it to the student to put them together over time. I remarked that students traditionally studied many texts with their khenpos, doing nothing other than putting the pieces together. Is this something only for Tibetans and not for us? Do the lamas not want to make it too easy for us or something like that? Or is it that the student hadn't sufficiently communicated with his teacher, hadn't asked the right questions at the right time, and therefore hadn't made the necessary connections earlier? If I'm correct, then the student was projecting his own lack of skill in approaching the teacher onto the teacher and imagining the miscommunication to be some bizarre strategy.

Probably the strangest and saddest example of this kind of non-communication happened to someone I knew in the East. He would ask his lama's advice, disobey it, and suffer as a consequence. He couldn't understand why his teacher was doing this to him! His logic: because of the omniscience of the teacher, he would know my friend would disobey and had, therefore, advised him accordingly. That it ended in disaster was the desired result of the teacher. Why did the lama want my friend to be unhappy all the time? This logic was as unbreakable as it was bizarre. I always found it difficult to help him.

I suppose one could say that there are many subtle communications between a higher being like a lama and their closest students. Students will report advice given through gestures, jokes, innocent comments, facial expression, and so on. Maybe I'm just too dim-witted to pick up on them. But I've asked lamas many times about things like this, and they always express dismay at the way Westerners misinterpret their actions. My teacher Chökyi Nyima Rinpoche says it's frustrating for him to have to be especially vigilant not to say or do anything that a Westerner will interpret as a sign. If you think I'm wrong and that you are receiving subtle messages from your teacher, that they're teaching you something nonverbally, simply check in with them. Occasionally ask them if your interpretation of their actions is correct. You have nothing to lose.

One of the reasons I feel the material in this chapter is important is that most readers won't be able to spend all that much time with high lamas. Your one interview may be nothing more than a quick question while getting your blessing in a reception line. With the spread of Tibetan Dharma in the West, the lamas' time is becoming more and more precious; it is becoming increasingly difficult to spend much time with them. So if the time isn't spent wisely, you may not get a second or third chance. Ask questions of high lamas that only high lamas can answer. Save your other questions for senior students, your therapist, or whoever you feel can help you.

One little trick I've learned is this: in teachings with question-and-answer sessions, word your personal questions in such a manner that they become questions of general interest. For instance, if I am seething with anger, I can request techniques for dealing with anger. If I feel my mind is opening up in some new and unusual way, I can ask a question about the relationship of space to emptiness. Among other things, this has the effect of keeping other students from feeling that I am taking up the teaching time with my personal problems.

Basically, it's up to you to establish a dialogue with a good teacher. Never forget why you're there, and don't lose sight of the goal—your recognition and stabilization of your own true nature. The lama is the only one who will be able to help you. Without them, you'll be completely lost.

CHAPTER 8

Getting Started

Now that we've received instruction on meditation, it is up to us to get started with a regular routine. In this chapter I will offer straightforward advice on how to begin a regular practice of meditation. Sounds simple, right? But how many really do it? How many people really maintain a daily practice? Not that many.

I read an analysis of meditation instruction once. The author had compiled statistics on the percentage of students still practicing after a certain period of time. The figures were abysmally low, and he commented that no other field of instruction would find such a failure rate acceptable. Actually, I don't find it acceptable either. Many of my students tell me that although they started years ago, they were never able to maintain a consistent practice, so they eventually gave it up. Coming to my class was a new beginning for them—I can only hope they will continue.

I try to teach, and now I'm trying to write this book, in a way that warns students of the most common mistakes they might make and prepares them for as many of the difficulties, obstacles, and misunderstandings that can hinder or derail their practice. At times it will seem rather gloomy as I go through one thing after another that can go wrong, but I feel that the most useful thing I have to give my students and readers is the lessons I've learned from my own mistakes. If you can learn from them, your path may be smoother and more delightful. I hope the advice in this and subsequent chapters will help you avoid the pitfalls that have caught so many of us. I have included some advice that is specific to Vajrayana practitioners, but most of what is here will be of use to anyone who is learning to meditate.

First, find a time to meditate. Morning or night, both have their adherents. Traditional texts generally recommend morning, although many of us are "night people." You should choose the time when your mind is most naturally clear and calm, your body fresh and rested, your environment relatively peaceful and quiet, and you're least likely to be disturbed. Don't be afraid to be creative—I just recommended to a student that he meditate during his work lunch hour.

Select a period of time for your meditation. Fifteen or twenty minutes is probably best for beginners. If you've read many books or heard many stories, you'll realize that the great practitioners of the past were extremely diligent, and you might be tempted to emulate their example: "I'm going to sit in the full lotus position for three hours. Whatever happens, I'm not moving!" Forget it; that isn't going to work. No matter how strong, tough, inspired, or disciplined you feel you are, you'll quit. It'll just be too much for you. You won't necessarily say to yourself or your friends, "Gee, this is a little too much for me." You will probably just find yourself getting interested in something else.

I would observe the following so often in the East that I became sadly cynical about it. A newcomer would meet a high lama, receive some teaching, and then go gung-ho into retreat, frequently into some famous cave, full of inspiration and vowing never to quit. Without fail, after a while they would return to town, usually with some excuse, saying that they were now ready to practice tantra (meaning they wanted sex).

So think of meditation like a physical exercise. You wouldn't start off jogging three hours a day, would you? Follow the same common sense. Start slow, gradually increase, and build yourself up. Develop meditation muscles. With time you'll be able to sit for longer and longer periods. The problem is both physical and mental. If you force your body too much, it will simply be too painful—you'll spend your entire session coping with the pain. If you force your mind too much, either you'll feel burned out, or you'll find you've been daydreaming for the last fifteen minutes of your meditation session.

When I was first taught meditation, the instruction was that your meditation session should be like visiting a friend. When you visit, you have your cup of tea and you chat. If you're skillful, you'll end the conversation before you run out of things to say and feel awkward. If the meeting ends on an unpleasant note, you might feel reluctant to see your friend again. It is the same with practice—end your session before it becomes unpleasant. If you don't, you won't look forward to practicing again. Although meditation can often be difficult and challenging, view your session as a special time in your day, a time you look forward to with joy and anticipation. If you do this, your ability to meditate for longer and longer periods will develop naturally.

One way I've developed for monitoring my duration and exertion has been to ask myself, "Can I meditate like this every day for the rest of my life?" If I have doubts about answering "yes," then I know I am probably pushing myself too hard.

The next major consideration is place. Many people like to meditate in groups and that is fine. I know it is common for Zen practitioners to go to their center to meditate before work. I certainly admire that kind of diligence. For now, I'll assume that you'll want to establish a daily practice in your own home.

If you're lucky, you might have an extra room to set aside for meditation. That's great. If that's not possible, select a room that's already in use. Most people choose their bedroom. Since we usually meditate either right before or right after sleep, it's a sensible choice. Also, since it's the room you've selected for sleeping, it's probably the quietest room in your house. Whichever room it is, it should be quiet, airy, and free of smoke.

If you really want to do things right, you can orient your house, room, shrine, or seat according to the traditional Chinese rules of geomancy, or feng shui. You can consult books or find an expert. There are many, many rules, and some of the lamas, especially H. E. Tai Situ Rinpoche, place a lot of credence in them. His Eminence is the overseer of the Samye Ling Tibetan Center in Scotland where I did my four-year retreat. He made sure that both the building and individual rooms conformed to feng shui. Doors were bricked up and new ones built. A pond was dug. Shrines and meditation cushions were moved about.

One rule of feng shui that I always try to follow is not to place my shrine in the direct line between my bedroom door and window. I try to put it in the last place I see when I open my bedroom door from the corridor.

Many people like to meditate with a view, perhaps looking out a large picture window. This sense of space can be expansive and is especially appropriate for certain kinds of practices or to counteract certain hindrances (such as dullness or sleepiness) in your practice. Others find this distracting and prefer to sit facing a shrine or a wall. Of course, many people meditate with their eyes closed so that none of this matters too much. Lamas generally recommend meditating with the eyes open; however, my teacher says that for beginning practices, it's acceptable to close the eyes. I personally find meditating facing my shrine too hectic, too overwhelming. But orientation is up to you.

Some people like to meditate on a special mat on the floor; others just sit up in bed. I've always meditated in bed; it's never seemed like a problem. Traditionally, of course, people generally didn't have enough room to meditate anyplace other than where they sleep. However, we can argue that the area normally associated with sleep and sex may not be the most conducive to meditative equilibrium.

I think you'll find that if you meditate in the same place every day, your seat will build up a special feeling, some sense of power or positive energy. I usually don't notice it until I've been away for a while; when I return, my seat almost seems as if it's humming.

I strongly recommend having a shrine where you practice. If you're a Vajrayana practitioner, a shrine is a necessity; instructions for its layout are contained in the commentaries on your practice. A shrine creates a sacred space in your room—it uplifts you and reminds you of the spiritual dimension of life. It also becomes both a repository and a generator of positive energy that will benefit your practice.

If you don't have the space for a separate piece of furniture, you can use the top of a bureau or chest of drawers. If you're doing a specific practice, the instructions will specify the shrine layout, but for now I'll give you the bare minimum. It's always nice to have the seven water bowls for offering. Traditionally, they should be made of the most expensive metal you can afford, but I've come to prefer the porcelain of Chinese teacups. You can also offer candles, incense, or flowers if you like. Next, place photos of the teachers to whom you feel closest. They will keep you inspired and motivated. It's nice to have one nice image, either a thankha (Tibetan scrolled painting with embroidery) or a statue of a buddha or deity, to remind you of your goal and to be a central focus for your practice.

The image should be clean and shiny; don't buy an old, worn-looking thankha or a dark, sooty statue. They might look like antiques, but they're not appropriate shrine objects. Our buddha-nature is not worn and sooty. Also, make sure it's a useful image for you. Is it a deity for a practice you've never heard of and probably will never do, or is it something more generic, like Shakyamuni Buddha, that will always be appropriate? The image must be iconographically correct or it cannot be blessed. If you're not sure, have it checked by a lama before you buy it. Finally, have it blessed by a teacher you respect.

You might also want to buy a rosary, or *mala*. There are many kinds, but except for small prostration malas, they all have 108 beads. The best are bodhi seed beads, which are made from the same species of tree under which Lord Buddha attained enlightenment, or lotus seeds, which generally come from China. Different practices might recommend different types of beads, but one of these two will probably suffice for quite a while. You'll also eventually want to pick up a vajra (Tib. *dorje)* and bell. They should be bought together as a matching set. Other ritual objects can wait.

Now that we've discussed the time and place, let's talk about you, especially your body. Try to stay healthy. If you're not already, try to get healthy. It's best to rely on more natural methods of healing if possible. Stop taking recreational drugs, especially anything that can be smoked—they're the worst. They block the subtle energy channels in a particularly pernicious manner.

Learn an appropriate posture. It's never easy for anybody, and you'll have to put up with a wee bit of pain. But as I said earlier, don't push yourself too much either. If sitting cross-legged on the floor is too difficult for you, use a chair. If possible, it is best not to lean against anything. Mantak Chia, a Taoist teacher in America, recommends sitting on a chair rather than sitting cross-legged. So don't feel shy or inadequate. Sitting on a chair has become more acceptable as the baby boomers age; temples and classrooms often have chairs now for those who can't sit cross-legged. Of the cross-legged positions, the full lotus position is preferred, and in some advanced practices it's mandatory. At least try. Other leg positions are acceptable. The most important factors are: you are able to sit comfortably for the duration of your session, the straightness of your back promotes mental clarity, your chest doesn't feel con-tracted, and you are able to breathe abdominally without feeling constricted. For the last, one needs loose clothing and a positioning of the legs that can be maintained without abdominal tension. For instance, the normal position Americans use when they sit on the floor, with their legs crossed in front of them and their knees slightly elevated, doesn't work well because it tenses the abdomen. Also, I've found that if people sit toward the front edge of their cushion, this tilts the sacral region forward and nicely aligns the spine and the rest of the body. If these postural factors are met, the energy flow in your body will aid the development of meditational experiences.

Many people seem to like these little kneeling benches. They are gaining in popularity these days, especially among those who have some physical problem prohibiting the cross-legged postures. I like them myself and really appreciate how positively they affect both my posture and my breathing.

Of course, you can meditate lying flat on your back. It's relaxing, but it's also easy to drift off and even fall asleep. So be a little careful with this.

Another consideration is whether to practice alone or with other family members. Once again, this is a matter of personal preference. I have almost always practiced alone and am very idiosyncratic, but I feel it would be both supportive and bonding to practice as a family. Practicing with another person can be a healing experience. If it's someone with whom you already feel close, it will make you feel even closer; if it's someone with whom you're having difficulties, it will help to ease those problems. It's hard to remain angry at someone with whom you've just meditated.

Having discussed the outer circumstances or conditions necessary—or at least helpful—to begin practicing, what then are the corresponding inner qualities? First is intelligence. Intelligence doesn't necessarily mean being brilliant or scholarly. In fact, overly intellectual people often have difficulty meditating. Intelligence means listening to the instructions, clarifying doubts and misunderstandings, and applying the instructions correctly. One must investigate one's own state of being and figure out how the teachings apply. Are you using the techniques correctly? Are you noticing your faults?

So many people never seem to resolve their doubts about the technique they are using, and they settle for a flawed meditation when conferring with a teacher, even someone like me, could really be of benefit. I have had this experience often since I began teaching—someone will finally reveal a problem with a practice that they think is unworkable or is due to some flaw in themselves. I am able to offer a relatively simple and straightforward solution based on my own experience that easily eliminates the obstacle. It's not that I'm a great or clairvoyant teacher—it's just that the error is so obvious.

A practitioner also needs faith or trust. In this case, I don't mean an emotional feeling toward the teacher or the Buddha. I mean confidence that the instructions will really do what they're supposed to do. It's like the trust a parachutist has in their parachute—they must have no doubt at all that it's going to open. If we don't have the same trust, we also won't be able to jump into the practice—we'll always be hesitating and hedging our bets. To stand too much outside the meditation, watching ourselves meditate, is a big problem.

It impedes our progress with our meditation. Too much of our energy is in the watching, which leaves little for accomplishing the meditation.

Guru Rinpoche said that we should meditate in the same way that a sparrow enters a nest. A sparrow spends some time investigating whether or not it is safe to enter. Once its examination is over, it then enters unhesitatingly. That's a wonderful metaphor for practice. First clear up all your doubts about your technique, then throw yourself into the technique with no separation or self-consciousness. Of course, that's easy to say, but it is the direction toward which we should be moving.

Another necessary quality is determination. It's easy to gear oneself up for counting mantras or prostrations. For some, physical discipline is also easy. But the determination of the meditator is different. We must be determined to strive to purify our obscurations until they're completely gone—in other words, until our buddha-nature unobstructedly shines through. When we sit, we decide to do our best not to be swayed by our negativities. We should cultivate this attitude at the beginning of our session. Otherwise, no matter how much we practice, we will daydream a lot, and our meditation will always be wishy-washy. I know this from experience—I may do my session of meditation, but it is tepid. Why? I don't have that inner strength to remain unmoved by the arising of various mental content.

We also need some renunciation. We may not be able to live in caves or become monks or nuns, but we have to be able to start saying "no" to the distractions of life. Otherwise, we'll never get any practice done. There'll always be something more interesting to do. We have to understand the impermanence and meaninglessness of most of what takes up our free time. In a later chapter, I'll talk more about the "four thoughts," contemplations to increase renunciation. For now it is enough to understand that some weariness with ordinary life and a willingness to give up a few meaningless things is necessary. Before we begin practicing, the day has twenty-four hours, and every minute is filled by some activity or another, whether working, sleeping, or watching TV. Lord Buddha does not have the power to add extra hours to the day; the only way to get any practice done is to stop doing something else.

Finally, we need the ability to face pain and hardship, to tolerate a little difficulty in pursuit of the ultimate truth. There will always be difficulties on the path. It's important to understand that, in general, your progress will be directly proportional to your willingness to endure these hardships. There's the hardship of giving up meaningless but fun activities; the hardship of separating and alienating oneself from family, friends, and community; the hardship of the difficulty of practice; and most important, the hardship of actually facing one's pain and negativities and dealing with them directly. Deeper, there is the hardship of giving up the ego. This can often feel like one is dissolving or even dying; experiencing this dissolution can be very threatening at first.

The point here is that the benefits of practicing the Dharma are innumerable and amazing. But for any one of them to be accomplished, we have to give something up. If we want to be disciplined, we have to give up some other activities. If we want solitude, we have to give up a little social life. On a deeper level, if we want calmness, we must abandon discursiveness; if we want to be compassionate, we must abandon aversion toward others. It's not going to happen that first you develop compassion and then that gives you the inspiration to give up your negativity. We must always take the first step, but once that first step is taken, there is always some reward, some benefit. And that encourages us to take that next little step.

A few words on meditation itself. Although there are innumerable techniques, especially within the Tibetan tradition, we can make a few general remarks for beginners. Whatever meditation you are doing, you will always experience it in the following way. You focus on the object, you get distracted, you notice your distraction, and you return to your object. What changes with time is the length and subtlety of the distractions. This process is unavoidable, and there are generally no shortcuts for making it easier. If you go to all the highest lamas and learn all the most profound techniques, none of them will tell how to recognize distractions sooner. You simply have to practice until it slowly improves.

That we all have some expectations of what we expect from our meditation makes it more difficult. When we find we are not doing much more than simply churning our thoughts, we can easily become discouraged or self-condemning. Don't. No matter how bad your meditation might seem, it's the effort that counts. Returning to your meditation time and time again will have gradual but deep benefits that a beginner can hardly imagine. Self-condemnation, feeling that you're the worst meditator on the block and will never get it, is simply indulging in more thoughts.

The experience of cascading thoughts doesn't get the credit it's due—it's actually a fantastic experience that we must acknowledge, respect, and appreciate. From beginningless time, all sentient beings have been completely identified with their thoughts. When they think, "I want a hamburger," for example, they really believe they want a hamburger. When we meditate, we progress from feeling we want a hamburger to knowing we had a thought about wanting a hamburger. Very, very different. I often call it a major step in evolution. The person who is aware of thoughts is a different being from the one who isn't aware. The meditator who experiences neverending discursiveness has made a significant breakthrough in development. One is definitely beginning the process of freeing oneself from the power of one's thoughts and their inherent negativity. I'll talk more about this in the next chapter.

Longchenpa summarizes the qualities of the successful student:

> ...the person who is going to experience for himself life's
>   meaning
> Must be one who has confidence, perseverance, and the desire
>   to escape from his present situation and the feeling of
>   disgust with it.
> Wearied of Samsara, he must deeply concern himself with
>   liberation,

Dismissing this life from his mind and looking to
 enlightenment henceforward,
Keeping excitement and distraction far away and having few
 emotions,
Being contented, leisurely, having visionary experiences, and
 being full of dedication,
Having a firm mind and a deep sense of reverence,
Such a person will realize most excellent liberation.[1]

Now you're ready to go. Remember that it isn't possible to get everything right. Don't give up or procrastinate if your room is too noisy, or you can't sit in a perfect position just yet. Not practicing is your loss. There is always some difficulty in practicing the Dharma; we'd all be buddhas by now if there weren't. If we put up with difficulties to accomplish the most mundane or trivial of things, how much more important is it to do so to accomplish enlightenment? So, if possible, perfect your conditions, but until then, don't procrastinate.

CHAPTER 9

Getting It Wrong

When I look back on my forty-five years of practice, I can't help but feel deeply disappointed by how little progress I've made in my meditation. In a sense, I've done most things right—I've played by the book, so to speak. Why then have the experiences of meditation, so tantalizing, been beyond my reach? Don't get me wrong, it's not as if nothing has happened; it's just that progress has been painfully slow.

What have I done wrong? Is it my fault? Basically, yes. I've zigged where I should have zagged a number of times. I haven't listened carefully to my teacher or neglected what proved to be a key point of instruction. Sometimes I simply didn't know the right question to ask. Luckily, I've had the leisure to flounder around for a while. Finally, I would right myself and bumble on to the next obvious pothole.

However, you may not have the leisure to make these kinds of mistakes. In that case, perhaps I can help you by pointing out where some of these potholes lie for beginners. On your part, you have to check yourself carefully. You need to monitor your style of meditation and your attitudes toward your practice. If you don't, subtle deviations can creep in. They can eventually be noticed and corrected, or they can grow until they are no longer so subtle and can completely derail your growth. So I'll point out a few common errors now and a few more in a later chapter. It will be up to you to check yourself and try to let go of them.

We all have a certain style of doing things—how we drive, how we cook, how we dress. Some of us are shy or cautious, others assertive or flamboyant. We've refined that style over the years based on how successful it is, but it's not usually something of which we're completely aware. As long as it gets the job done, as long as we get the appropriate feedback from others, our style goes unnoticed, and when questioned we'll say, "That's just the way I am." When we begin meditation, it is inevitable that we will meditate with the same style with which we do everything else, because it's who we think we are. Furthermore, this style has proven to be reasonably successful in our other activities. However, in this case, it is not at all appropriate. If there is any style, there is a hidden agenda and an implicit judgment of the various phenomena of meditation. We don't have the true detachment or choiceless awareness of real meditation. Our style contains our unacknowledged attitudes toward meditation. Also, a significant amount of energy goes into maintaining our attitude or style, resulting in less energy available for the meditation itself. This is obviously highly limiting to the progress of our practice.

For example, if you are aggressive and ambitious, you will meditate aggressively and ambitiously. This is not correct. It is not the same as being aware in the present moment. I've always been a shy person, so my meditation has had some of that timidity—a very limited approach.

Of course, no one is a perfect meditator. It's not like we have to wait until we have a perfect attitude before we begin. If that were the case, we would never start. This in itself is another obstacle—"I really want to meditate, but I can't until my attitude changes." So we try the best we can, but we don't want to be stupid either. Don't bash your head against the wall; get up and walk through the door. With time, the purity of your attitude will grow. The Japanese founder of Soto Zen, Dogen Zenji, often taught that practice and enlightenment were the same thing. "Perfect practice is perfect enlightenment." Not so perfect is very little enlightenment. From this we can see that refining one's approach is a lifetime's work and is, at the same time, the practice itself.

What's the problem in meditating with an attitude? First, a large amount of energy goes into maintaining the attitude. To make this clearer, if we are trying to be aware of our breathing, 100 percent of our attention should be on our breathing. If we're thinking, "I'm a shy person and I'm a little afraid of what's going on here," even if we're not consciously aware of that thought, it will be taking energy away from breathing and keeping it tied up in the world of ego. Consequently, this energy is not available for our practice. This also holds true if you're meditating competitively—you're spending most of your energy looking over your shoulder. It's like the old saying of trying to do something with one hand tied behind your back. You're trying so hard to be pure or disciplined or whatever, meditating assertively or cautiously, you have very little energy left to be aware.

With these attitudes, you'll be heading in the wrong direction. Your evaluation of your practice and progress will be based on your agenda rather than on the Buddha's teaching. You'll be more interested in maintaining your flamboyance, for example, than in true spiritual growth. If your practice starts to undermine your flamboyance, you might feel you're doing it wrong and abandon it.

Finally, to meditate incorrectly, with an uptight mind or with a particular style, creates a certain tension between your volition and the natural unfolding of meditation. When done correctly, meditation results in the unfolding of the mind. As it expands, its repressed contents come to the surface. But your attitude might prevent this. So you have this clash—the rising of buried feelings, bumping into the harsh, unrecognized qualities of various attitudes. These buried feelings are often the same ones that propel your incorrect attitudes to begin with. An aggressive meditator may have a lot of buried rage and pain that needs to be released in order to progress, but the aggressiveness will always be in conflict. I used to think my timidity was a lack of aggression, and I mistook it for true detachment. When my practice started to undermine these patterns by revealing them, I would feel uncomfortable and look for a way out.

You might find this discussion of attitudes threatening or insulting. No one wants to be told they're practicing incorrectly. We don't want to hear that we are uptight or repressed, that we are unskillful in dealing with our pain. We just want to continue doing what we are doing. But there's a Tibetan saying that the highest teaching is the one that reveals our hidden faults. So if you can be made more aware of your faults in practice and any mistake you might be making, it will only result in what you most truly desire—progress in your spiritual development. Remember, I know of these mistakes because I've made them all myself. Practice involves a radical transformation of our being, and we have to learn to face and eventually dissolve all the attitudes we have about everything, not only meditation. So check yourself out.

We can summarize all these styles and agendas by saying that most people, including me, meditate with too much effort. The way you meditate and the effort you apply is an expression of your ego on a deep level. By reducing the intensity of the effort, the personality of the meditator will change for the better. What was once unconscious drive will be recognized and then released by simply making the effort to meditate more subtle. If we meditate gently, with a certain kindness toward ourselves, we will become gentler, kinder people. It is less important that our meditation improves; it is better that we as meditators improve. But I think you will find that if the meditator improves, the meditation will follow along naturally.

This discussion may sound a little depressing, but I assure you that when you can let go of these strategies, you will really begin to make progress with your practice. There will be a lot more space and energy in your mind with which to meditate and a growing sense of openness as you demand less from your practice.

With that as a lengthy introduction, let's discuss the faults themselves. Some people see meditation as a form of punishment or feel guilty about not meditating. If you come from a very religious upbringing, you might have this attitude. Meditation becomes a burden, a cross to bear. This attitude constricts the mind and prevents any joy from entering it. And guilt is rarely beneficial—we usually feel guilty as a way to compensate for doing something we shouldn't have. "If I feel really bad about not meditating, perhaps that's almost as good as doing the meditation." That's how guilt usually works. If you realize you haven't been as diligent as you should, don't feel guilty. Just practice.

Your meditation session should be a time that you should look forward to. Of course, there will be times where sitting will be difficult for you. Nonetheless, even the worst times can be experienced as a challenge, and the best can be a sheer joy. Don't make it into a punishment. If you think of meditation as a kind of punishment, a penance, it will eventually become one. It will be something heavy and depressing, and you'll have no option but to give it up. If you practice with a happy mind, you'll do much better.

My retreat master at Samye Ling, Lama Yeshe Losal, said, "If I were making you build a building, I could push you and, at the end of the day, count how many bricks you had laid. However, meditation isn't like that. Two hours practiced with a happy mind is better than sixteen hours practiced as a burden."

Don't practice to please or seduce your teacher. Although they will express pleasure with your diligence, don't be coy about it. They are already enlightened; they're not your proud parents. You're not going to hurt their feelings if you don't practice. They are beyond all that. What kind of habitual pattern are you acting out with this one? It's almost impossible not to project your parents onto your teacher, but it's up to you to be aware of it as it happens. We practice because our buddha-nature demands it; we practice to purify our minds and heal our being; we practice to liberate all motherly sentient beings. We don't practice to please anyone else.

Many people have strong self-discipline, to the point where they always seem to be competing with themselves. With some practices such as the preliminaries, where you have a set number to do, this attitude seems almost unavoidable. "I've done three hundred prostrations today. If only I could push myself a little and do four hundred, I could be finished in March." I've counted how long I could hold my breath, how long I could sit in the full lotus position, how little sleep I could get by on, how often I lost semen in my sleep. So what? Does it really matter? Maybe a little. But the attitude becomes overwhelming. Everything becomes a test; everything becomes measured and quantified. If it can't be quantified, how do we know how we're doing?

The basis of this pattern is a separation of oneself into a good mind and a bad body. The good mind is always monitoring and controlling the bad body. "If only I could control my [fill in the blank], then I'm sure my practice would take off."

Of course, discipline is necessary. It's the attitude that's problematic. There's actually nothing inherently wrong with the body—it's just our temporary guesthouse. Our watching, judging mind is an altogether different matter. That is the real problem. This is exactly what we're trying to *eliminate* in our practice—not to glorify or worship. This kind of discipline trip can only reinforce the ego. Then, as your practice starts to undermine your ego, you are torn in two. Be forewarned—this can become dangerous if carried to extremes. You might even become schizophrenic.

A similar pattern is to meditate with a competitive attitude. The person next to you is sitting in full lotus, so you sit in full lotus. Your friend finished their ngondro, so you break your neck trying to finish yours. You might even do a three-year retreat just because others have done one or try to accumulate as many empowerments or teachings as your friends. How silly. I've noticed this a lot among Western followers of the Nyingma lineage—we're always finding out about new termas. Be the first one on your block...

Or we can compete with historical characters. All Tibetan Buddhists, but especially the Kagyupas, are inspired by the example of the great yogi Milarepa. His biography and songs have been available in English for a long time. When reading them, it's difficult not to measure yourself against him. But how much do we really know about him? What was a sane and successful style of practice for him may not be so for us; we are very different people. Also, did Milarepa practice the way he did to compete with someone else, or was his diligence a natural expression of his own character and understanding? Let our diligence be the same—a sincere expression of our deepest aspirations. Once again, practicing based on competition can only enforce our ego, not undermine it. Don't do it.

We all have different past lives and different propensities in this life. Why would meditation unfold in the same way for everybody? If you deem your meditation to be inferior to that of others, try to understand that we all have separate paths to follow. If your friends seem to be doing better than you, rejoice and think you will have fewer sentient beings to liberate once you're a buddha.

If you are really stuck feeling like a failure, pray to your guru. Also you can do tonglen for all the other beings struggling with their mental states. It is better to feel compassion for others than to feel sorry for yourself.

Obviously, another fault or wrong attitude would be to meditate chiefly for worldly benefit. You might meditate for the traditional benefits of long life, good health, and prosperity. Although these are helpful for practitioners, if they become ends in themselves, they become obstacles. Also, you could be practicing to appear more spiritual. Perhaps you'll have better luck finding a partner! You might want to be famous as a meditator. The needs of our ego are vast, and this list can go on and on. It becomes more and more subtle too. An attitude that's appropriate for newcomers would be an obstacle for older practitioners. To learn more about this, you can read Trungpa Rinpoche's excellent *Cutting Through Spiritual Materialism*.

Many people come to meditation to relieve themselves of stress or anxiety. As a teacher, I have found that students with this motivation usually don't succeed. There's nothing wrong with wanting to be free of stress and anxiety, but if that wish isn't conjoined with a sincere interest in spiritual transformation, it won't carry the student along. There are probably better ways (at least in the short term) of dealing with stress or anxiety, and anxious practitioners might find that their practice simply throws them right into the center of their anxiety.

If I had to name one fault as the most prevalent and dastardly, both for my friends and myself, it would be using meditation to escape from psychological pain. Let's face it, we all hurt. If we didn't, we wouldn't be contemplating something as weird as getting involved with Tibetan Buddhism. Then we think, "If only I could find a nice peaceful space inside where I could hang out, free from my depression, my sadness. If I were to meditate, I would feel bliss-ful and would, therefore, have no time or place for the pain." Don't we all think like that? So we use meditation as an escape from pain. It seems we're doing everything right, following the instructions perfectly. We might even become successful in creating an inner sanctuary for ourselves. When we sit down, the pain and stress dissolves, and we feel calm. We start thinking about changing our conditions so we can become even calmer and hurt even less.

What's wrong with this attitude? We are never addressing the cause, the source of our pain. We are not purifying it, we are not understanding it, we are not transforming it. We are simply using spiritual techniques to ignore and run away from it. Our pain is still there. It will stay there until we decide to do something about it other than pretend it's not there and hope it will somehow go away. No matter how long we meditate like this, it'll catch up to us.

One way your pain might manifest is in psychosomatic illnesses. Your blocked energy will start to hurt your health. Another is through projection; you'll project your unfinished business onto others by judging them. I was celibate for a long time. Although this can be a wonderful discipline, freeing oneself to practice more, for me it was an escape from all sorts of relationship problems. I would, therefore, judge any noncelibate practitioner as not really serious and then feel myself superior. It was my way of not dealing with my issues. I feel that many of the difficulties at centers and of "Dharma politics" come from projections similar to this. It's especially diffi-cult for people who are trying to be spiritual to acknowledge their anger; as a result, that anger is frequently projected outward. Everybody is projecting everything onto everybody else. What a mess!

Sooner or later, something will happen that upsets your calm in such a way that you can no longer ignore your patterns. You start to see yourself for who you really are. It's insulting. For me, it was doing a group retreat. Try living with seventeen other men in a claustro-phobic environment for four years! It is impossible to pretend to be calm and peaceful for too long. My faults would eventually annoy someone else; others' faults would always annoy me. There was no place to hide. Also, you can no longer use the Dharma as a weapon against others—they'll throw it right back on you.

When we practice, we must always practice into the pain. If you are angry, go into the anger. If you're depressed, go into the depres-sion. It's the only way to purify it. Your courage and ability to jump right into your pain will determine how fast you progress, how quickly you heal. Remember, there's really nothing to your pain. What are its characteristics? Where does it live? What can it really do to you? Resisting it, trying to run away from it, gives your pain a certain solidity and a hold over you. A brave friend of mine repeats to herself, "It's only pain," almost like a mantra.

When you turn around and begin to face your pain, you discover there's really nothing to it. It's strange—from one side, it looks so solid and formidable; from the other, it's only a light mist. Your resistance is probably a remnant from an earlier period of your life when you had no resources to deal with your feelings. You had no viable options other than denying the pain or dissociating from it. So it just sat there in the back of your mind, seemingly out of the way but secretly running your life.

Things have changed. You're older, stronger, and wiser. You don't have to escape pain anymore; it's simply an old habit that you've outgrown. Now you have the best resource possible—the Buddha-dharma. Now when you look at your pain, it may hurt for a little while, but so what? It slowly disappears, and you wonder what the big deal was. Each time you do this, you heal a little more. You reclaim a little more of your lost self. You become more confident in your ability to cope with life. And your deep trust and confidence in Buddhism and the path of meditation will only increase.

At this point, you will be happy when garbage comes up, when situations provoke hidden flaws to come to the surface. You will have gotten into the rhythm of dealing with them, and each time you do so, your mind will open up more.

You might be wondering that if what I'm saying is so important, why don't the lamas speak of it more? When I last saw Chökyi Nyima Rinpoche in Nepal, I asked him about this point. He agreed with my analysis and added that lamas assume that when they teach the Dharma, listeners will apply the teachings correctly to their own minds. It takes a while for the lamas to learn that Westerners are not necessarily able to do this immediately, that the issues of personal problems and woundedness must be addressed distinctly and explicitly.

As I have gained the confidence to practice in this way and gotten to know more people as a teacher and friend, I have learned that we all have a tremendous burden of pain and unresolved issues from the past. It's not just you and me; it's everybody. We're all carrying this big bag of shit around. It's universal—nobody is special or exempt. Of course, we have a hard time meditating. Who wouldn't, carrying this bag? So open the bag up and go through it, turd by smelly turd. As any hiker can tell you, the lighter your pack, the faster and easier your walk will be. Throw away those turds! Why would you want to keep them?

Check carefully. When any negativity arises in your mind, how do you deal with it? Do you use the Dharma to go toward it, or do you run away from it?

Related to attitude is our intention or motivation. Why are we really embarking on this journey? Why are we giving up our precious sleep to get up a little earlier to do our practice?

In theory, if we're Hinayanists, we are practicing to escape the suffering of samsara, and if we're Mahayanists, we are practicing to bring all motherly sentient beings to buddhahood. However, to develop even a sincere Hinayana motivation is actually difficult.

The essence of the Hinayana view is egolessness. In other words, the Hinayanist meditates to unravel their mind in the same way that we might unravel a blanket until it is nothing more than a pile of yarn. Everything we think we are dissolves in that process. How can we, as beginners, possibly aspire to do something so utterly radical and seemingly suicidal?

For now, we must always check our motivation. For most of us, it is likely that our motivation is still quite worldly. Let's examine a few of these possibilities.

We may want to have magnificent experiences. If we took LSD when we were younger, we might imagine that the purpose of meditation is to reproduce those kinds of experiences. Similarly, we may want to sedate ourselves. Instead of being a substitute stimulant, it takes the place of alcohol, marijuana, or tranquilizers. We might want ecstatic experiences, cures for illnesses, or feelings of being loved by a higher being, or we may simply want to have a more relaxed, simple, mellow life.

Who doesn't want experiences like that? I sure do. Unfortunately, none of this has anything to do with unraveling the mind. It is simply creating entertainments for the ego.

Also, we might want to meditate to become a certain type of person or to fit a certain kind of role. We may meditate to gain respect, admiration, or power. We see this in the worst spiritual scandals all the time. People always ask, if so-and-so has been practicing for so long, how could they act this way? The answer is that so-and-so was practicing with the wrong motivation; they didn't check up, and they got the wrong results.

Here is where we need to think about the Mahayana motivation of compassion. We're not practicing to become rich, powerful, or respected. We are practicing to become the perfect servant of all motherly sentient beings. So the dissolution of the ego must be even more complete than in the Hinayana school—we can't just sit back and watch ourselves dissolve. Toward the end of this book, we will discuss the dissolution process and how it relates to our Western ideas of self in greater detail. Here I want to emphasize that although we, as ordinary, flawed human beings, may have real needs that we feel meditation can address, we can't separate our practice from the view. As we hear teachings and read books and contemplate them, our understanding of the spiritual path will deepen. We must take that understanding and work to bring our meditation in line with it. It's a slow, gradual process. A good motivation is a sign of practice; a truly compassionate or egoless being is already highly accomplished.

A more subtle or, one could say, somewhat more advanced mistake deals with mindfulness. Mindfulness is the basis of any meditation, tantric or not. If we're not attentive, how can we possibly meditate correctly? However, we can still make mistakes while being mindful.

If, when you were young, your strategy for dealing with pain was to dissociate, separating from your experience to diminish its intensity, then you may have developed a personality that observes your life rather than living it. In this state of observation, one does not feel one's pain. When people with this tendency meditate, they appear to be doing well and always seem mindful, calm, and meditative. The fault here is subtle but important, as it applies to many of us. In a sense, we are too distant, too detached. Our detachment is based on fear. We feel that if we were really to experience what is happening, it would be unbearable in some way or other—too intense, too painful. So our detachment is not real detachment or mindfulness; it's a kind of habitual frozen fear or paranoia. We think we are being mindful and meditating in the present when, in actuality, we're fearfully dissociating and living in the past. We can go on like this for a long time and in the meantime feel drawn to the Buddhist tradition with its emphasis on detachment.

Many Westerners are this way. I certainly am, although I'm trying hard to break this pattern. People who are very cerebral or intellectual can be like this. We feel Buddhism gives us permission to be dissociated. Other people will see us as meditative and will compliment us. We'll feel we've finally found what we've been looking for—Buddhism will seem so right to us. Why? Because finally our negative patterns seem to be supported. And meditation can serve to enforce this pattern almost indefinitely.

A good test to see if this applies to you is to check if you're capable of true feeling. Do you ever cry? How do you feel about your teacher? How do you react to the suffering of others? Can you love, be passionate? If you don't think your feelings are very strong, you might be this kind of person. You need to have a capacity for true, deep feeling and its attendant responsiveness, as well as an ability for real detachment. Remember, true detachment happens in the present and is born of choice—you choose to observe, to be mindful. Detachment should be free of judgments, free of condemnation, and free of fear. Fear is something from which to detach yourself; fear is something to purify, not to indulge in as a kind of meditation. But you must be able to feel. Without this ability, you will never be able to generate compassion, and your development will always be stunted.

This is a mistake that takes more than noticing to correct. You actually have to try to be emotional. Whatever makes you feel, try to cultivate it. Notice how it feels to feel! Get a puppy, fall in love.

I will tell you the story of how I overcame or at least began to overcome this problem. It's rather long; I hope you don't mind.

I had been a fairly diligent and consistent practitioner for about twenty years before I began teaching. Also, I seriously believed in the value of living a celibate, solitary lifestyle. Underneath, I was dissociated, although I was hardly aware of it.

Almost as soon as I began teaching, I was approached by a lovely woman who was seriously interested in my guidance. Her physical beauty was matched only by the beauty of her heart—I had never met such a loving being. I immediately fell in love despite every effort not to do so. I kept my feelings to myself but saw her frequently as we were living in the same small spiritual community.

How did I feel? Believe it or not, the unrequited love was wonderful. Although at times the longing was painful, and it was excruciating to see her with another man, it was the most transforming experience of my life. I was able to feel, able to love. The joy of opening up was far greater than the pain of longing. I was able to see all the negativity I had been holding behind my veneer as a detached meditator. And I was able to let go of these negativities. I became a very different person—the change was also obvious to my friends.

Circumstances changed, and we started contemplating becoming partners. We consulted Gyatrul Rinpoche, who said to me, "You've lived in a shell all your life. You haven't hurt anybody, but you haven't been of any benefit either. Now you have the chance to take care of someone." This was his commentary on my twenty years of serious practice!

Since we've been together, the shell continues to break. I continue to grow, and my meditation is also much stronger. I'm not putting down retreats or celibacy, but sometimes I feel that you truly have to love samsara before you can renounce it; otherwise, your renunciation is simply fear or aversion. So if you feel drawn to celibacy or solitude, I'm just warning you of some possible hidden attitudes behind that attraction that could undermine your practice the way they undermined mine.

The opposite of being too detached is to be "too merged," another common mistake made by Western practitioners. Some people identify or seem to become one with whatever they place their minds on. They are extremely empathetic with others. When this identification focuses on our inner world of thoughts and emotions, it can become problematic. Being too merged means becoming absorbed in one's inner landscape, the thoughts and emotions. The merged meditator becomes fascinated with the thoughts and feelings that arise through practice and prefers the fascination to a true meditation experience. Wonderful insights keep arising, the time flies, and we feel we could practice all day. Or else we become intoxicated with our feelings. We wish we could stop sitting so we could write a poem about the weather or the back of the head of the person in front of us. We could rush to our therapist and spend hours sharing our experience. Trungpa Rinpoche said the two groups of people who had the most difficulty meditating were poets and therapists—the two groups most identified and merged with their thoughts and feelings.

Another aspect of this fascination is what I call "emotional enthrallment." When we look at the mind, it is often in one of two states: a strong defiled state, such as anger or anxiety; or a prolonged heavy state, such as depression, grief, or sadness. We become aware of this state (let's take depression as an example), and as a result, we feel that we are being mindful. But somehow the depression persists. With time, not only does it persist, but through our attention, we notice more and more about it and eventually start analyzing the various causes of it. We might spend a great deal of time discussing our depression with our friends, and we might even write about it. Many years of valuable time and practice can be wasted in this manner.

The purpose of Buddhist meditation is to purify the mind of suffering (such as depression) and the causes of suffering (such as anger), but our practice doesn't seem to be working. We feel we are being mindful, yet the depression persists rather than dissipates. What are we doing wrong?

Our fault lies in confusing attachment with mindfulness. Of course, we are aware of our depression; if we weren't, we wouldn't know that we were depressed. We are not, however, aware of how "sucked in" or enthralled we are by the depression. We are similar to zoned-out TV viewers who are barely above the drooling state. Although we are aware, all of our power, life force, clarity, and so on has been surrendered to our emotion. Our depression has taken all our energy, leaving none for us, the supposedly mindful practitioner. No wonder the state persists, and we are unable to do anything about it. We have been weakened and drained through our fascination.

Obviously, this is not the correct practice of mindfulness. What can we do? Based on my own experience, I can make several suggestions. Try any combination you feel may help:

- First and most essential, notice that you are in a state of enthrallment rather than mindfulness. Otherwise, nothing else will work.
- Rather than being aware of the emotion, be aware of your attachment to it. This will lead to a clear detachment.
- Be aware of the situation energetically. Breaking enthrallment involves pulling energy from the emotion back toward the aware practitioner.

· Try to create a spacious, clear state of awareness. Notice your emotion from that perspective.
· Try to visualize something—for example, a clear light or a letter in your heart. Notice your emotion from that perspective.
· Pray. Once again, notice your emotion.

With any of these techniques, the more correctly they are done, the more you will find the strength of the emotion decreasing. It will start to be purified. In the beginning, it will take tremendous effort to have even a momentary experience. But with that momentary experience, you will see the contrast between the enthralled state, originally believed to be a form of mindfulness, and a more correct and pure state of mind. With time, it will take less effort, the positive state will persist longer, and the habit of enthrallment will slowly be broken.

One thing about correct mindfulness is that there should be a gap between the meditating mind and the disturbing emotion. Learning to recognize and cultivate this gap is something I find very important and teach in classes and retreats. For more details, see Dzogchen Ponlop Rinpoche's excellent book *Emotional Rescue*.

Many times I've heard lamas asked why it seems Westerners make so little progress with their practice. Rather than talking about things like laziness, differences in upbringing, or lack of faith, lamas almost always say that Westerners are using their practice time for self-psychoanalysis rather than for correct meditation. As I've become more aware of the enthrallment in my own mind, I see how easy it is to become stuck for long periods of time and have come to agree more and more with their assessment.

Both the detached and merged attitudes have their positive aspects. The detached meditator has a sharp, nonjudging awareness. The merged practitioner has a greater capacity for opening ego boundaries and developing a sense of oneness and compassion. Both of these qualities are needed on the path.

As we practice, we notice more and more of these hidden agendas. They're all based on using meditation to prop up the ego rather than to undermine it. Each time you notice one of these mechanisms, you'll feel shocked and a little embarrassed that you have been fooling yourself. But once you release it, your meditation will deepen.

Another problem most of us have, especially in the beginning, is unrealistic expectations. We need to deal with them. Expectations and misunderstandings regarding the teachings are as numerous as the teachings themselves. Therefore, I would like to address the most prominent expectations regarding meditation.

One is the belief that there is a special technique that, if you could only discover it, would rapidly transform your mind. Especially if you have gathered information about Tibetan Buddhist techniques, you may believe that if you searched from one lama to the next, you could find this magic teaching. But in reality, it is something like searching for calculus while we are in the third grade. Powerful techniques may not be that powerful for everyone; they all have their prerequisites that most of us haven't met. If there were one technique that was the most efficacious for everyone, that would be the only one Lord Buddha would have taught. I have found that some basic Mahayana practices have been wonderfully transformative, while the more esoteric Vajrayana ones have often been beyond my capacity and therefore not very useful. So it is probably counterproductive to pine away for some secret instruction while ignoring the present opportunity to practice a technique that might be the best thing for you. If you are fortunate enough to have a close relationship with a good instructor, accept their advice on this matter.

The reality is this: no matter what technique you are using, the mind is habituated to go in one direction, while you want it to go in a new one. The struggle between these two directions is the real process of meditation.

The main preconceptions I have to address as a teacher of meditation involve the relationship between meditation and thoughts. First, there's "I should be able to eliminate my thoughts." Probably not going to happen. The main cause of thinking is the stimulation caused by the parts of the day when you aren't meditating quietly.

Therefore, the main cause for eliminating thoughts is isolation. If you are unable to isolate yourself for long periods of time, your meditation will be filled with thoughts about what you just did or what you are going to do. It is natural and unavoidable.

Second is "Everyone else is sitting so quietly. I'm the only one whose mind is in turmoil!" Nope, we're all the same—see the preceding paragraph. A friend of mind quoted Alcoholics Anonymous, "Don't judge your inner by someone else's outer." Very good advice.

Third is "Until I stop thinking, I will not experience the benefits of meditation." This one is almost universal in the beginning, so I will address it at length. As Buddhists, we believe we have been in some sort of existence since beginningless time. Over the course of all those lifetimes, we have been thinking. And we have made some basic but erroneous assumptions about those thoughts that have gotten us into a lot of trouble.

The first assumption is "I am thinking these thoughts; these are my thoughts." If thinking were the product of a real self, then two things should be true: we should be able to apprehend that true self—recognize its nature and characteristics—and that true self should be able to stop and start the thought process at will. Neither of those is true.

The second assumption is "I believe those thoughts. Their content is valid. They refer to something true." Well, most Buddhist philosophy is a refutation of that notion. For now, we can notice that the thoughts, "I need another piece of cake," or "My partner is really a sociopath," are probably neither true nor helpful.

The third assumption is "I need to do what my thoughts tell me to do." If I think, "I need another piece of cake," then I really do need another piece of cake, it would be beneficial to have another piece of cake, and I should stop what I'm doing to acquire and eat that cake.

If you think about these points, you can easily conclude that a great deal, if not all, of the world's suffering is caused by how we misapprehend thoughts and then get hooked by them. We completely lose ourselves to them, forget our enlightened nature, and become unconscious.

So let us view meditation as a process of not getting hooked by thoughts rather than eliminating them. Really, they are never going to stop. But over time, we can train ourselves not to be seduced by them but to observe them and let them pass through the mind and move on.

Now when we meditate, thoughts arise, we get hooked, we realize we're hooked, we reestablish our meditation. Over and over and over. It seems boring. It seems like nothing is happening. We get discouraged.

But something is happening! Every time we reestablish mindfulness and awareness, we break the chains of samsara, of bondage, of suffering. We are breaking an eons-long, negative habit and building an extremely positive new habit—being aware. Until we began meditating, our thoughts and the negative emotions that drive them were mostly unconscious. Meditating brings them into awareness and allows us to break the strong hold they have over us. What could be more important than that?

It might not be apparent what is truly going on. But imagine you have been meditating for a while. Thoughts, awareness, thoughts, awareness. Boring. Then perhaps, one day at work, a coworker loses their temper at you as they have done on countless previous occasions. And just like on those countless other occasions, you prepare your rebuttal.

But this time as your oh-so-clever comeback is about to go hurling out your mouth toward your antagonist, you notice, "Gee, that's a thought." You watch it go by and feel absolutely no need to express it. So you smile at your coworker and shrug your shoulders. Your coworker is taken aback at first, shocked at your lack of retaliation. But what can they do? You just smiled and shrugged. They smile back sheepishly, and perhaps over time you learn to get along with each other, communicate and understand each other, and eventually become friends. Your life has just become more workable and enjoyable.

The cause of this change? Your boring meditation. Every time you meditate, you are breaking the habits of negativity. If you simply wait for the thoughts to stop so you can begin to meditate properly, that attitude might prevent situations like the one with co-workers from taking place.

With time, because you are reacting to your thoughts less and less, they lose their energy. Instead of someone blasting loud rock music at you, your thoughts become more like boring but quiet elevator music. What a relief! You feel a lightness and a freedom arising from this lessening of clinging to thoughts that permeates every aspect of your life. You become a calmer, happier, and kinder person. Other people notice it too, and your relationships with others improve significantly. You look forward to your meditation; it is both pleasant and rewarding to do, and you are appreciative and grateful for its effect on the rest of your life. *All the while, when you meditate, you have lots of thoughts.*

Here's another way to look at thoughts. Most of us have a bad habit of being overly critical and judgmental toward ourselves. We have a cruel taskmaster inside that's constantly flogging us with a barbed whip of self-condemnation. Of course, when we meditate, we think, "Why can't you do this simple task? Everyone else can. You're a failure at this just like everything else."

Now imagine this scenario. You meditate. The thoughts arise, the self-criticism arises. But instead of getting hooked by the criticism, you let it go. You train yourself to treat the thoughts, distractions, and emotions that arise in your mind the way you treat your precious puppy that just urinated on the carpet. You don't get truly angry at the puppy; that's just what puppies do. Likewise, thinking and emoting are just what minds do. We can train ourselves to view our mental processes in a more accepting, loving way.

After several months of meditation, we still have lots of thoughts, the same as before. But when we notice these thoughts, we embrace them with acceptance and self-love rather than criticism. How would this shift from criticism to love affect our lives? In so many positive ways!

You get the picture; it's not the thoughts that are the problem, it is how we view them and deal with them. Don't wait for them to end; embrace them in your practice now.

There are worldly benefits we shouldn't place too much emphasis on: improved health, the ability to magnetize wealth or people, and so on. You might be going to a Dharma center with the hope of meeting people. You may want to cure yourself of excessive anger or shyness so you function better with others. Or you could be meditating with the thought, often unconscious, that you want to feel better about yourself by having a self-image of being a "spiritual person" or wanting others to see you in that light.

Not all expectations regarding meditation are incorrect, misplaced, or obstacle-creating. In fact, the only reason anyone meditates is because they expect positive results. However, these expectations should be reasonable relative to the diligence of the practitioner and the way meditation really works. We will be discussing the benefits of practice later.

Another common mistake one can make is to mistake mastering some aspect of Tibetan Buddhism like ritual or academics for spiritual progress. This expectation is especially pernicious because it is so hard to recognize. I have fallen prey to it myself. Instead of genuinely reducing the power of negative emotions, I feel good about myself because of attaining a certain mastery over the details of Vajrayana practice.

Consider the following scenario. As a newcomer, you attend a ritual at a Vajrayana center. When you first attend, it is overwhelming: how to prostrate, how to follow the text (which often skips around seemingly randomly), how to recite the Tibetan and Sanskrit words, and so forth. Later, when chatting with the other participants, you hear a bewildering number of names of lamas, lineages, deities, and practices. It's mind-boggling, and you sense everyone must be very accomplished.

But you stick it out. You learn your way around the texts. You learn the background information and theory, you learn the *mudras* (hand movements), and eventually you learn to, say, play the drum or make tormas.

You start to feel a sense of accomplishment. You start to feel good about yourself, that you are no longer a complete beginner. New students start to ask you questions, and you answer with confidence and kindness. You imagine they look up to you. When you look back over the several years this process took, you have a sense of progress, and you feel positive, happy, and optimistic about your involvement in Buddhism. You look forward to continuing this process.

But nothing has happened. These positive feelings are pride at mastering the outer forms of Buddhism. Once again, they have nothing to do with overcoming the five negative emotions and real spiritual growth. But because you feel more and more positive about your involvement, this confusion is hard to recognize.

I truly hope you can avoid the mistakes I've made in practice. I also hope that these few tips can be of help.

CHAPTER 10

The Four Noble Truths

After attaining enlightenment, Lord Buddha began teaching. His first teaching was that of the Four Noble Truths. Most readers are probably familiar with these already, and it's easy to understand them on a basic level. I've taught them to American high school students without a problem. However, thorough insight into these truths is tantamount to a high degree of realization. Thus, if we're really going to understand the intricacies of tantric Buddhism, we should start here, at the beginning.

The Four Noble Truths are the truth of suffering, the truth of its cause, the truth of its cessation, and the truth of the path. I read somewhere that they follow the same formula that Ayurvedic doctors use when talking with their patients: the disease, its cause, its cessation, and the treatment. That's how Lord Buddha saw himself—as a doctor for the suffering of humanity.

I think this is a clearer way to explain it: the first two truths are suffering and the cause of suffering, the second two are happiness and the cause of happiness. This illustrates that we are definitely aspiring to a life of greater joy and not simply numbing our pain by being detached.

We all have bad times. It's amazing how miserable we can be. Even when most things are okay, just a small thing can ruin our day. Lama Tsering said we are like someone with a beautiful cup who only notices the small chip in it. We're just waiting for the next bad thing to happen.

Suffering can be gross, such as when we're really sick or in pain, or it can be a subtle mental pain. Whatever it is, we're not operating optimally, and the focus of our attention is not on the positive. We're like the princess with the single pea under seventeen mattresses.

Some people say that Buddhism is wrong for concentrating on this unhappiness. To this, Chökyi Nyima Rinpoche replies, "If people were happy and the Buddha said they were suffering, that would be an error. But we should examine closely our real condition. Did the Buddha make it up, or was he simply describing the way things really are?"

To really understand and appreciate the first noble truth, we have to dive a little deeper into the meaning of suffering. Traditionally, it is divided into three kinds.

The first is the suffering of suffering. You're sick, you're depressed, you're in pain. Your significant other dumped you. We are all familiar with this; everyone knows this is suffering.

The third form of suffering is often translated as "all-pervasive suffering." It is so subtle that only bodhisattvas are aware of it. We need not concern ourselves with it here.

It's the second form of suffering that's the key for us. It's usually called the "suffering of change." It applies to what most people refer to as happiness. Why is ordinary happiness suffering? There are two reasons: first, our happiness is impermanent and will always change into the suffering of suffering. We work hard, save for a lovely vacation. We go away and have an amazing time. But we come back home, go back to work, and what happens to all that happiness we just experienced? It has vanished.

Second, in the moment we are happy, we cling to it. We want it to last forever. That clinging to something that is impermanent as if it were permanent is suffering; recognizing this gives us greater confidence in the noble truths.

If we don't appreciate the suffering of clinging, we will still harbor hope that while we sometimes suffer, sometimes we are also happy; maybe we can win this game. Maybe impermanence can be our friend; our misery is also impermanent. But we should remember that we experience either a gross unhappiness in the first suffering or a subtler unhappiness in the second suffering. Both are far from the cessation of suffering!

What is the cause of suffering? Traditionally, the Buddha said that desire is the cause, but there are many slightly different variations. Sometimes we're taught that the disturbing emotions in general are the cause; sometimes karma is also included. Chökyi Nyima Rinpoche often explains the cause of suffering in terms of the yanas: Hinayanists consider desire to be the cause of suffering; Mahayanists, aversion; and Vajrayanists, ignorance.

Whatever poison you are more aware of will color your approach to the path. If you are more aware of desire, you will feel more drawn to a renunciate's life. You will see ordinary life as an indulgence in desire and attachment, and you will always be trying to simplify your life, to find contentment in whatever situation you find yourself.

If you perceive aversion as the cause of suffering, your approach will be the opposite. Renunciation will seem like avoidance, indulging in aversion. You will try to lead a normal life and use the experience of work and family as a way of overcoming aversion and generating compassion. Retreat might tempt you, and it is always beneficial, but you will find normal life challenging, rewarding, and rich.

The Vajrayanist tries to overcome ignorance, the lack of recognizing one's buddha-nature in all mind states. This practitioner may lean toward a life of either renunciation or involvement and may occasionally become wild or nihilistic in an attempt to eradicate the conceptual mind. Such people, no matter how lofty their view, must also eventually settle down and apply themselves to the disciplines of the lower vehicles.

I think there's a little of all three in all of us. We don't really have to make any rigid classifications or barriers in our lives. In fact, we must always work on all three poisons, and we must deal with any situation in which we find ourselves. There's no question that a simple life provides greater opportunity for formal practice and the cultivation of deeper experiences in our practice; however, daily life, especially its conflicts, gives us an opportunity to discover our blind spots, unconscious attitudes to which we are holding on that can block our meditation. For me, Chökyi Nyima Rinpoche has always advocated a lifestyle that alternates between practice and being with others. With time, I have come to appreciate his wisdom. Each facet touches a different aspect of our being. We can see that all three poisons are always present; all three poisons cause us to feel this constant dissatisfaction.

To repeat, the third truth says that the cessation of the causes is the cessation of suffering. Easy to understand, right? But when we practice, aren't we trying to create experiences (desire) or escape from our annoying present mental state (aversion)? It seems like we're doing it right, but aren't we really indulging in the three poisons? If we are, can we ever hope to attain freedom from suffering?

Milarepa said that the first main deviation for a practitioner is to drift into Hinayana quietism. I did it for years. I wanted a peaceful environment so that I could cultivate blissful experiences; I was lucky (or unlucky!) enough to find them in the mountains of India or living near my teacher in the Kathmandu valley. When there was some disturbance, I longed for an even quieter, more peaceful and removed environment. Rather than dealing with the disturbance, I blamed everything on the conditions—never myself. If only I could find a place free from mosquitoes, traffic noise, or whatever, *then* I could really meditate. Disturbances were to be endured with a sense of self-righteous patience, hoping to get back to the bliss as soon as possible. When some experience or conflict with a person intimated that I was still holding on to a truckload of neuroses, I avoided dealing with it and dismissed the problem as "only" psychology. I was above all that. I reasoned that if only I could stay in retreat and continue to bliss out, the problem would automatically disappear, that meditation itself would uproot it. After all, great yogis who attained high levels of realization were hardly neurotic people.

There is both truth and value in that approach. It will work for some of the people some of the time. I certainly benefited from those years. But it took more active involvement with others—in a group retreat, as a teacher, and as a husband and stepfather—for me to start to confront my deeper layers of defilements. For me, these take the form of strong aversion, resistance, or negativity toward most people, activities, and situations. This aversion has hidden behind my yearning for solitude and retreat. By dealing with this negativity, much growth has resulted. And I'm not talking about a purely psychological or therapeutic growth; by dealing with aversion as it manifests in ordinary life, my meditation has deepened in a way it never did in a more idyllic retreat. Why? Because I'm working on the defilements that create suffering, and as they slowly abate, I'm experiencing a more wholesome and less samsaric life. From the outside it might seem that I've given up my practice and become more worldly, but internally I know I'm practicing more sincerely than before, that my practice is in harmony with the noble truths and not some sort of hippie fantasy.

I'm not putting down retreats themselves. Twenty-five hundred years of Buddhist history speaks for itself. If you have the opportunity to do a retreat, great. In fact, I would suggest even going so far as to take on some hardship so that your retreat can take place; that would be wonderful. I would, however, like to emphasize this: make your practice harmonize with Lord Buddha's teaching, not with some idealized dream you have. In retreat or in the world, we always have to deal with our minds and with who we are. When in retreat, we are always longing for the pleasures of the outside world in the same way that many people who are seemingly trapped in endless busyness long for the serenity of retreat.

How do we eradicate the defilements that cause suffering? For that, of course, we need to follow a path; this is the fourth and last of the noble truths. The path can be subdivided into eight parts, which are called the noble eightfold path, or into three parts, which are called the three higher trainings. I will discuss the latter since it is briefer and I'm more familiar with it.

The three higher trainings are morality (Skt. *sila*; Tib. *tsultrim*); meditation (Skt. *samadhi*; Tib. *ting nge dzin*); and wisdom, alternately called knowledge, understanding, or intelligence (Skt. *prajna*; Tib. *sherab*).

One can say a lot about morality. Western philosophers certainly have, and one of the main collections of the Buddhist teachings, the Vinaya, is a compilation of ethical dos and don'ts. Briefly, morality means ceasing to harm others and engaging in helping them. Negative acts are usually subsumed under the ten nonvirtues, which are divided into three of body, four of speech, and three of mind. The three of body are killing, stealing, and sexual misconduct; the four of speech are lying, harsh words, slander, and idle gossip; and the three of mind are covetousness, ill will, and wrong views. Greater detail can be found in many available sources; *The Jewel Ornament of Liberation*, mentioned in the introduction, is a good place to start. Also, we may decide to take the five precepts for laypersons: refraining from killing, stealing, adultery, lying, and the use of intoxicants. Again, more details about these can be found in *Jewel Ornament* or elsewhere.

Besides the obvious merit of not harming but instead aiding others, I think we can look upon morality as the first step in eradicating the poisons. If we can't bring our gross behavior under control, how can we hope to settle and purify our minds? Can we meditate well while stealing or cheating on our partner? Many nonvirtues require considerable work. Imagine committing a crime and keeping all your stories and alibis straight; when meditating, you would find yourself having to review them in your mind. So first we have to act in an outward way that conforms to our aspirations. We do so as much as possible, and as we progress in our practice, we become aware of subtler and subtler aberrations and develop increasing strength to remedy them.

We should check our lifestyle. Is it sane? Are we holding down a job, maintaining a stable relationship, staying healthy? If not, we are probably blocked somewhere. Many people practice with the naive idea that others will take care of them. Some people are lucky that way (I have been), but for most, it is not going to happen. Don't regard those you meet who are wealthy and prosperous with greed.

We have already become somewhat familiar with the second training, meditation. It consists of calming, settling, relaxing the mind into a state of serene clarity.

But that serenity is not enough. We need wisdom, prajna. We need to understand, contemplate, investigate. We need to know if our behavior is appropriate and that we are meditating correctly. We need to listen to and read teachings and clearly discern what the point is. It's not enough to receive teachings from a high teacher as if it were some foreign ritual where mere attendance assured benefit. We must listen carefully, remember as much as we can, check up with ourselves about what the teaching implies, and integrate the knowledge with the other teachings and books we have assimilated.

I'm always surprised by how little most Westerners understand the teachings they've just listened to. I'll leave a teaching and ask a friend for clarification only to find he doesn't remember the part I'm talking about or didn't get it and just shrugged it off. Perhaps people assume that the teachings are supposed to be over their heads and impossible to comprehend. Perhaps they see the teachings as a social event, a place to be seen and a credential to accumulate. Or perhaps they feel that the connection or blessing is sufficient, and clear understanding is not the purpose.

But I'm afraid that a clear understanding is, indeed, the purpose. All these teachings given by high lamas are for one purpose only, to benefit your mind, and they will only do that if you listen carefully and contemplate the meaning deeply. Many teachings begin with instructions on how to listen, explaining the faults in terms of the three pots. The student who is completely distracted during the discourse is likened to an upside-down pot; the student who doesn't remember is a pot with a hole in the bottom; and the student who mixes what they've heard with their own ideas is a pot filled with poison.

When you leave the teaching, discuss it with your friends. How does their understanding differ from yours? What did they hear differently? Be clear about how the teaching fits into the bigger picture. Was it a Hinayana or Mahayana teaching, one on relative truth or absolute truth, a traditional teaching or one specifically for Westerners? This is why I present all of the classifications in the appendix; one must know how all the pieces fit together or they remain just that—pieces. If you have done all this, you should still have questions or doubts; if you haven't examined the information in this way, you probably wasted your time by attending the teaching or reading the book. With your questions, search out someone who knows more than you: a high lama, a local teacher, or perhaps a senior student whom you trust. Check those books sitting on your shelf. This process of understanding is endless, but rewarding and enriching. Your insight will deepen and deepen, and you will begin to understand the underlying simplicity and logic of the Buddha's teachings. By going through this process, you will eventually be able to share your insights with others in a way that can really benefit them.

The most important function of prajna is in refining your meditation. Is it going as well as it should? Do you really understand the instructions, the technique, or are you meditating with a sense of blind faith, believing that although nothing much is happening, you are receiving some sort of blessing that will ripen for you at some time in the uncertain future?

As I mentioned before with the teachings, I'm repeatedly surprised by how easily many of us will settle for second-rate practice. As a teacher, I've seen this often: while engaged in the practice of a meditation technique, a person will simply accept a mediocre experience of meditation, without questioning whether that practice could be improved. We would never do this with our other pursuits—if our car couldn't go over twenty miles per hour, we would certainly get it fixed. Perhaps questioning the meditation experience would open too many doors: our own unwillingness to delve deeper into the practice, the lack of real communication between us and our teacher, our real aspirations and self-image as practitioners, and so on.

Never settle for second best. It's your meditation, and it should be as good as it can be. You should understand what you're doing and why you're doing it. If you don't ask, you might stay stuck for a long time. That lack of knowledge could be what's keeping you from the very growth you yearn for.

Meditation is always a progression from stuckness to stuckness. We make effortless progress for a while, but we get stuck again. The more quickly we identify the problem, of course, the more quickly it will be remedied. Generally, it is stepping back and asking, "At this moment, where am I stuck?" that will provide the clues we need to make the next step. All this is the functioning of prajna.

At its deepest level, prajna is what discerns rigpa—self-cognizing awareness of buddha-nature—from its opposite, *marigpa*—ignorance or, more precisely, the lack of recognition of buddha-nature. Through insight and the application of all that you have read and heard, you evaluate your experience to determine whether genuine realization has arisen. Without a sufficient study effort, you will not be able to recognize buddha-nature unhesitatingly nor will you be able to communicate your understanding or lack of it to your teacher.

All of these examples show the use of wisdom, which is perhaps the single most important cause of enlightenment. It should be clear by now that neither morality nor meditation on their own are sufficient to progress far on the path. However, with these three—morality, meditation, and wisdom—the path can be traversed, the causes of suffering eradicated, and the cessation of suffering (nirvana) approached.

CHAPTER 11

The Four Thoughts

Kalu Rinpoche was considered by many, including His Holiness Karmapa, to be a fully enlightened buddha. He was often compared to Tibet's greatest and most famous yogi, Milarepa, having spent twenty-seven years in retreat, both in solitude and later leading group retreats at Palpung Monastery.

I met him at his monastery in Sonada, near Darjeeling in northeast India. At an altitude of seven thousand feet, the almost constant thick fog obscured any of the available views. The spiritual atmosphere was similar; one could feel Kalu Rinpoche's power as a constant, strong presence, like being in a magnetic field.

Almost every day he would teach whatever Westerners were gathered there. One day, he began his talk by saying, "Just up the hill is our monastery's retreat center, and there are a group of monks diligently engaged in a three-year retreat. Right now, they are practicing dream yoga, which means they are training to be consciously aware in their dreams so that they can manipulate and even develop the ability to go to the pure lands and see the buddhas and receive teachings from them."

"Oh boy!" I thought. "This is going to be great! From Tibet's greatest living yogi, I'm going to receive some really juicy teachings!" I was completely awake and attentive.

He continued, "Their ability to practice dream yoga is based on their practice of tummo, inner heat. That practice is based on their deity practice, and that is based on having completed the preliminaries, the ngondro. That, again, is based on only one thing: their understanding of the four thoughts that turn the mind. So today, that is what I will talk about: the four thoughts that turn the mind."

Actually, that is what he talked about every day, and I was getting bored. I wanted the deep and esoteric stuff. Nobody wants to hear about the different hells over and over.

But hear about them we must. Kalu Rinpoche knew what he was doing, and he was exactly right in his talk; all subsequent progress is based on one thing and one thing only: your realization of the four thoughts that turn the mind.

You may already be familiar with these contemplations. If not, many excellent books contain extensive discussions of them. Both *The Jewel Ornament* and Patrul Rinpoche's *Words of My Perfect Teacher* contain excellent material on them. I won't go into that much detail here; I just want to highlight some points and perhaps mention some areas where Westerners get stuck.

First, what are the four thoughts? They are precious human rebirth, death and impermanence, karma and its result, and the suffering of samsara. The basic logic of these thoughts is that we now have a wonderful opportunity to practice the Dharma, but it won't last long. Death will come soon, and unless we've practiced a lot, it will most likely propel us into a rebirth a lot more miserable and longer lasting than what we experience now (which isn't all that great anyway) due to all the negative karma we've accumulated in both this life and others. Therefore, we must be extremely diligent in our practice if we don't want this fate to befall us.

This argument is very persuasive if one is raised in an Asian culture with the appropriate belief system. Otherwise, it's not so convincing. When I teach the four thoughts, I always introduce the hidden assumptions first. If we can accept these assumptions, the subsequent presentation of the four thoughts themselves will have much more power.

I feel there are three main assumptions: rebirth or reincarnation, the law of karma (cause and effect), and the existence of realms invisible to us. None of these three can be logically, rigorously proven, but if we allow ourselves to examine them, they seem sensible.

Also, many intelligent people in our culture hold one main belief that limits their ability to accept these arguments: the belief that the mind is something like a biochemical computer, that we are really our brains, and all mental experience can simply be reduced to physical or chemical activities. Thus, when the body dies, so do we. This view has great appeal, especially as more and more is learned about the brain. However, we are dealing with reductionist reasoning here. This is not the place to try to refute this view. Let me just advise adherents that reductionism itself is a belief, not something provable, and that clinging to it will be a great detriment to delving deeper into spiritual topics. Remember our discussion of buddha-nature in the first chapter? To what can buddha-nature be reduced? Neurotransmitters? Quarks? If you are someone who holds strongly to this materialist view, at least be willing to question it or suspend it for a while.

I'm sure we all know what rebirth means. It seems pretty weird at first—the idea that we go from life to life, body to body. It's hard to imagine being reborn as a fish or that the dog keeping you awake at night with its incessant barking could be the rebirth of your uncle Irving. But weirdness isn't refutation, and neither is the lack of remembrance, which is often cited as an argument against reincarnation. We are unable to remember deep sleep or being in the womb, yet no one would dispute that these events occur.

What are the reasons to accept this belief in rebirth? First, highly realized beings assure us that it is so. This is not proof, of course, but neither have most of us personally proved that the speed of light is 186,000 miles per second. We believe it because we trust the intelligence, integrity, and expertise of the scientific community. The Buddhist community has the same qualities within its field of expertise, which is the mind. Buddhist scholars and teachers have repeatedly demonstrated their trustworthiness. Lamas accept nothing on faith; many of them just love to debate. It's embarrassing to consider yourself reasonably intelligent, as I do, and then be defeated in a simple debate by someone who hardly speaks English. With this kind of refinement of their discriminating, critical faculties, any major flaws in their doctrine would have been discovered ages ago. I think we can believe what they say about such a basic principle.

Second, many people remember their past lives. Although most don't, that's hardly a rebuttal against those who do.

Who remembers past lives? We probably all know some open person, perhaps someone who is generally psychic, who speaks of their past lives. That might not be very convincing. People have remembered their past lives through hypnosis and have even described buildings that were at the time buried but upon excavation corresponded exactly to the descriptions. Many children remember their past lifetimes, and this has also been carefully tested and documented. Professor Ian Stevenson, in his books such as *Cases of the Reincarnation Type*, has devoted considerable research to investigating the claims of young children regarding memories of past lives. Of course, practitioners and realized beings remember theirs relatively routinely. We all know the story of how the Dalai Lama's recognition is confirmed by his recognizing his possessions from the past. Some tertons remember whole teachings from previous lifetimes. The opposite is also true: some lamas predict exactly where they will be reborn, and it always results in the discovery of a remarkable child.

There is a subtle argument that I once read was presented by the Dalai Lama. It is convincing to me, but somehow it rarely seems to touch others with whom I share it. (Could it be that I'm not His Holiness?) Anyway, here it goes. If we examine the mind, does it have shape or color? Does it have any discernible physical qualities? Some reflection reveals that no, the mind has no physical qualities and, in fact, resembles space. This argument closely relates to the earlier discussion of the brain. If you firmly grasp the belief that the mind is simply the brain, this argument will seem obtuse. If you directly ascertain that the mind is indeed formless like space, the remainder of the argument will make sense. One must look directly at the mind rather than just repeating beliefs.

If the mind is like space, what could cause it to come into existence? Can the union of our mother and father bring something like space into existence? If you answer "yes," then there is no relationship between a cause and its effect. If parents can cause something like space to be created, then anything could cause anything else to arise. There would be no rhyme or reason to our world or our experience. A little reflection reveals that there must be some similarity between a cause and its effect. Sheep always give birth to sheep, rabbits to rabbits. What can give birth to something space-like?

The answer is nothing. There is nothing material in our world that could possibly be the cause of our space-like mind coming into existence. Therefore, our mind has always existed (it's the only other option) and will always exist. More precisely, we can say that not even this mind is permanent but is a momentary phenomenon caused by the previous momentary mind. Of course, that mind was caused by the mind one moment before it, and so on since beginningless time. I've found that if one believes in either one permanent mind from beginningless time or a succession of momentary minds from beginningless time, one will be able to grasp further arguments, although the latter view is most likely closer to the truth. Once we accept the logic of this, it's easy to see how the mind merely identifies with each life's body from birth to birth, endlessly, until it realizes its own true nature.

On a gross level, there is some connection between mental contents and the body. We're not happy when we're sick. In addition, I don't experience your body's pain in the same way that I experience mine. But again, if we didn't have some sense that there was something deeper to our nature, something more basic and profound than the body-mind connection, we probably wouldn't have developed an interest in Tibetan Buddhism. We should consider whether the relationship between our mind and body is immutable, or whether it is something based on habit and open to change.

What propels this mind, and what gives it its unending display of myriad experiences? Karma. Karma means activity; when we do something with either body, speech, or mind, it creates causes that we will later experience as effects. This law cannot be proved. Although the word *karma* is used often in everyday English, it's really the most difficult Buddhist concept to comprehend. Lord Buddha himself said that karma was more difficult to understand than emptiness; emptiness can be demonstrated logically, karma cannot. A total understanding of karma exists only in the mind of a fully enlightened being, but simply put, all we need to trust is this: virtuous actions of body, speech, and mind will yield positive results; nonvirtuous actions will yield negative ones. That's it.

Once again, we can accept this through trusting our teachers and because it seems sensible. How else can we give some meaning or value to the countless types of experiences people have? How else can we view the patterns that flow through our lives and gain some acceptance and understanding as well as perhaps some meaning and direction? To develop more faith in karma, we can examine the way life experiences unfold for people. Is it coincidence, or is there a deeper underlying cause? Consider, for example, identical twins. They have the same upbringing and the same genes. However, their lives can often be quite different from each other. Here's another example: Someone close to me was once accused of a serious crime simply because he was "in the wrong place at the wrong time." If he hadn't stopped to urinate, the police would never even have known he existed. We all know of many cases like this. They can never prove karma, but they make it seem sensible.

The third assumption that may cause us trouble is the belief in realms or kinds of beings that we can't see. As we gain more and more scientific knowledge of the universe, none of these realms has been discovered. Also, many of them seem quite fanciful to us; for instance, we talk about beings who live in the clouds or live off odors. The variety of such beings is almost endless. They are generally invisible to us, but some have the ability to interfere with our lives in one way or another. When I lived in Britain, I was amazed at the number of stories people told: fairy circles, haunted houses, unhappy spirits in the woods, and so on. The storytellers were always credible, and all were convinced of the veracity of their stories. One was an Olympian wrestler turned plumber, a man of incredible strength and gentleness, whose down-to-earth manner made his experiences completely believable.

In Buddhism, especially Tibetan Buddhism, we are presented with a vast array of nonhuman beings—gods, ghosts, water spirits, smell-eaters, and so on. At the end of most Mahayana sutras, some of these types of beings in Lord Buddha's audience voice their approval of the teaching and vow their willingness to embrace it and protect others who also practice it. In tantra, nonhuman beings are referred to even more frequently. Various tormas are offered to a wide variety of spirits and gods. In both sutra and tantra, pure lands or buddha-fields are frequently mentioned.

Once again, we might find this difficult to believe. Where are these beings? If they can influence our lives, why can't we see them? Where are the hells and pure lands? Are the hells in the hot core of the earth; are the pure lands somewhere in outer space?

None of this can be easily understood if we solidly grasp this world as being real and concrete. If, for a moment, we can accept the primacy of mind, we might be able to understand how the mind could create any of an infinite variety of worlds, beings, and types of experience. Could you dream of being in hell? In a pure land? That's not so difficult to accept. The next question is the obvious one—what's the difference between waking and sleeping? If you can demonstrate some real fundamental difference, the other realms of being might seem implausible, but if waking and dream are basically similar in nature, then it's easy to understand how other realms can exist: we simply dream them.

I tend to think of these various realms like different TV channels. None of the channels is more real than the others. The events on one channel have no spatial relationship to the events on another; the characters in the soap opera cannot influence the basketball games I'm fond of watching. This makes it easier for me to imagine that there are different realms filled with many kinds of beings, each realm existing within its own space and time.

As I mentioned in a discussion of scientism in chapter 6, another way of looking at resistance to accepting these beliefs is the very real difference between a scientific and Buddhist perspective. Even if we don't have much scientific background, our culture is saturated with it. Briefly, science is concerned with third-person, objective reality. Buddhism is concerned with first-person experience. Allow yourself to make the switch. If you wanted to learn Tibetan, the fastest way would be to leave the English-speaking world and go live with a Tibetan family. That doesn't mean there is something wrong with English. To delve deeply into Tibetan Buddhism, we must learn when a scientific perspective is useful and when to immerse ourselves in the Buddhist worldview.

Therefore, if we can resolve our doubts about rebirth, karma, and other realms, contemplating the four thoughts will have real power. With these assumptions cleared up, we can talk more about the thoughts themselves.

As I mentioned, the first of the four thoughts is the contemplation of the precious human birth. That does not necessarily imply that being human is, in itself, precious; rather, there's a subset of human beings that is called precious. Why? Because these lucky few, including you and me, have the opportunity to follow the Buddhist path and reach a state free from suffering. That's precious!

We take so much for granted. You go to a bookstore and buy a book of profound teachings; you drive into town and receive an empowerment from a special lama. It seems to happen with so little effort. How can this be special? Perhaps your seat wasn't so good during the empowerment, or your mind drifted due to a fight you had earlier at work. It can seem like no big deal.

But it is. How many beings have the opportunity to participate in something like an empowerment? How many different causes and conditions must come together for this to happen? If you had simply been born one generation earlier, the chances of your receiving a tantric empowerment would have been very slim indeed. Do any of your friends or family have any interest, even though it's just a short drive and a few dollars? "But Mom, if you take this empowerment, you'll never have to be reborn in lower realms again!" Does she believe you? Does she care?

You have to be at the right place at the right time with all the right internal qualities. If the place is wrong, it won't happen. No matter how ripe you are, you're not getting any empowerment in Iran. You also wouldn't have been able to receive any empowerment in the West only a short time ago. Fifty years ago, Tibet was perfect for practicing the Dharma; a hundred years ago, so was China. Now, in both places, it's very difficult. Due to politics, circumstances have changed. Who knows when or where it will change next?

You must have the interest, the leisure, and the intelligence to benefit from your external circumstances. If you don't care, are too busy, or are not bright enough to understand, it also won't happen. Traditionally, there are eighteen circumstances and qualities like those we've discussed; if just one is missing, forget it. No path, no practice, no chance to escape from the terrible sufferings of cyclic existence. An incredible, mind-boggling confluence of conditions must come together to produce the life we have right now. It is indeed rare and precious.

No matter how wretched our life seems, we have that chance. I remember being in my cloistered group retreat feeling very sick and very sorry for myself. I kept comparing myself to all the other men who seemed healthy and strong enough to glide through the physical demands of such a strict retreat. But after contemplating the precious human birth, I was humbled. Compared to the most glorious, exalted worldly life, mine was much better. I had a chance to reach permanent happiness and do something completely meaningful for both others and myself. What did it matter if I was sick?

How often do we whine, if not to others, at least within our own thoughts? But we have the precious jewel of this life, a chance to progress on the spiritual path. We may feel our conditions aren't perfect, but were they ever? They're good enough. Who doesn't have the opportunity to be mindful during the day, to silently intone OM MANI PADME HUM as we go through our activities?

Being as plugged into the world as we are gives us manifold opportunities to consider our lives. Whenever I watch a movie or read the news, I become acutely aware of how different life can be.

I could be a refugee in Rwanda, moving in a human wave of a million destitute persons, with no real place to go. Am I really better or different than those poor folks? I just feel very lucky.

A while ago I saw the film *Braveheart* for the first time. Imagine living in a place where your wife gets raped by the local ruler. Could I maintain my mindfulness? Could I control my anger and refrain from nonvirtue? If someone approached me and told me to watch my mind or to pray to Guru Rinpoche, would I have the reason to listen?

Needless to say, there are countless opportunities to reflect like this. Be happy to be alive, to be able to think, to be aware, and to love. It's an amazing situation. Life can be hard, and I'm no stranger to self-pity either. But waking up is worth it all.

Unfortunately, this amazing opportunity will not last long. We will die.

Traditionally, death contemplation has three parts: the certainty of death, the uncertainty of the time of death, and that only Dharma will be of help when one dies. The first two seem obvious enough. None of us knows anyone who is approaching immortality, and we all know of people who have died young, suddenly and unexpectedly. But do we live our lives in harmony with that understanding? If you examine what you've done today, what would you have done differently if you knew you were going to die in a year, a month, a week, a day? Many of us have friends who, when they found out they had a fatal illness, became diligent practitioners.

We had someone like that in retreat. Al had been a long-time student of Akong Rinpoche in Scotland, but he had never practiced much. However, when he was diagnosed as having colon cancer with only a few months to live, he was admitted to our retreat even though it was already in progress. He practiced diligently and was extremely grateful for every day he had. When he died, he left us cheerfully and with love. Both Akong Rinpoche and H. E. Tai Situ Rinpoche were there with him with prayers and blessings. He was a true inspiration to us all.

But it's always "not me." It's always the other guy who gets cancer, isn't it? Recently, someone at our center came down with a vicious cancer, and that's exactly what he said: "I always thought these things happened to someone else."

As my mom got older, she moved to a senior citizen's apartment in Sacramento, California. It was run by a Jewish agency under HUD, and most of the residents were Jewish ladies. Being a good Jewish son and feeling more than a little guilty for all the time spent abroad away from my mother, I visited her often.

It was a pleasant and well-managed place with many caring people on the staff. Most of the residents were still healthy, although I'm sure they all had their aches and pains. But the sense of meaninglessness and depression was palpable. People seemed to be just sitting around, waiting to die. Very little seemed to interest anyone. They had no Dharma, something that could give both their lives and their deaths meaning. Although they had every reasonable comfort Western society can provide, they were lacking in this one thing. I vowed that this would never happen to me, that I would never abandon the one thing that gives my life meaning and value while also preparing me for death.

On the opposite side of the coin, in the East I was acquainted with older Tibetans, both lay and ordained, who, although they were both ill and destitute, faced death joyfully because they had their practice and an unwavering faith in the power of the Three Jewels. When I was living in Kathmandu in the eighties, my cook told me about her mother. Her mother lived in her attic, eating one meal a day and reciting *mani* for eighteen hours a day! Who do you think was more prepared for death, that woman or my mother and her friends in Sacramento?

It's especially difficult to take death seriously in this country. I just heard of a luxurious senior condominium where those who need care are placed in the basement where the others can't see them. Prospective buyers are not shown that part! Television shows and movies are filled with young, beautiful people. We're always trying to look younger. As Albert says in the movie *The Birdcage*, "When you say I look good, what you really mean is that I look young. When you say I look tired and need a rest, what you mean is that I look old and am no longer attractive."

Inwardly, we defend against death by the very structure of our ego. The ego claims to have the ability to provide us with happiness based on its belief in its own permanent existence. On the one hand, to believe in ego results in denying death. On the other, to accept death is to question the very nature of ego as a permanent, ongoing structure and to confront strong defense mechanisms. As a result, we have fierce resistance to contemplating death. This resistance is the same resistance that comes up when we meditate. Recognize it for what it is and move on.

What happens when we die? We are no longer grounded by being in a body; we are blown along by the winds of karma. If we have acted virtuously, we will have positive results; nonvirtuous behavior will bring negative results. So we need to check up: What actions have predominated in this life? Have our actions been motivated by positive mental states, or have most of them been propelled by desire, anger, and ignorance? I don't know about you, but I rarely have a good thought; it's all garbage. Every one of these thoughts, verbalizations, and actions will bring a result. I haven't liked it much in this life when my negative actions from the past have resulted in unhappiness; I'm pretty sure I also won't like it in the future when the negative actions I've taken in this life ripen.

Even relatively virtuous, kindly people have done things worth regretting. Who hasn't killed ants or mosquitoes? Who hasn't hurt a relative or a dear friend with an unkind or thoughtless word? If your actions are not purified by your practice, their result will be experienced later.

Contemplation of the four thoughts can be our best friend on the path. When we begin our practice, we must find the time for such contemplation. Unfortunately, nobody is going to add an extra hour or two to the day just so they can practice; even the Buddha doesn't have that ability. That leaves two alternatives: sleep less or do less. In the long run, sleep is hard to do without. Understanding the four thoughts gives us the impetus to examine our daily activities to see which ones are really essential and which ones aren't, to learn the difference between "want" and "need." We should always be asking ourselves, "Would I be doing this if I knew I were going to die next week?" I'm afraid you probably won't find much time for practice without at least some restructuring and reprioritizing of your life.

I'm always amazed by how busy Americans are! I read recently that the average American works two months a year more than the average German or French person and one month a year more than they did thirty years ago. This seems insane to me. We're the world's most prosperous country; it shouldn't be that difficult to restructure our lives to trade some hectic activity and the accumulation of goods for time to practice something that would bring true, permanent happiness.

For example, British citizens have a per capita income that is 62 percent of the average income in the United States. This means that if we worked an average of 38 percent less, we could still live as well as they do in Britain; it certainly wouldn't be like India or Tanzania. I know this is easier said than done, and some of you are truly busy with no flexibility in your schedule, but I think my point is still valid and clear. If we can't work less, at least we should be saving money for a time when we can.

I feel strongly that our understanding of the four thoughts manifests in how we spend our money. Do we buy more or better stuff, or do we put some money aside so we can work less now or possibly enter retreat in the future? The problem is that many people take a certain standard of living for granted and often confuse yuppie values with spirituality. Consequently, our time and wealth go toward maintaining that standard, and practice time always seems far away.

In Buddha's time, monks begged for food and ate whatever was placed in their bowls. One day, a leper's finger fell into a bowl, and the monk ate it. Contrast that with our lives today. How many of us are satisfied with ordinary Western fare, Western clothes, or Western housing? Sometimes spiritual people seem to be even fussier than ordinary folks. For example, when I was young, my father was successful, and we were prosperous. That prosperity was reflected in my parents' purchase of Yuban coffee. I would never do that now—I always purchase the much more expensive whole-bean coffee. I'm always apprehensive about going to a potluck—I'm afraid the food I'm bringing will be rejected.

The point is there is a lot we can do to simplify our lives. Always remember death!

Even once we have found time and have established a regular practice, temptations and distractions will arise. Even Milarepa was tempted to leave retreat to go to a nearby village for some entertainment and companionship. If Milarepa was distracted by a simple Tibetan village, how can we resist the countless distractions of modern Western life? Your best friend, your most trustworthy advisor, will be the four thoughts. Always examine your actions in their light; always remember death.

Beyond that, there will come a time when practice is just too hard or painful. It's not that we're distracted or that we desire something else, it's merely that doing the practice is agonizing. You begin to see things about yourself that you've always ignored. You experience mysterious kinds of physical pains while sitting that make every moment unbearable. At times like these, the four thoughts may be the only things that pull you through. You understand you are ripening previous negative karma and saving yourself from possible rebirth in the lower realms. If you don't have any previous meditative experience with these four thoughts, you will have no allies to cope with these difficulties.

These winds of karma can blow us to places beyond our imagination. Unfortunately, most of these places aren't much fun. Remember all those gruesome hells we've either heard or read about? Why do these miserable states predominate? Because most of us are driven by the three poisons of desire, anger, and ignorance most of the time. It's like trying to play a computer game at a higher skill level than we have: those little black stones keep accumulating faster than we are able to eliminate them or able to accumulate the white ones. There doesn't seem to be much we can do about it on our own; we need some help.

That's where the four thoughts come in. Their purpose is to turn our minds to the Dharma. What exactly does that mean? In my original training back in Nepal, it meant to meditate more and more, which of course implied I would do other things less and less. So for me, turning my mind to the Dharma means giving up nonmeditative activities so I can practice for longer periods of time with fewer distractions. This book always has the slant that practicing the Dharma means meditating. I apologize for this because it is misleading. Thus, I would like to discuss the value of practicing as a layperson, which I alluded to earlier.

I like to call the layperson's path "plan B," where plan A would be the more traditional path of the meditating renunciate. Plan B is perhaps the most common and paradoxically the most interesting path these days. All the other paths are more obvious, have traditional roots, but require a significant investment of time, often to the point of uprooting one's life, disregarding any sense of financial security, and distancing oneself from one's loved ones.

But what about people who are either unable or unwilling (or both) to do that? Are they doomed, somehow beyond the reach of Lord Buddha's compassion? What about the single mother who is trying to work, go to college, and raise her child? What about the middle-aged couple who still have kids at home and whose parents also need a lot of care as they age? What is the path for people like this (and I think this applies to most of us)?

When I first started teaching twenty-five years ago, I was returning from a cloistered retreat in Scotland and many years of intensive practice in Asia. I assumed that those who became interested in Buddhism did so with the intention and aspiration of becoming "serious practitioners," people who were thinking of simplifying their lives and orienting themselves around the reality of doing retreats.

Then one day I was talking to a student of mine. He meditates regularly but also is a dedicated parent, has a meaningful helping career and valuable relationships, and engages in healthy physical activity. It dawned on me that he had absolutely no interest in going on retreat. It never even seemed to occur to him. Yet—and this was an important insight for me—*his meditation and other Buddhist training gave everything else in his life deeper meaning and value and was extremely precious to him.* Honoring that led me to coin the term "plan B."

Often people feel frustrated that they can't do retreat. They whine about their lives, feeling they're spiritually cursed because of the conditions they live in. Or they use these conditions as an excuse not to try their best and to rationalize negative or indulgent behavior.

There have always been laypeople in Buddhism; however, their primary practice has been to support the ordained and the monasteries. For the first time in twenty-five hundred years, we have educated laity who have at least some leisure to study and practice the Dharma.

Plan B is new. Plan B is evolving. It's an exciting development. As I see it, Plan B requires no overt lifestyle changes. Of course, simplification and giving up bad habits never hurt. It requires no outward expression of being Buddhist. Plan B'ers do a regular meditation practice. But it is just that. It's practice. What are they practicing for? The rest of their lives. What they gain in their sitting practice, they apply in their work and family relationships. That means they do what everybody else does, but they do it with the intention and effort to bring constant mindfulness and a kind heart to whatever it is they are doing. They are trying to wake up in everything they do! This is radical, this is revolutionary, both for Buddhism and the world at large. It will be fascinating to see how it unfolds over time.

When contemplating the four thoughts, our minds turn toward the Dharma. How that turning expresses itself is unique for every individual and should be embraced, whole-heartedly, with joy.

CHAPTER 12

Ngondro: Refuge and Bodhichitta

Ngondro is Tibetan for the preliminary practices that begin one's career as a tantric practitioner. They are divided into two sections: the common, or ordinary, and the uncommon, or extraordinary. The common preliminaries are the contemplation of the four thoughts we discussed in the last chapter. The extraordinary practices are taking refuge and generating bodhichitta, which are generally done in conjunction with prostrations, the purification practice of Vajrasattva, offering the mandala, and guru yoga. These four preliminaries are always done; sometimes the practices of *chod*, offering one's body, and *phowa*, the transference of consciousness, are also added.

For every practice lineage, there is a set of preliminaries. For instance, within the Karma Kagyu tradition, there is a ngondro for mahamudra and a different one for the Six Doctrines of Naropa. Other Kagyu schools have their own systems of ngondro. Although they are similar, it is preferable to do the ngondro that corresponds to the lineage, root lama, and practice you will most likely be following. If you change lineages, you may be asked to do a new ngondro in order to make a connection with your new school. You generally don't need an empowerment to do ngondro, but having the Vajrasattva empowerment certainly can't hurt. You definitely need the *lung*, or "reading transmission," as well as the oral commentary for the ngondro practices. In addition, there are many fine books on the preliminaries.

The manner of doing the ngondro varies among the different lineages of Tibetan Buddhism. I'm most familiar with the Kagyu and Nyingma approach. There, the preliminaries are done in one block from beginning to end. Completion of at least one set of preliminaries is often necessary to begin a deity practice, attend more esoteric teachings, or even participate in some empowerments. I've heard that the Sakya approach is quite similar—one completes the preliminaries in one big bundle. However, the Gelugpas, who formed the largest tradition in Tibet, have a different manner of working with the ngondro. Completion of the ngondro sets is not a prerequisite to tantric practice for Gelugpas; instead, the ngondro practices can be done alongside tantric practice throughout the practitioner's life. However, Gelugpas often complete the full set of ngondro practices at the beginning of a three-year retreat, just as the practitioners of the other Tibetan Buddhist traditions do.

Refuge

The ngondro begins with taking refuge. Refuge has three levels: outer refuge in the Buddha, Dharma, and Sangha; inner refuge in the lama, yidams, and dakinis and protectors; and secret refuge in the dharmakaya, sambhogakaya, and nirmanakaya.

What does taking refuge mean? The image that always comes to mind is that of a shelter in a storm. It's raining heavily, you are getting soaked, and you look for something to protect you. Recalling the discussion on the four thoughts, we are being buffeted by the winds of our own karma, which are threatening to blow us into the miserable realms of existence. We need help!

Who can help us? Obviously, someone who isn't being blown about by karma. Such a being is called a buddha. Only they can help. For anyone else to try is dangerous—a drowning person cannot save another drowning person. The help itself is called the Dharma. Dharma refers to both the teachings and the truth they represent. The Sangha comprises those who help and support you while you are practicing the Dharma.

After deeply contemplating the four thoughts, our appreciation of how wretched samsara really is should be indelibly etched in our minds. We will never find lasting happiness until we can escape. Lord Buddha is offering us a way out; if we don't avail ourselves of his offer, there will be no other way and no other chance to free ourselves from suffering. The Buddha is someone who has freed himself from sorrow and who knows how to guide others to that freedom. When we think of his qualities, we will gladly entrust ourselves to his guidance. That is taking refuge in the Buddha.

The Dharma is the exposition of everything we need to know to progress to freedom. Although taught twenty-five hundred years ago, it has been maintained lovingly and painstakingly through all sorts of cultures and all sorts of calamities. After being practiced mostly in Asia for centuries, it is now easily available in our own country. Understanding how these teachings can bring us and all sentient beings to ultimate freedom, we will joyfully entrust ourselves to practicing these teachings. This is taking refuge in the Dharma.

For centuries, teachers have passed on these precious teachings to their students. The teachers and students have formed communities that provide instruction and support for those yearning for liberation. Without the support of the Sangha, what chance would we have? Acknowledging this, we take refuge in the Noble Sangha.

Entrusting yourself to these three is taking refuge. Let's face it, we haven't done so well on our own. Sometimes we can keep our heads above water; sometimes we cannot. When things are going well, we might feel we're doing fine; but a little difficulty, a small reversal, and suddenly we seem completely unable to cope. If that happens now, what will happen as we die? What will happen in the *bardo*, the treacherous and dangerous period between death and our next birth?

Some people have an aversion to the idea of taking refuge. It seems too religious or too weak. Only a wimp needs someone else's help. I don't buy it. We are always taking refuge. The main differences are that our present ways of taking refuge are poorly thought out and our objects of refuge are not very useful.

Ask yourself: In whom or what do I take refuge now? To whom

do I turn when things are rough? What will I do when I die? If you believe in another spiritual path and take refuge in that, that's fine. If you think you're strong enough to handle death and the transition process by yourself, you are probably fooling yourself. If you prefer not to think about your death, you are simply taking refuge in your own ignorance.

We take refuge in many things, such as our intelligence, our beauty, our aggressiveness, or our wit. A friend of mine once said, "When I have a problem, I just throw money at it." These methods can all be called "taking refuge in the ego." By now you should be convinced that this is probably not a good idea. The ego is not doing a great job right now; it will only do worse when we die.

The point is this: we all take refuge all the time. Now it's time to do so intelligently.

I think we have to admit to ourselves that the ego can be a good minister, but it makes a lousy king. Taking refuge is the first step in the ego's descent from that throne. There is probably no better way to embody that understanding and demonstrate a willingness to restructure one's inner landscape than by prostrating. Prostrations become the physical expression of the willingness to dethrone the ego and enthrone a king who is wise and compassionate. Each prostration should be accompanied by the sincere feeling of taking refuge and giving up a little of ego's domain.

You must learn how to practice prostrations and refuge from a teacher. How to recite the liturgy and what to visualize varies from practice to practice. I will try to make a few general observations.

Since you will be doing 100,000 of them, you will need a method of keeping count. A small rosary of twenty-seven (one-fourth of 108) that fits over the palm works fine. Then you need to count the groups of twenty-sevens and so on.

You will need a place to do prostrations as well as some gear. (We're Americans, aren't we?) But remember, prostrations are supposed to be difficult and painful. Each one becomes a test of your commitment, and the more difficult they are, the more committed to your own unfolding you will be when you complete them. Also, prostrations are said to purify physical karma, the karma created by violence, stealing, and sexual misconduct. So it's better to have sore knees than to be reborn in hell. Of course, a little common sense is necessary. We don't want to wind up in a wheelchair or abandon our practice because it was too gruesome.

Lama Thubten was the lama who sealed us into retreat in Scotland. When he was young, he did the three-year retreat at his monastery, Palpung, the seat of H. E. Tai Situ Rinpoche. Lama Thubten was diligent and truly believed he was purifying his bad karma with his exertion. Therefore, he prostrated until his knees became bloody pulps. Situ Rinpoche (the previous one) spied on him and discovered his condition. He called all the monks in retreat together and told them that Lama Thubten was the only one doing it correctly; by taking care of themselves too much, the other monks weren't purifying their karma. What did he do? He had them all hung from hooks like slabs of meat and whipped them!

Now when we prostrate, we like to have special pads for our knees, something for our hands, and a smooth board. I recommend firm foam for the knees, myself. On the other hand, I have prostrated many, many times until I was so weak I couldn't lift myself off the board anymore. I prostrated until blood ran down my legs, and I prostrated (and did other demanding practices) until I had arthritis in my knees and had to walk a while with a cane (I'm better now, thank you). It's up to you how diligent you are, how much suffering you're willing to take on to complete the practice. I understand that after a grueling day at work, whiny kids at home, and a fight with your spouse, the last thing you might feel you need is an hour of pain. It's not exactly why you got involved in the first place.

Also, with all the ngondro practices, you have a quality-versus-quantity payoff. You can try to do them perfectly, or you can try to do them quickly. The implications are obvious; if you sacrifice speed for quality, you might never finish, but if you really exert yourself to complete them as fast as possible, you might find yourself unprepared for the next practice without having changed or having had any real experience.

I did my first ngondro when I was twenty-five. I practiced diligently. My roommate, Jeffrey, was an extremely gung-ho practitioner (he's now in retreat in the woods somewhere in Canada), and my competitive nature forced me to try to keep up with him. He would slap himself in the face in the late evenings to keep from falling asleep. I think I learned a lot from him about discipline and the value of pushing, just doing the practice no matter how difficult. I was almost continually sick with mysterious ailments that no doctor could treat, but I never quit. I would prostrate and do the other practices until I simply couldn't do them anymore.

I think it's good to push yourself like that sometimes. You discover what your limits are and what you can really do. At other times, you can balance that kind of fanaticism with greater quality. But you start to know where the lines are within your being. Also, you will please your teacher.

Pushing like that gave me an unshakable desire to practice. Before then, I was somewhat wishy-washy; afterward, I was much more consistent with my discipline. I owe whatever subsequent benefits I've derived from my practice to that year of militant pushing and the example of my good buddy Jeffrey.

We often come to Buddhism with an inflated sense of how spiritual or committed we are. But our rosaries don't lie. We get constant feedback on our level of commitment simply by looking down at our beads.

I did my second ngondro in my cloistered retreat at the age of thirty-eight. It was a whole retreat full of Jeffreys, all militantly disciplined practitioners. One is great, but a whole building full of them?! Anyway, because the retreat was already so structured that there was no real way to lose one's practice, I tried to do the ngondro as best as I could from the quality perspective. That is, I tried to do each practice to the best of my ability without worrying about the numbers. I found that this could be broken down further into two techniques.

First, I could try to perfect the visualization. I could make that my main focus and judge my success by the clarity of the various images I was producing.

Second was to emphasize the emotive, devotional aspect. That is, to take the open-hearted feelings that come with devotional practice; focus on them; and try to maximize their power using whatever techniques, images, or associations that evoked them. Personally, I feel the latter has more power and benefit than the former. Visualization can become a dry exercise without the devotion. Devotion without the connection to the visualization can really open your heart but can also lead to becoming overly emotional. For a while, I felt like a rhythm-and-blues singer singing emotionally about something completely silly and trivial. It was close to cultivating feeling for its own sake, divorced from any kind of meaning. Visualization grounds the feeling in context and value; the devotion elevates the visualization into something real and meaningful. Once again, we have things that we must learn to balance.

It would be nice if we could easily integrate those two—visualization and devotion—into one practice, but I have found that they are two different mental functions. Hence, I start by alternating between them until they begin reinforcing each other. Having some sense of presence through the visualization can increase your sense of devotion. And devotion can convince you of the reality of the visualization, making it clearer.

Reminding yourself of the qualities of the Three Jewels also helps. One quality of the buddhas is their unconditional love for all sentient beings. While taking refuge, and in many other practices, if you remind yourself of this love and do your practice within its field, your practice will benefit greatly.

To return to the discussion about quality versus quantity with the ngondro: both approaches work, and like other aspects of practice, some balance is necessary. It is also necessary to try it yourself. What happens to you if you push yourself? Does it raise you to a higher level of commitment, or does it burn you out? Does it open you up, or does it make you more uptight? Does an allegiance to quality become an excuse for not practicing, or do you monitor yourself to do the very best you can?

With prostrations, expect a real drama to unfold. All the issues of commitment to the Buddhist path and to commitment in general will well up completely and intensely; the warring voices will be screaming inside your head, "Push harder!" and "Stop!" I hope you listen to the right one at the right time.

Bodhichitta

Usually accompanying the refuge and prostration practice is the generation of bodhichitta. *Bodhi* means "enlightenment"; *chitta* means "heart," "thought," or "mind." *Bodhichitta* means "the thought for enlightenment" or "the enlightened mind." It's hard to define the term precisely as it has several related meanings. "Ultimate bodhichitta" is the enlightened mind itself; "relative bodhichitta" is the desire to attain that enlightenment. The idea here is that we aspire to attain enlightenment to benefit all sentient beings. We are no longer practicing for the sake of our own liberation from suffering; our motivation encompasses all that lives. Thus, generating bodhichitta means to train oneself away from a selfish motivation and toward a completely altruistic one.

That's easier said than done. Luckily, in Tibetan Buddhism, there are simple, direct, and effective techniques to make that transformation. These teachings are called lojong, which can be translated as "thought transformation" or "mind training." They change the mind from self-centeredness to the altruistic motivation of bodhichitta and were introduced into Tibet in the eleventh century by the highly revered Indian pandit and saint Atisha. The teachings became incorporated into all the lineages in Tibet and have proved to be quite popular in the West. I've given classes on lojong many times and feel they have been the most beneficial I have taught. I'm always deeply touched by the real and meaningful changes and breakthroughs my students make in this class.

Most techniques in Tibetan Buddhism are deep and profound. Unfortunately, they are also difficult to practice in terms of both the spiritual acumen of the student and having the proper conditions in which to practice. Lojong excels in being down-to-earth and completely suited to our times and the lifestyle of a layperson—hence, its great effectiveness. However chaotic and miserable your life, the lojong teachings have a technique that will enable you to use that experience for growth. No more whining about not being able to go off to retreat; here is a teaching perfect for your busy and stressful lifestyle.

The original lojong teachings are lists of slogans—for instance, "Be grateful to everyone." Various lamas have written commentaries over the years; so have a few Westerners. Without going through all the slogans, I'd like to say something about what I feel is the main point and then mention the main formal practice from lojong: tonglen, or "taking and sending."

The slogans of lojong reveal a profound psychological insight into how the ego develops, maintains its territory, and refuses to consider others. The slogans demonstrate how we have a strong tendency to accumulate positive experiences, to push away negative ones, and to get angry with anyone who interferes with this process. This would be fine if the ego's strategy worked, but for a variety of reasons, it doesn't. Among the reasons are, of course, that experiences are only temporary, and the ego doesn't really exist. The ego is playing a losing game here. It may occasionally seem to be winning, like someone who wins a jackpot at a slot machine. But over time, it's inevitable that, like the player at the slots, the ego will come out a loser.

Hence, with lojong we take those three processes—hoarding the good, pushing away the bad, and blaming others—identify them, and exert ourselves to reverse them. How can we do that? Because the ego doesn't really exist. The lojong teachings start with a short explanation of absolute bodhichitta, which, if you remember, is the ultimate nature of the mind; by having a little familiarity with that, the mind develops both the courage and the flexibility to undertake reversing its bad habits.

Let's use the slogan mentioned earlier, "Be grateful to everyone," as an example. When you find yourself thinking, "If so-and-so weren't getting in my way all the time, I could really...," you first recognize the thought and its attendant aggression. You then cultivate a sense of gratitude: "If so-and-so hadn't been obstructing me, I never would have seen what an aggressive and obsessive jerk I am. Thanks to them, I have this new self-knowledge and am able to change."

Each slogan is really saying that we are its opposite; they are actually a list of our flaws. When we hear, "Drive all blames into one (our ego)," we know we have the tendency to blame others for our trouble; if we don't, we can ignore this particular bit of advice.

What does this have to do with compassion and bodhichitta? Our selfishness and aversion cover up our own intrinsic compassion. It is natural for us to feel loving and compassionate toward others, but as we grew up, we learned to defend ourselves more and more. Defending means pushing away or denying pain. Because we are always pushing away pain, we push away others who feel pain. Therefore, we must first break the habit of pushing pain away; only then can we acknowledge others' pain. When we remove the defense, we automatically begin to feel the compassion. Once we feel the compassion, it's easy to take the next step, which is generating bodhichitta.

Once you let go of blaming others and getting angry with them, you will naturally feel some love toward them as you experience gratitude. Once you experience that love, consider that others are also suffering; you will feel the wish for them to be free of it. Then resolve, "The only way to completely eradicate suffering is by becoming enlightened. If I want to remove the misery of others, who have helped me learn about myself, I must become a buddha." That thought is bodhichitta.

In the beginning, it all seems contrived and artificial. After a while, it becomes more natural, and eventually, applying the slogans is almost automatic; they start to replace all the usual voices in your head.

This whole process can be greatly accelerated by doing the meditation of tonglen. Briefly, the practice of tonglen means to breathe in others' pain, then while you breathe out, you give your happiness and virtue to them. Having practiced tonglen as a one-month retreat during my longer group retreat, and having taught it many times since then, I have developed a certain style or technique for teaching and practicing it that seems to work.

It's easy to sit back and have compassionate and loving thoughts toward the world, all humans, nature, or something like that. This doesn't really threaten us; in fact, we feel good and a little high from that kind of thinking. But this kind of thinking doesn't actually change anything. You can check for yourself: do those expansive feelings really change how you relate to others in your everyday life, or do old patterns return? If you're like me, the old thought patterns return.

The reason is those feelings are not really connected to the structure of the ego, which is about pushing away pain while accumulating happiness. You must be precise in your observation of that process before it can truly be changed. Because of that, the lojong teachings recommend that you begin the exchange with yourself.

Many students who are somewhat familiar with the teachings have ignored this advice, but I feel it is the real key. We must learn to see our strategy of denying pain before we can truly generate the strong wish for beings to be free of it. By pain, I primarily mean mental pain, even the mental pain of having physical discomfort. If you try to do tonglen for others while denying your own pain, your practice becomes a technique for perpetuating avoidance and will never yield any meaningful results. So first, simply be aware of your pain at the moment. Notice your awkwardness, your wish to squirm away from it somehow. Allow yourself merely to feel it.

Now you are ready to begin tonglen. You might want to imagine an unhappy version of yourself standing in front of you; this can make the visualization flow better. Take in your suffering; give yourself healing white light. Link this with the breath: breathe in the suffering as black gunk; breathe out the goodness as healing white light.

Do it until it works! You should "get it" and have some definite sense of healing, acceptance, and transformation. You should develop the insight that blocking out or denying pain is actually what keeps you in a place of pain, that it is entirely within your power and ability to do something simple and effective to change this. Your ego mechanisms developed when you were younger and had no other defenses for dealing with difficulties; now you're older and have had the great good fortune to meet the Dharma. Thus, although it is everyone's habit to push away discomfort, there's no practical or logical reason to continue to do so.

This is also a wonderful way to deal with the self-loathing many of us feel. Associated with that feeling is a sense of being unlovable, unworthy of love. If you can see yourself in front of you with your sense of self-loathing and being unlovable, you can send that person love and healing white light. Slowly, the unlovable you blossoms in the absorption of that love, and the self-loathing falls away. Doing this can change your life!

Here, the teachings say that we should focus on the suffering we will experience in the future. I prefer to deal with the past. As Westerners who have been raised, educated, and immersed in the psychoanalytic tradition, we are accustomed to thinking of our present discomfort as being caused by events in our past. So here is a chance to do something about it. Many people will find that this method provides the kind of healing they would expect from a long and costly program with a therapist.

Let your mind drift backward in time. Remember the pain of being younger. When the feeling is there, do tonglen practice conjoined with the breath. Spend as much time as you can remembering different incidents. You can definitely heal yourself of the wounds of your earlier life by doing this practice. You will recall the roles others played in bringing you sorrow. When you remember them, you can do tonglen for them also. Everything they did to hurt you was their attempt to escape their own misery. The effects of practicing in this way can be profound, but proceed carefully—the memories you invoke might be overwhelming.

I once asked my teacher what practice wounded Westerners should do. He advised either the practice of tonglen or meditating on the nature of the mind. The latter is difficult and requires the close supervision of a high lama; the former is relatively straightforward and easy to do.

I had one student who had been raped as a child. Through this practice, she was able to forgive her rapist. It was an incredibly moving moment in class when she recounted her experience and really convinced me of the power of Lord Buddha's teachings, not only to help people attain the highest levels of awareness possible, but also to heal the deepest wounds and sufferings that ordinary people experience right now. I gained a certainty that for all but the most deeply disturbed, Buddhism is the perfect medicine; we needn't think of combining or mixing it with anything else. It works just great on its own.

After you've opened up to yourself in this way, you are ready to move on to the sufferings of others. Start with the one person to whom you feel closest. Traditionally, this would be your mother, but as many Westerners have problems with their mother, it can be anyone—a parent, a spouse, a friend, or a child. Feel their pain and do the tonglen practice, taking that pain on yourself. Do you feel yourself shutting down? Can you open up through the experience?

When I did the practice in retreat, I spent a lot of time doing tonglen for my mother. I was only partially successful. I felt a lot of resistance to feeling her pain, probably because I felt like I had abandoned her to go to Asia and into retreat in Scotland. However, I felt it was necessary to do the practice. Wherever we are shut down is where we must work to open up. It's not simply a question of becoming compassionate; anyplace where we are blocked will limit our meditation and our overall growth. It's not possible to develop strong meditation while maintaining a coldness toward others. I think one of the main lessons of Buddhism is that it is in our own best interests to be compassionate. We won't become boundaryless slobs; we will become open and loving.

After our loved ones, whom I recommend taking on one by one, we can move to all those toward whom we feel neutral, those people we pass every day and hardly notice and about whom we don't care. They are suffering as well. We cannot remain insensitive to their pain.

The most difficult and potentially the most powerful objects are, of course, our enemies, the people who may have harmed us and toward whom we harbor ill will. Is it in our own best interests to hate these people? Are we happier hating them and obsessing about them or forgiving and loving them? Your ego will scream that it's not fair to forgive these people and give away your goodness to them, but by now I hope you're becoming a little suspicious of listening to your ego. It has been wrong before! Because this is where the greatest resistance is, this will also be where the greatest change will occur. Once again, I recommend taking your enemies one by one so you can completely unblock your mind from the aversion that's constricting it.

Once you've done that, it's easy to move on to animals and the beings of other realms. We have no real unresolved issues with any of them. We can then conclude with all sentient beings in the universe. Having worked through at least some of our blockages, it's now appropriate to cultivate those expansive, loving feelings.

Some people are afraid that when they do tonglen, they will literally develop the symptoms of their object. For instance, if you do tonglen for Aunt Betty who has cancer, you might develop cancer or at least get a little sick. This is a common worry.

I've been told that although it's theoretically possible to literally transfer another's suffering onto oneself, it seems to happen with only the most spiritually gifted practitioners. Those who are actually able to do this don't resent it at all—they are really delighted to suffer for others and to purify themselves by doing so. For the rest of us, the practice is mainly about generating compassion and bodhichitta rather than taking on beings' actual suffering when we practice. If we are able to remove others' suffering through the power of our practice, that is a wonderful bonus, but we should be content with the inner transformation that will result in our attaining buddhahood, with its ability to remove *all* beings' pain.

CHAPTER 13

Ngondro: Vajrasattva Practice and Mandala Offerings

The next two ngondro practices are the Vajrasattva purification practice and offering the mandala. As I mentioned before, it's not necessary to have the Vajrasattva empowerment to do the practice, although it would be beneficial.

The Practice of Vajrasattva

To summarize the practice briefly, you imagine Buddha Vajrasattva above your head. In some practices he's alone, in some he has a consort. You invoke the wisdom beings, imagining that they merge into the visualization. You then pray for purification. Nectar flows from Vajrasattva's body and enters yours, pushing out your defilements, obscurations, and transgressions in the form of various gross things. As you recite first the long hundred-syllable mantra and then the short six-syllable mantra, you continue to meditate on this nectar flowing through you. At the conclusion of the mantra recitation, which occupies the bulk of the session, you recite a confession prayer. Then Vajrasattva dissolves into you, and you rest in a state of being merged with him.

This practice is based on applying what are called the four opponent powers. These are four techniques taught in the sutras for purifying nonvirtuous activity. Visualizing Vajrasattva above us is the power of reliance. Recollecting our nonvirtue and repenting is the power of remorse. Resolving never to repeat these nonvirtues is the power of the vow. Visualizing the nectar while reciting the mantra is the power of the remedy. When these four are complete, the purification is effected.

Some people really like this practice; others never connect. I've listened carefully to what other Western practitioners have said about it, and I've discerned a clear pattern. Those who, while reciting the mantra, consider all their nonvirtues item by item or even do some sort of life review eventually find the practice tedious. Those who focus instead on the flow of nectar and get into that experience enjoy the practice and find it beneficial.

I'm fortunately among the latter. I can't say it's the superior method; I just know that most of us prefer it. I've done Vajrasattva as my main practice for many years. I've been satisfied with the results, and I feel it's an excellent beginning practice for Western Vajrayanists.

By focusing on the flow of nectar, one brings one's awareness into one's body and also into one's energetic system, the inner body of channels and energy. As many of us know from Western concepts of body armoring and bioenergetics, we hold unexpressed emotions in our musculature. This is experienced in practice as a sort of tension and solidity in the body. Letting the nectar flow through the body slowly releases this chronic tension. It's an important process; so much is held in the body. As one perfects the practice, the flow of nectar becomes stronger, and one can direct it into more and more blockages. More negativities are released, and the practitioner develops one of the main signs of progress: a lightness of body, or what in English we would call suppleness.

Many of us aren't even in our bodies. We are either dissociated, lost in fantasy, or "in our heads." We might even feel that spiritual practice should serve to enhance that kind of separation. I'll talk more about the body in a later chapter, but for now let me say that this is not exactly the correct attitude. Doing Vajrasattva and visualizing the flow will help you greatly integrate your mind and body.

Although the flow of nectar is important, don't neglect the other powers. Reliance on Buddha Vajrasattva generates a feeling of surrender and letting go. Contemplate his qualities, including his unconditional love for you. Remember his omniscience; he knows everything about you and has the love and ability to cleanse you of your shortcomings with his nectar. Through your reliance, bask in his presence and the flow of nectar.

If you consider that all your limitations in this life are due to nonvirtues in the past, you should be able to feel deep remorse. Hold that feeling as the nectar washes away any remaining trace of your actions. This will help you to let go at an even deeper level and will aid you in abandoning yourself to the nectar's flow. Then you don't have to hold on to that feeling anymore.

What I'm emphasizing here is to make the practice experiential and devotional rather than conceptual. Your stains exist at a level deeper than the chatter of your thinking mind; to remove them, your practice must go deeper as well.

There are many ways to visualize the flow. One lama told me to imagine it like a waterfall flowing through me. That kind of visualization develops a lot of power and brings awareness to the area associated with the central channel.

Chökyi Nyima Rinpoche told one student to go slowly and carefully. The student was instructed to take about half an hour imagining one downward movement and carefully to feel the nectar in every part of his body, such as into each and every finger.

I've done a combination of both. I'll usually start with the waterfall. When I feel it getting stuck or blocked, I'll work very carefully, imagining the nectar permeating the blocked area.

Some teachers recommend visualizing the nectar filling the various channels and chakras; you must learn this directly from them.

Whatever way you do it, it's up to you to make it effective. Not only should you feel physical benefits, such as a lessening of chronic tension and a lightening of the body, but you should feel that whatever you are mentally holding on to is washed away, just as sticks are dislodged in a strong current. Therefore, the stronger the current, the more numerous and larger are the sticks that are washed away. Feel free to throw everything into the stream: your previous non-virtue, your present defilements and ego-clinging, even your sicknesses and physical pain. It's an amazing practice—simple and easy to do but very effective.

After you have completed your mantra recitations for your session, you recite confessional prayers. You don't have to remember everything; since you're not enlightened yet, you must have done a lot in the past to obscure you. Even if you don't remember specific acts, all your suffering, limitations, and slowness in spiritual progress are due to previous nonvirtue. When you contemplate its real and present effects, you can feel strong remorse even without knowing exactly what you did. Of course, when you do remember those acts that you truly regret, it is a time for sincere confession.

Vajrasattva is especially effective and is generally considered to be mandatory for purifying transgressions of tantric samaya, the vows that accompany Vajrayana practice. It's up to you to find out what they are, but be assured that you're breaking them all the time. It's daunting to consider, but we are taught that doing twenty-one of the long Vajrasattva mantras daily protects us from experiencing the results of these numerous infractions.

Lord Atisha said of himself, "I never violated the smallest of the monastic vows, not even in a dream. I occasionally considered something that would be a violation of the bodhisattva vows. But my violations of the tantric samayas were like rain." If that were true of Atisha, how much more true is it for us? Samaya can be broken merely by thought. If you, for a moment, consider someone with whom you have taken an empowerment to be a jerk, you have broken your vow. Therefore, once you have entered the gate of the Vajrayana, even if you don't do any other formal practice, try to do a little Vajrasattva daily without fail.

At the end of the practice, Vajrasattva melts into light and dissolves into you. Your mind and his mind merge. You enter a state that is completely free of the stains of defilements, transgressions, and nonvirtue: the mind of Vajrasattva.

Mandala Offerings

The next practice is that of offering the mandala. It takes an enormous amount of merit to become enlightened; it even takes a huge amount simply to have the appropriate conditions to practice. We make mandala offerings to accumulate this merit so we can progress along the path in a smooth, obstacle-free manner.

The practice is as follows. Using an ordinary or specially constructed plate, one offers the whole universe, filled with all that is positive and precious, to one's guru and the other objects of refuge. This is done by placing piles of rice and other substances on the plate to represent the various components of the universe while reciting an appropriate verse 100,000 times. There are concluding verses that mention deeper levels of offering followed by the usual dissolution and dedications.

In this practice, we use the ancient Indian concept of the universe being made up of certain similar units. The basic unit has a central mountain with continents, islands, and seas symmetrically arranged around it. The central mountain is called Mount Meru and is the home of the gods. Other god realms are located above Mount Meru. A billion of these units make up the universe.

As modern, scientific Westerners, what are we to make of all this? It's definitely the teaching of Lord Buddha that the universe is constructed this way; do we have any hesitation in accepting it? Of course, we can think of it as an Indian legend that Lord Buddha didn't want to challenge, so he just played along. That's the simplest explanation.

What I've come to believe is this: The universe appears differently according to whether one investigates it physically or mentally. That is, if you get into a spaceship and probe far into space, you will never see any Mount Merus or discover any pure lands. However, if you expand your mind in meditation, the realms that become apparent conform to Buddhist cosmology. These two universes exist on different planes, and an attempt to reconcile them, or to reduce one to another as is frequently done these days, will never be successful.

Another point of view would be to consider the actual construction and structure of the physical universe as completely irrelevant; the purpose of the meditation is to generate the merit of giving away everything wonderful and imaginable. There is no particular need to make the representation resemble the physical universe as we perceive it scientifically; doing the practice in its traditional form brings blessings.

When I do this practice, the issue of clarity of visualization versus feeling becomes very clear for me. The last time I did mandala offerings was during my group retreat, and I was able, at least for a while, to generate a clear and detailed image by keeping the visualizations growing. I would imagine something I wanted to offer as part of the wealth of the universe, and when my mind started drifting, I would use that mental energy to add more details to my visualization. For instance, I would imagine a beautiful lapis lazuli stupa. When my mind couldn't hold the image and wanted to move on to something new, I added butter lamps on the stupa with sweet yellow light. Next, I added gardens with pools reflecting this most beautiful of stupas; then I filled the paths in the gardens with people who were devotedly offering it to the lama or circumambulating. And on and on.

But this can become a mental exercise devoid of feeling. So I would try to conjure up images that were the most touching to me and then offer them to my precious teacher.

Before the retreat, I had an extremely difficult time helping to construct the retreat facility. It was hell for me. Finally, I had a day off and was able to go to the nearby city of Dumfries to go shopping. I was completely burned out and exhausted from building and experiencing a lot of apprehension about the retreat and my ability to do it. Dumfries, however, is like many Scottish cities, very gray and damp. Through it flows a river, and on the river floated several swans, trying to find food. The sight of these swans moved me deeply. Something about finding such beauty and grace in the midst of both this internal and external grayness left a profound impression on me.

So when doing the mandala offerings, I remembered the image of those beautiful swans on the river and would devotedly offer it to my lama. It always had an opening effect on my heart. Another method that had this effect was to offer a chorus of sweet-faced youths singing praises to him. During the break times, the monks in retreat would compare the various offerings we were making; it was fun hearing about all the marvelous things that my friends were imagining in their offerings.

It's also nice to get pretty little things to add to your rice. Since I've spent so much time in Nepal, I always use the plastic beads that Nepalese women love to wear. It makes my rice colorful and sparkling. I also try to use a few semiprecious stones. Some people like to add things that have special significance for them.

However you do it, it can be wonderful to spend your time making offerings to your teacher. What they have given you is priceless! Gyatrul Rinpoche emphasizes cultivating the ability to offer without holding back. You offer your possessions, body, and merit without any hesitation. It is a practice that can truly open your heart and prepare you for the next stage of ngondro—guru yoga.

CHAPTER 14

Ngondro:
Guru Yoga and Devotion

Guru yoga is the final and most important part of the preliminaries. It might also be the most important practice you ever do. It is the key or hub of the Vajrayana, around which everything else is oriented. I've repeatedly referred to the importance of the teacher-student relationship. Here, we are consciously endeavoring to open and broaden that channel for greater blessing and transmission.

Let me describe the practice. As usual it varies from lineage to lineage, liturgy to liturgy. In the Nyingma, the guru is visualized as either Guru Rinpoche or Samantabhadra (Tib. Kuntuzangpo); in the Kagyu, as Vajradhara (Tib. Dorje Chang), either with or without consort. The practitioner visualizes themself as a deity, usually as Vajrayogini. By visualizing yourself in a divine form, it's easier to make a connection between the guru's enlightened qualities and your own incipient ones. You can imagine the guru in the space in front of you, on the crown of your head, or more rarely, in your heart.

A series of prayers follows, invoking both the guru and the lineage from which they descend. A mantra, such as the vajra guru mantra, may also be repeated. The prayers and/or mantra are counted and accumulated.

At the conclusion of the session, you imagine the guru bestowing the four empowerments on you. In chapter 4, we talked about receiving these empowerments in person. That is the empowerment of the ground. Here, the principle and visualization are similar, but you engage in the process as you practice on your own. This is the empowerment of the path. The actual attainment of enlightenment is the empowerment of the fruit. The actual procedure varies slightly from liturgy to liturgy but is basically as follows:

1. White light flows from an OM at the lama's forehead to your forehead. This bestows the vase empowerment, purifying your body and enabling you to practice *kyerim*, the development stage. This results in the attainment of the nirmanakaya.

2. Red light flows from an AH at the lama's throat to your throat, bestowing the secret empowerment, purifying your speech, and enabling you to practice tsalung, the meditation on the channels and energies. This results in the attainment of the sambhogakaya.

3. Blue light flows from a HUM at the lama's heart to your heart, bestowing the wisdom empowerment, purifying your mind, and enabling you to practice the meditation of union. This results in the attainment of the dharmakaya.

4. White, red, and blue (or sometimes a fourth color from a fourth center) lights flow together to your three centers. You receive the fourth empowerment, purifying your body, speech, and mind, and enabling you to practice mahamudra and dzogchen, resulting in the svabhavikaya.

5. At the conclusion of the empowerments, the lama dissolves into light and merges into you. Your body, speech, and mind become the lama's body, speech, and mind. You then rest in that state.

Everything I've heard, read, or studied in the past forty-five years has emphasized the extreme importance of this practice. Let me quote Jamgon Kongtrul at length:

In general, in order to follow the Mantrayana or Vajrayana, especially to receive instructions in the meditation of the Fulfillment Stage, you must first receive the guru's blessing. Until you have received it, you will not be on the true path.

It is said that a disciple who is intensely devoted and reverent toward a fully qualified Vajrayana master with whom they have formed a sacred bond will achieve supreme and worldly *siddhi* without doing anything else. But a person who lacks devotion and reverence for the guru, even if they perform a great (number of mantra recitations) for the yidams of the four tantras, will obtain no supreme siddhi whatsoever.

As for worldly siddhi, they will not achieve long life, wealth, power, etc., no matter how hard they may strive. Anything they do achieve will have been won through great hardship. This is the "non-profound path."

On the other hand, if he or she develops true devotion and reverence, all obstacles will be cleared, uprooted, and expelled from his path, and they will obtain supreme and worldly siddhi by this method alone. Therefore, we call it the "profound path of the Guru Yoga."[1]

The practice of guru yoga goes hand in hand with the path of devotion. I've mentioned devotion often in earlier chapters, but I want to treat the subject more extensively now, especially warning you of many of the pitfalls that can easily befall the average Western devotee.

What is devotion? It's a practice that constantly changes for me the more I practice. How I define it today is different from how I did five or ten years ago. It is a complete opening up to the state of enlightenment as embodied by our teacher. All our longing for liberation merges with all our love, appreciation, and gratitude toward the teacher to produce a tremendously powerful force. This force can truly cut through our conceptual mind. In that moment of openness, we are receptive to the lama's blessings, and our own buddha-nature is very close.

All of our samsaric mind, our ego, is an inward contraction, a fascination and identification with some particular content of our minds. Devotion provides the strength to fight against that contraction, to locate the focal point of awareness outside the usual restricted confines of our own small minds. So true devotion is expansive and thought-free.

Devotion has often been compared to falling in love. When we fall in love, the mind opens up and focuses outward. The experience feels blissful and liberating. With ordinary love, however, expectation, desire, and attachment soon creep in. We see our beloved, and we feel this tremendous wave of openness, bliss, and love. But in the next moment, more ordinary thoughts fill us: "I want to snuggle. She doesn't seem so happy to see me today." This kind of love leads only to more ordinary states of mind. I sincerely believe that romantic love can be used to produce many of the benefits of devotion if the lovers conscientiously will it; however, the main emotional difference between romantic love and devotion is that our lover seems to have the potential to satisfy our desires. Because those desires can be satisfied, it is easy for us to let them go unexamined.

Gurus won't do that. Not only won't gurus make love to us or marry us, but they won't give us the adoration we come to expect from our partners. The guru may be kind and affectionate, or they may be distant and wrathful, but we will never feel completely satisfied or consummated. Trungpa Rinpoche said, "Devotion is unrequited love for the guru."

It's that unrequitedness that provides the path. We open up to them, feel the surge of love, but then immediately stumble upon our desires: "I hope they acknowledge how good my meditation has been." "Will they smile at me?" We all go through this. Letting go of these ordinary desires and attachments and deepening the love is the path. We must always remember that the gurus are buddhas who have impartial love toward all. If they smile at us today, it's their skillful means; if they are wrathful toward us but affectionate toward someone else, that's also their skillful means. This interplay allows us to see and subsequently deal with deeply conditioned parts of our minds as we persevere in our attempt to open.

As our openness becomes freer of our emotional needs, it becomes purer and approaches a state of true devotion. In that state of true devotion, it is easy for the lama to transmit buddha-nature to you.

It is much better than a pat on the back. And this naturally intensifies your devotion and encourages you to persevere further on the devotional path.

The real key in the beginning is to have the intelligence and wisdom not to get stuck in emotional states, not to confuse them with true devotion. They are not. They are simply needy, unconscious states that we have never properly dealt with before. If we get trapped there, our devotion will always be off, and we'll simply be indulging in old habits rather than receiving a transmission of buddha-nature. Many of the problems we've seen in the West over the past several decades related to the issues of gurus, cults, and devotion have been because of this very theme—the confusion of unconscious emotion with conscious devotion.

I want to take some time and expand on some of the emotional states that may arise for you as you deepen your devotion for your teacher. Because they represent some of our deepest conditioning, they are often difficult to recognize. I know this because I've been trapped in all of these states many times.

The key concept here is the one of transference. We learned our habits of love from our parents when we were infants, so when we fall in love again, either with a teacher or a lover, we unconsciously reproduce those habits and patterns. In psychological terms, we are unconsciously projecting our feelings toward our parents onto our new loved one. I prefer not to think of it so much as projection as simply the repetition of our habits of love. If it always rains where we live, we will habitually reach for our umbrella whether it is rainy or sunny; if our parents expected us to act a certain way to receive their love, we will habitually act that way when we want to be loved.

You can see here one of the differences between the devotional and the romantic relationship—your teachers have no emotional needs of their own and are aware of the process you must go through to get beyond your emotional needs and habits. They will act in a way that will enable you to do so. Your lover, on the other hand, is just as confused and needy as you are and will most likely keep you reinforcing your old patterns.

Whether we see it as transference or as habit, when we become devotees, we are in a sense regressing to infancy. What are some of the emotional patterns that may arise?

We might want to be taken care of, either spiritually or materially. We may feel that we don't have to do anything, that the guru will provide whatever we need. We might feel we no longer have to take responsibility for our behavior since we're under the guru's umbrella. I even met one fellow who wouldn't ask his teacher any questions. He expected his teacher to provide the answers automatically from his omniscience.

We fear either losing our autonomy, our sense of being a distinct, strong individual, or autonomy itself because we sense it will anger the guru or lead to separation from them. The latter goes back to our original separation from our mother and colors many of our relationships. Actually, our teachers want us to develop into strong, self-sufficient individuals. It is the habit of our infancy that we can't be autonomous and simultaneously merged with another being. As we practice devotion, we learn that the two are not in opposition at all. The stronger we become, the cleaner is our opening to a state of pure love. We are now strong enough to surrender because we have confidence in our ability to cope with the dissolution of our boundaries. Our inner autonomous strength actually enables us to merge more deeply; the blessings of our union with our teacher gives us more self-confidence. At this stage, these tendencies positively reinforce each other.

We must always remember that, although our parents weren't buddhas and our lovers aren't buddhas, our teachers are. They don't fear our growth; it isn't threatening to them in any way.

When I first started teaching, the first thing I taught, at Gyatrul Rinpoche's request, was the ancient text *Fifty Stanzas of Guru Devotion* by the Indian saint Ashvaghosha. We spent a long time discussing it, and my friends asked many questions. Much later, well after the end of the discussion, I realized what the key, unspoken issue was. All of us were afraid of being rejected by our teacher. If we didn't prostrate right, if we were too serious, if we weren't serious enough—whatever the issue was for each particular student, it always boiled down to one thing: the fear that if we made a serious mistake, the guru would take us out of his heart.

It was an interesting insight; I'm sure I had many of the same fears. But how can a buddha possibly reject you? You might have felt rejected by your mother or your childhood sweetheart, but your lama will never reject you. It's quite a relief to realize that. It's okay to make mistakes, to experiment a little, to learn from experience. Sometimes you can try being formal, like a Tibetan attendant; at other times, be friendly and playful. Your lama will understand what you are trying to do internally and, if you are sincere, support your efforts and guide you with appropriate feedback. Feeling confident that your teacher is truly committed to you provides a lot of space. Your fear of rejection is simply one more of the habitual emotions you must learn to relinquish. Beyond that fear is a very open state.

Some people use devotion to surrender common sense. Either they think the guru has all the answers and they don't have to think for themselves anymore, or they feel that if they think or question, it will incur the guru's wrath. As I said before, gurus won't reject us easily. If we are habitually thinking too much and not getting on with our practice, our teacher may comment on this. But a clear intellect is part of the independence they are trying to cultivate in us. So if you find yourself becoming an unquestioning follower, be careful. You won't be able to penetrate the depths of the teachings without a keen mind. If the lama asks you to do something that doesn't make sense or seem appropriate, there is no rule prohibiting simply inquiring as to the reason behind their request.

Another mistake is to exaggerate the lama out of all proportion in your mind. They are already buddhas, but if you start to consider one the greatest yogi or the greatest scholar or whatever, you have a secret agenda somewhere. Either you're identifying with your guru and feeling proud of yourself ("My lama is the greatest, and I'm their favorite student"), or you're using their greatness to diminish yourself.

The latter is especially disturbing. If we have low self-esteem (and most of us seem to), the exalted nature of our teacher may reinforce that. The higher they seem, the lower we seem; the lower we seem, the higher they seem; it's an endless cycle. It feels like devotion, but is it? It is simply reinforcing our wretchedness.

Some students idealize their teacher to such a great extent that they become quite disillusioned when they perceive what they consider to be a fault. For instance, you might feel a high lama should be celibate and after a while discover that your teacher has a consort no one knew about. This can be upsetting to many.

Before you make a firm commitment to a teacher, consider what your nonnegotiable demands are regarding the behavior you consider to be appropriate or inappropriate. Check them out thoroughly. Once you've made that commitment, if you then discover things about your teacher that you don't like, be willing to work with them. Those things could be an indication of some attitude you are clinging to.

A teacher to whom I feel very close appeared as a monk. After many years, when I discovered he wasn't, I was a little upset. Now, looking back, I can see it was my own unresolved issues related to sexual activity that made me uncomfortable. I felt safer with a celibate teacher as a role model; it didn't threaten my own repressions. When this discovery became painful for me, I reasoned, "I know this teacher has been skillful and kind to me. Why shouldn't I feel he will be the same to the women in his life?" Later I thought, "When I was immature and needed a celibate teacher, he manifested as one. Now my mind is more flexible, and his manifestation has changed. How amazing!"

When you find fault with your teacher's behavior, try to see what this says about you, and try to have pure perception. If that doesn't work, admit to yourself you aren't really qualified to judge the behavior of an enlightened being. If that still doesn't work, and you have sincere doubts about their behavior, remember that the teachings of the Buddha are pure and can be transmitted through less than perfectly pure vessels. Try to learn what you can from them, and don't make a big deal about their faults.

Akong Rinpoche addressed this issue when he said, "The difference between a good and a bad student is this: When a good student sees a pile of gold and a pile of rocks, he takes the gold. When the bad student sees the piles, he takes the rocks and complains."

By now I hope that you have understood my point and are not too deeply offended. To reiterate, our teachers are not parents or lovers. They will not reject you; they are not afraid of your growing up. They also will not be seduced by your offerings, your praise, your groveling, or your flirtatiousness. Always check: With whom am I relating? The key here is to remember one of the main points of the devotional path—always consider your teacher to be a buddha.

There's a famous Kagyü saying:

> If you see your guru as a buddha, you will receive a buddha's blessing. If you see him as a bodhisattva, you will receive a bodhisattva's blessing. If you see him as a siddha, you will receive a siddha's blessing. If you see him as an ordinary person—a good spiritual friend—such is the blessing you will receive. If you feel no devotion or reverence for him, you will receive absolutely no blessing.[2]

If we act in a flirtatious or infantile manner, are we really regarding our teacher as a buddha?

One thing that has helped me greatly with my relationship with my teacher is falling in love and marrying. Many of the needs I once unconsciously expected my lama to fulfill are now being met by my wife. I don't expect my lama to say I'm wonderful—that's my wife's job. This has made my relationship with my teacher purer and even more wonderful. By having fewer expectations and needs, I can remain more open. Every moment with him is special and blessed.

As you purify your many unconscious needs through the path of devotion, you will heal some of the deepest and most difficult conditioning. You will grow stronger and more independent while developing a greater capacity to love, and your mind will open to the true blessings and transmission of your lama, the transmission of rigpa.

An important component in guru yoga, and indeed many Tibetan Buddhist practices, is prayer. I've stuggled with that word for forty-five years! First it has an association with theistic Western religions toward which I feel no connection. Also, it connotes weakness to me, like I'm some sniveling stray dog or beggar.

I don't think there is a right or wrong way to pray. For me, it has become a means of really focusing my most powerful, heartfelt intentions joined with the power of the object of prayer. It's also a way to change a wishy-washy aspiration or hope ("I kind of want to be a better person") into something much stronger. If I want, *yearn*, to develop a more loving, compassionate heart, I can invoke Chenrezig, the buddha of compassion, and sincerely pray, "Lord Chenrezig, please grant me your blessings that I can become a more compassionate person." It's important for me to believe Chenrezig is there before me and has the ability to aid me. By this stage in our practice, believing shouldn't be too difficult. Aligning my intention and aspiration, my trust and devotion toward Chenrezig, with his blessing creates a powerful transformative energy.

Most of the prayers we do in Tibetan Buddhism are done in Tibetan. As I said earlier, we believe the Tibetan words contain great blessings. But when we are feeling raw or inspired, praying with whatever words arise in our hearts can be inspiring.

Now we have finished ngondro. By "finished," I mean I have finished my brief description of the practices; hopefully you will finish the recitations. But what does it mean to finish ngondro? A simple answer is that ngondro is a preparation for doing Vajrayana practices; when we are indeed ready to do Vajrayana practices, we have finished ngondro.

What are the signs of having finished ngondro? According to Chökyi Nyima Rinpoche,

> When we begin these practices we will notice that our minds begin to change. The way we react is different from before; clarity, warmth, and strength blossom from within. We are more

balanced and flexible and our impulses and emotions have less of a grip on us. Gradually, we become more caring, devoted, and intelligent. These are the surest signs that the preliminary practices are working as intended.[3]

As you can see, some of a ngondro practitioner's important shifts will be in character, not experience. Our character can change in many wonderful ways without necessarily developing deep or profound meditative experiences. We may develop a warmth and an ease that feels meaningful. We may be more content or work harder.

Nowadays in the West, meditation instruction is easily available. It makes it seem like anyone can walk in off the street, take a class, and begin meditating. Although that is true to a certain extent, and a person will receive some benefits, if they try to meditate more intensively, obstacles and deviations will arise (the main obstacle—they never stop thinking).

As I mentioned earlier, this has been recognized for thousands of years in many spiritual traditions. In a monastery, monks or nuns are trained in the monastic routines until they are mature; aspirants of recluses become apprentices or servants of their masters; Zen monks "chop wood, carry water"; Milarepa built houses for Marpa. We can even say that in our culture the challenges of family and work, or the use of Western healing modalities, are forms of preparation.

These are all examples of ngondro in the sense that they are preparatory activities that come before more intensive meditation. Where we are so lucky is that the Tibetan masters have created simple practices to achieve the same benefits that these apprenticeships did in the past.

If we have become more caring, devoted, intelligent, or any of the other qualities that should emerge and grow through the ngondro, we should feel a great satisfaction with our lives and profoundly grateful that we have been able to connect with Buddhism. If this is indeed the case, then our ngondro is working.

There are two kinds of positive change—change in character and change in meditative experience. In the long run, both are necessary. In general, character comes first, then meditative experience can change character as well. But real progress in meditation is difficult. Let's approach ngondro as a wonderful opportunity for growth and transformation.

Many people take ngondro as a lifelong practice. Probably half of my practice for forty-five years has been ngondro. Tulku Urgyen Rinpoche recommended completing ngondro four times; his wife completed it eleven times!

The practices in the following chapters will be much more challenging. If you don't do ngondro properly, they might be too much. If you do complete ngondro properly, you will be amazed by your transformation and ready to move on.

CHAPTER 15

Kyerim

Perhaps the most obvious aspect of Vajrayana practice is the meditations associated with the various deities, called *yidams* in Tibetan. Even the most casual observer of Tibetan Buddhism has noticed these striking iconographic representations—flawless statues and minutely detailed scroll paintings called thankhas that show all manner of yidams. Some are beatifically peaceful with loving, serene smiles and gazes; others are incredibly malevolent, surrounded by flames and brandishing a wide variety of weapons from a multitude of arms. Then there are the deities in sexual union—what are we to make of that?

Practices associated with visualizing these deities and reciting their mantras are called *kyerim* in Tibetan. *Kyerim* has been variously translated as "arising yoga," "generation stage," or "development stage." It is contrasted with the completion stage, which will be discussed later. Briefly, in kyerim, you use a liturgical text called a *sadhana* that is related to the specific yidam you are practicing. You recite the text, visualizing as you go along. At the mantra section, you pause and recite the mantra, then you conclude the practice. There are many stages within a sadhana, and not every sadhana has every possible section; nevertheless, all sadhanas follow a fairly typical format, and this allows us to discuss them in a generic way.

When do we do kyerim? In other words, at what stage of our practice is it appropriate? As I mentioned before, in the Kagyu, Sakya, and Nyingma systems, we begin a serious yidam practice only after we have completed the preliminaries (Gelugpas alternate some deity practices with their ngondro practice). It is important to complete ngondro before commencing kyerim, especially if we aspire to practice a wrathful deity or a deity in union, or if we are interested in the completion stage practices of tsalung. Ngondro prepares the mind in a number of essential ways that enable subsequent practices to be efficacious.

Some lamas in the West prefer that their students do some simple sitting practice for a while before beginning Vajrayana practice. The flexibility and insight that arise from sitting also enables the kyerim practice to be more effective. I agree wholeheartedly. With its visualizations and rituals, there is a danger that kyerim practice can become a kind of dissociative fantasy unless the student has a strong background in working with the mind. I will talk more about this later when we consider the dangers of kyerim.

A few teachers give their students kyerim practice—almost always in the form of a peaceful deity's practice—right from the start. For instance, Kalu Rinpoche had all his students practice Chenrezig, the buddha of love and compassion; Chagdud Rinpoche instructed all his students to meditate on Red Tara. It's nice when all the students of a lama know the same practice; whenever they meet, there is a practice they can do together. In general, it is necessary to have the appropriate empowerment; these days, however, that requirement is being loosened for some of the peaceful deities.

Many Westerners have great difficulty with the deities and their attendant rituals. We are usually attracted by the depth and profundity of Buddhist philosophy and the charisma of the great teachers; the existence of these deities and their practice does not seem to fit in our scheme of things. "I thought Buddhism didn't have any gods and believed in egolessness. If there is no ego, no creator, and everything is empty, what are all these deities anyway? This must be some kind of Bonpo or Hindu perversion." I imagine we've all thought like that at times, especially while trying to navigate an especially long and confusing sadhana.

When we try to understand what these yidams are, we usually formulate two categories or answers that we then assume are mutually exclusive. The first is that the deities are basically symbolic, representing our own latent qualities and buddha-nature. If we're familiar with Jungian psychology, we may regard them as archetypes. This approach is more satisfying to the more intellectual, nontheistic practitioner. It's safe and appealing. We're not actually worshipping an external deity as the folks down the street are doing when they go to church; it's much more esoteric and profound than that. In other words, it doesn't threaten us, our autonomy, or our conceptions.

The other approach is to consider the deities external to ourselves, powerful enlightened beings with the ability to manifest and bless us at our invocation. For the more devotional, it's quite comforting to know someone's out there watching over us. Even if it seems that nothing is happening in our practice, we know they will reward us later. This is similar to the lay Asian view but seems difficult to reconcile with Buddhism's nontheism.

You wouldn't believe how often I've heard this subject debated (often within my own mind). From one viewpoint, some rituals just don't make sense, whereas other rituals or different parts of the same one flow perfectly well. I will be doing some long ritual or puja and thinking the deity is just a symbol of my buddha-nature; it all makes sense, and I even feel inspired and somewhat pleased with my high view and for having figured it out. Then I will have to imagine the deity within some strange Hindu god or something, and the whole edifice I've been constructing and congratulating myself on will come tumbling down.

The answer is that both approaches are partially true; their union—the deities are both symbolic of inner states to be developed and tangible external beings who can intercede and help the practitioner—is the real solution. I would like to quote the great modern meditation master Bokar Rinpoche. Although he is speaking of one deity in particular (Chenrezig), his words can be applied to any of the other myriad yidams:

Who really is Chenrezig? . . .

First, we need to know that Chenrezig is both an appearance, the divine manifestation, as well as an essence, the inner reality, with one not excluding or contradicting the other. The appearance of Chenrezig is the symbol of his essence made manifest. Through this appearance we can approach the essence of Chenrezig. The appearance does not exhaust the essence anymore than the essence negates the appearance. To pretend that Chenrezig only has an existence outside ourselves would be a mistake. But it would also be a mistake to see him only as an abstraction. Grasping the link between the two aspects (appearance and essence) is necessary in order to understand both his nature and meditation....

Chenrezig is within us because love and compassion are not qualities added to the mind. These qualities are part of the awakened state even if, for the moment, this state exists only as a potential for us....

Saying that Chenrezig is the ultimate nature of the mind does not negate his form manifestation. The essence expresses itself through an appearance.... He is the visible expression taken by all the buddhas to help us activate the love and compassion that are presently only a potential in us and to reveal the ultimate Chenrezig in ourselves....

The relationship between Chenrezig as the potential of compassion in our mind and Chenrezig appearing as a divine form is the real foundation of the practice:

- On one hand, Chenrezig as a manifested deity is charged with and transmits the power of the grace and compassion of the mind of all buddhas;
- On the other hand, our mind is endowed with the potentiality of love and compassion;
- Thirdly, the ineluctable interconnection that links everything causes the first factor to necessarily act on the second one and reveal it.[1]

I think this is the clearest description of the yidam I have ever read.

There are three key points while practicing kyerim: the clarity of the visualization, the pride of the deity, and the recollection of the meaning. In theory, visualizations are supposed to be clearer than real life. In extended commentaries, the minutiae of visualization are taught with amazing detail. In one practice, I had to visualize myself as a deity. Inside that deity were the subtle energy channels. Inside the channels were more deities. Inside the deities were Tibetan letters. Light circulated from letter to letter. In retreat, it is possible to spend a lot of time building up a visualization like this, and in the process, I've discovered a trick or two that helps.

In general, visualization can be extremely difficult, if not impossible, for most people. But some people are natural visualizers. Without effort or training, they can visualize clearly. A friend of mine can visualize so clearly that he can mentally walk around the visualization, viewing it from all angles. According to research, about one in ten people are natural visualizers, and of these, three out of four are women.

Here are some of the tricks I've stumbled across while trying to master this skill. First, believe that the visualization is real. If you're trying to visualize a deity in front of you, develop the conviction that the deity is actually there and you're just trying to see it rather than trying to create it from scratch. It's as if you are tuning in to a radio station that you know is already broadcasting.

Second, emotion helps. If you feel devotion toward the deity in front of you, that also helps to make it clearer. Yearning brings it closer. Also remember that the deity loves you and has the power to grant spiritual accomplishments. How does that make you feel?

Third, try to keep the visualization moving. Scan it; move from top to bottom, adding details as it fades. If you're visualizing the Buddha, start with his hair. When that starts to fade, add the eyes, the ears, and so on. Work down to the lotus seat and then scan upward. Most people find this easier than trying to hold and stabilize a static image. This also makes use of our tendency to indulge continually in discursiveness. When you feel the beginning of a thought welling up, use that energy and momentum to add another feature to the visualization. With the Buddha, for instance, if you feel a thought coming, add some folds to his robes. If you really like to think, you can add the wheels to the soles of his feet or decorate his robes with brocade-like patterns. This can be a lot of fun. You can really get lost in it, and the time can fly by. Lamas feel that complicated visualizations are completely appropriate for Westerners because we are so discursive. We may long for simple practices, but simple practices require that we block the tendency to be discursive. In these practices, we are using that tremendous momentum of the mind to progress instead of squashing it.

The fourth trick is similar to the previous one. Make the visualization more elaborate. If I visualize a Tibetan letter, I try to make it three-dimensional and glistening, as if it were made out of ice. It's actually clearer that way than if I try to visualize a flatter, more lifeless letter. Hence, an important point is that the more complicated and difficult the visualization, the easier you may find it and the clearer the resultant image will be.

Fifth, remember the emptiness aspect. We may not be completely clear about what that means at this point, but there are a few things we can keep in mind that may enhance our ability to visualize. We've already dissolved our ordinary body at the beginning of the practice; therefore, we shouldn't allow ourselves to refocus on our physical sensations. Also, we've dissolved our ordinary mind; therefore, our visualization should exist without a strong sense of a watching, judging, manipulating mind. The visualization just hangs by itself in space. I'll talk a bit more about this idea in a while.

Perhaps none of these suggestions will help. Your visualization might still be exceptionally hazy, almost completely nonexistent. Don't despair. Lots of us have the same problem. Luckily, these practices are so rich that even if visualization doesn't work for you, another aspect will give the practice meaning and value and will provide a technique for your growth and development.

One technique I have found to be amazingly successful is the deity's pride. The general instruction is to consider yourself as the deity rather than as your usual identity. For many years, I had great resistance. Who was I fooling? I knew what a hopeless jerk I was. What was the use of pretending?

Then, while in retreat, I read a quote from Je Tsongkhapa, the great founder of the Gelug school. Tsongkhapa said that in the beginning one's pride is conceptual; it is simply the thought, "I am this deity!" But one should check one's mind and notice the ordinary or nondeity aspects of it. These are to be abandoned as one returns to the deity's pride.

This quote in an obscure book really opened a gate for me. Instead of thinking "How could I possibly be a deity?" I saw that I could use this technique as a method to abandon the very self-images that were keeping me from feeling like a deity in the first place.

Like most Westerners, I have been plagued by many intense and well-entrenched negative self-images. "I'm unlovable," "I'm not attractive," "I'm weak," and so forth. Sound familiar? Well, these self-images are nothing more than clusters of thoughts, albeit with a tremendous amount of energy invested in them. We spend our lives crippled by these images, and we view all our experiences through these distorted lenses. I know from my own experience that these images make us completely miserable.

But the images have power only if we identify with them. And the buddhas have been insightful and compassionate enough to give us an easy technique to overcome this tyranny. We simply acknowledge how we are identifying with a self-image and then recollect the pride of the deity. When we disidentify with the self-image, its power completely evaporates. And the thought, "I am the deity," gives us something to hang on to. It's like jumping out of a sinking ship into a shiny new cruiser. Once you get the hang of it, it's an easy and effective method for dealing with a variety of problems and negativities. It requires no skill in visualization, simply the intelligence to identify where you're stuck and a willingness to change. Believe me, it is a most effective technique.

When you're not crippled by negative self-images, your invocation of divine pride can be subtler. Tsoknyi Rinpoche explains deity pride as that which holds the disparate parts of the visualization together. Without that pride, you have only parts. Tulku Urgyen has said that invoking divine pride has more merit than having a clear visualization;

from my own experience, I completely concur. Chökyi Nyima Rinpoche told me that during rituals, divine pride is more effective than visualization in realizing the ritual. For instance, if you are doing a ritual for long life, believing that you are really Amitayus, the buddha of long life, even without clear visualization, is more effective than visualizing clearly but still harboring some doubts about pride.

Traditionally, clear visualization precedes pride. In fact, when done properly, visualization elicits pride. The imagery gives you a sense of being the deity. We all know how good we feel about ourselves when we're nicely dressed—it definitely affects our minds. Here, we are allowing the visualization to work in the same way. Having the various forms and attributes gives rise to the appropriate sense of being the possessor or inhabitant of those forms. I often teach divine pride first so my students get some sense of it before struggling with the visualization, especially since so many of us can take ages before we feel really comfortable with this process. Then the visualization can flow out of the pride: "Since I'm this deity, I must have this body."

The third aspect of kyerim that one must embrace is recollection of the meaning. Remember, the first is clear visualization, and the second is divine pride. All deities are made of rainbow light. They're not flesh and blood like you and me, nor are they clay or brass like statues. They are completely pure. Also, they don't have ordinary insides, such as livers or small intestines. They're either completely hollow, or they contain subtle energy channels, moon disks, mantra circles, and so on. There's a deep and pure symbolic meaning to their attributes, weapons, and ornaments. It is not that they are in union because they're horny; they're not brandishing swords because they feel angry and they want to get even. Their union represents the union of skillful means and emptiness; the swords cut through duality or ego-clinging; and so on. If you think they're just like us, that's a big mistake.

Understanding the discriminating wisdom that cuts through dualistic conceptions is difficult; visualizing a sword is much easier. But because of the blessing of the practice and the power of symbols to act deeply on the mind, visualization brings the symbolized reality closer. You really start to feel that you are cutting through ignorance and that this is truly happening rather than being imagined. Other deities are depicted trampling on representations of the ego or one's negativities; visualizing yourself like this can be quite empowering and a great aid in overcoming your limitations. When you have experiences like these, you can genuinely appreciate the profundity of the techniques.

Although it may be difficult to remember or to practice perfectly, never forget the connection with emptiness. We can easily comprehend that the deity is no different than the mind; they have no separate existence. Can we truly distinguish between a mind that is doing the visualizing and the visualization itself? Where does one end and the other begin? The visualization should be merged with our experience or understanding of rigpa. If that is too difficult, remember the advice of Jamgon Kongtrul:

> Though a beginner has difficulty in realizing [the correct view], he or she can, however, understand that the mind appearing as the deity is the generation phase, that knowing the deity to be one's own mind is the completion phase, that realizing these two to be inseparable is the yoga of union.[2]

If your visualization and pride are both stable, but there is no recollection, there is the danger of taking the whole setup too literally: "I am the Great Wrathful One crushing all enemies." Remember that what you're really crushing is your ego. If not, you can become demonic, taking the whole thing literally and using the images to fortify your ego and project it out against others. You might become like the yogi who couldn't leave his cave because he believed he had grown all these extra arms and horns.

When one begins a deity practice, it is good to receive as much commentary on that practice as possible. For any kyerim practice, there will be instruction manuals explaining the shrine setup; the appropriate visualizations for each stage, especially what's to be visualized while reciting the mantra, which can become elaborate and sometimes juicy; and how to do retreat on the practice. There will be notes on subsidiary practices; signs of progress, both in your sitting and in dreams or visions; and how to deal with various obstacles. The preceding quotation, for instance, comes from Jamgon Kongtrul's commentary on a Guru Rinpoche practice called Konchog Chidu. Although many of these commentaries are not yet translated, they're worth seeking out. They contain some of the most useful information on Vajrayana practice.

There are also some good general commentaries on kyerim, such as Gyatrul Rinpoche's *Generating the Deity*. A manual of teachings for one deity may contain good general advice for any practice. The earlier long quotation of Bokar Rinpoche came from *Chenrezig: Lord of Love*, but obviously, his words can be applied to any deity. Be somewhat discriminating, however, in mixing advice; visualization details cannot be transposed from one sadhana to another, even for the same deity. These books and other teachings you receive will not only teach you the visualizations, but also clarify the meaning of the practice as a whole and of each individual stage, such as refuge and bodhichitta, throwing a torma to the obstructers, and so on.

The main concept of kyerim is *dagnang*, which is usually translated as "pure perception" or "sacred outlook." Dagnang means to regard all beings as deities, all sounds as mantra, all thoughts as the play of the deity's awareness. What does this mean? That the objects of perception change form? That your friends are walking around with consorts in their laps and swords in their hands? That when they ask how you're doing, they're really saying OM MANI PADME HUM? How would you reply?

The exact meaning and method of practice of pure perception is elusive and subtle. It is true that advanced practitioners do have experiences of the world as a mandala. Devoted students would see Je Tsongkhapa as Manjushri, for example. On the other hand, it's difficult to fake. How can we twist what we're actually perceiving?

We can start by being willing to concede that our judgments are merely that—judgments. They don't necessarily correspond to the outer world. Let go of them and then see how the world appears. When you are not judging appearances quite so heavily, you may notice a change in their quality; your perception will shift somewhat. It will give you a clue on how to proceed. Keep trying to see through your rigid judgments. The world will be much more open.

One problem that always arises is how to deal with difficult people in that nonjudgmental state. Are we breaking our samaya by having a clear understanding of what they're doing? Chökyi Nyima Rinpoche answered me as follows: "No matter how much people seem to be careening off the road, they always have good hearts." Later, he added, "The negative things that they do are due to their *not* having pure perception."

Rinpoche has further explained to me that there are two aspects to pure perception—contrived and absolute. The former is the fabricated visualization of deities and the recitation of their mantras. The second is how the world actually appears to someone experiencing absolute reality. The former is valuable, because with time and cultivation it leads to the latter.

Some of the difficulties we have with deity practice and pure perception can be clarified by examining a little Tibetan Buddhist philosophy. If we believe emptiness means reducing everything to a kind of neutral grayness, it's hard to understand where deities come from. But the philosophy of emptiness, especially its presentation by the Kagyupas and Nyingmapas, emphasizes that when we overcome conceptual designations generally associated with the explication of emptiness, what remains are the inconceivable qualities, the wisdoms and embodiments. In deity practice and in the cultivation of pure perception, we connect with these inconceivable qualities.

What are some of the dangers of kyerim practice for Westerners? First, kyerim can be an indulgence in dissociation or fantasy. If you have problems you're not dealing with, it can be pleasant to escape into this world of deities and magic. Of course, this merely reinforces the underlying problem by giving it a reality from which it is necessary to escape. By always trying to be "pure," you repress anything that you perceive in yourself or in the outer world that seems impure. This can feed what the Jungians call the "shadow," the dark, repressed side of the mind. It takes a considerable amount of practice and spiritual sophistication to be able to use kyerim to deal directly with our negativities. If we try to have pure perception of our worst faults, we can open up to their twisted energy and free ourselves from their grasp in a quick and powerful manner. This is quite different from trying to be "pure" in too literal a way. Detailed instructions for this kind of transformation are not usually included in the commentaries, and we're pretty much left on our own.

Chökyi Nyima Rinpoche says lamas assume that practitioners will use the techniques to benefit their minds. When the lamas discover the instructions have been poorly applied, it may be too late. That's why a period of sitting meditation before beginning Vajrayana practice can be extremely beneficial. When we do simple practices, we develop the habit of dealing directly with our stuff. We get the point, and as a result, our subsequent Vajrayana practice can be especially effective—it is an even more direct technique. The techniques I mentioned earlier of using the pride of the deity for confronting negative self-image is an example of that directness.

It's easy to forget the association with rigpa, or buddha-nature, while doing kyerim. Our visualizations or experiences can be very solid and cause us to forget the connection. Or we may get lost in detail, trying so hard to perfect the endless details of the visualization that we forget we are actually trying to benefit the mind and realize our buddha-nature. We can also become absorbed in the broader details of the tradition of kyerim and tantra, the different tertons and terma, different lineages, outer aspects of rituals, and so forth, so that tantra becomes more of a hobby than a spiritual path.

We might also be naive about pure perception. A friend of mine bought a real lemon of a car and drove it coast to coast because he happened to have pure perception of the man selling it. Somehow we have to balance our yearning to perceive others purely with the need to function effectively.

We can confuse ordinary purity or beauty with pure perception. We might consider organic food to be more spiritual than nonorganic food, the woods to be purer than the city. While there may be some truth in these views, they are not the correct meaning of pure perception. Pure perception is always pointing to the absolute.

By developing the skills of deity practice, incredible transformation can take place. We can leave all those painful negative self-images behind and begin to connect with the reality embodied by the deity. Kyerim practice is sometimes mystifying and confusing, but our effort to penetrate the truth that the deity manifests is extremely rewarding.

CHAPTER 16

Rituals

The life of a typical Vajrayana monastery revolves around its cycles of rituals. At Ka-Nying Shedrup Ling, the monastery where I lived and studied in Nepal, an extensive purification ritual is done toward the end of the Tibetan year. It lasts nine days and includes tsok, the offering of food, powerful music, and lama dancing. There are different shifts of people practicing all night so that the mantra is being recited continuously. Many great lamas will "drop in," and I've been fortunate enough to see H. H. Dilgo Khyentse Rinpoche, H. E. Kalu Rinpoche, and other great masters at this puja.

This is followed by a several-day protector ritual that ends right before Losar, or Tibetan New Year. Most Kagyupas practice Mahakala before Losar, while Nyingmapas usually perform Vajrakilaya rituals. During these rituals, all negativities and obstacles are repeatedly driven into a huge torma, which is fashioned into a human-like form, that is burned on the last day. The highest lama present, wearing full ritual regalia, starts the fire by shooting a flaming arrow at the human effigy. It is quite powerful, and one can certainly identify with what is going on—everything negative and unpleasant being burned, going up in smoke.

Then comes Losar, the biggest holiday for Tibetans, consisting of three days of constant partying. Even the monasteries get into the spirit of things. Everyone puts on their finery, including jewelry that looks as though it should be used for weight training rather than ornamentation, and visits the lamas to offer them huge trays of (for us Westerners) almost completely inedible food.

This is followed at Ka-Nying Shedrup Ling by a nine-day ritual for long life. This is also extensive, including lama dancing. And on it goes.

Sometimes I go; often I don't. It's nice to sit with my teacher, even in a room with hundreds of others. There's an undeniable power—it is obvious that something is going on. But in the end, especially because it's all in Tibetan, I feel a little confused and alienated. I know something is happening, but I don't know how to connect.

During our retreat in Scotland, we spent approximately one quarter of our time in pujas. Some of us liked them; many like me were overwhelmed, bored, or alienated. Our rituals were almost as elaborate as in Nepal. Here in Oregon, Tashi Choling has a yearly schedule of three long pujas. Since I've moved into town, I rarely attend.

Like many Westerners, my main tool for dealing with life is my intellect. Especially when confronted by a situation I do not understand, I try my best to analyze and examine it until I have a tool for coping, a gateway for entering. Unfortunately, it is currently difficult to receive sufficient instruction in the theory behind rituals so that an intellectual person like myself actually feels comfortable with what is going on. Although there is a power and profundity to Tibetan rituals that can speak to us in a language much deeper and more basic than logic, the rituals themselves have clearly delineated meanings that are clearly explicated in traditional Tibetan sources.

Because so much of what really happens at Dharma centers is ritual, it's a subject we really can't ignore. So although I'm not the best person to speak up for this tradition, I have given it a lot of thought. Also, rituals have, at times, been very moving and powerful for me. I'll be discussing my interpretation of rituals here; much of it I've gleaned from my teachers, some from other Buddhist readings, some from more general Western sources, and a little from my own struggles. If you're a person with the same difficulties or resistance, I hope this will help.

First, let's discuss the ritual itself. Although each one is different, they follow a similar format. Different rituals emphasize different sections.

Rituals, or pujas, are all centered around a major deity. For example, the three major pujas at Tashi Choling are focused on the three deities of Vajrakilaya, Vajrasattva, and Tronma Ngagmo, a wrathful dakini. Two are from the termas of Dudjom Rinpoche, and the last from his predecessor, Dudjom Lingpa. Other centers do other pujas.

Each ritual is associated with a main text. Different sections of the text are chanted in each session. In addition, commonly known prayers, such as the lamas' long-life prayers, are occasionally inserted. The chanting is punctuated by the playing of music. The chant leader (*umdze*) plays the cymbals; someone else plays the drums. The high lamas, here called the dorje loppons, play the small hand drum, the *damaru*. If your center is more established, or if there are Tibetan monks in the community, there can be additional instruments: the *radong*, the longhorn, an oboe-like reed instrument called the *jaling*, and a trumpet-like horn called the *kanling*.

Every ritual has a shrine master, or choppon. It is their job to prepare the shrine and make sure all the tormas are made. The choppon must also prepare the tsok so it's ready to be shared during the puja itself. During the puja, the choppon usually runs around acting out what is being chanted—lighting incense, making offerings, taking tormas outside. That person has to make prostrations at certain times and probably gets very little sleep.

During the ritual, all participants without other jobs are expected to chant, play their bells occasionally while holding the vajra, do the visualizations, make the beautiful hand gestures called mudras, and recollect the meaning while the chanting and the rest are going on. It is, however, especially the job of the dorje loppon to maintain the visualization. Therefore, the dorje loppon will be the highest lama present. If there are many high lamas, they will all be loppons; playing damarus, they sit higher than the other practitioners on the shrine side of the umdze. If no high lamas are present, the job can be done on a rotational basis along with the other jobs. It is also obviously everyone's responsibility to help with the preparation and the cleaning up.

Learning the various jobs is a great way to learn the puja itself. As the umdze, you learn the chanting and the order of the ritual. As the choppon, you actually act out the visualization, which makes it more real and deepens your understanding. And, of course, as the dorje loppon, you learn the visualization, the main part of the practice.

The more familiar you are with the ritual before it begins, the more you will get out of it. At least try to read the English translation before it begins so you have some idea what is going on. In retreat, we did different practices on our own. At their conclusion, we would meet and do more extensive rituals together, but by then we were already familiar with the visualizations and most of the liturgy, greatly enhancing their power.

Most pujas follow a fairly standard format. They begin with offering a gektor, reciting the lineage prayers, taking refuge, and engendering the enlightened attitude of bodhichitta. There is a section on purifying obscurations and accumulating merit. This usually takes the form of a seven-branch prayer, but it may involve a short ngondro. Next, a wheel of protection or vajra tent is erected. Within that vajra tent, the environment, practitioners, and offerings are all blessed. These sections are very similar to those that take place at the beginning of an empowerment; they are the preparation.

The next section is called the "main part" and is similar to the deity practices one would do on one's own. It entails developing the visualization of the deity, inviting the wisdom deity, making offerings and praises, and reciting the mantra. These stages as well as the preparatory ones are extremely important, and you should learn the meaning and appropriate visualizations.

Next come the stages that are unique to each specific puja. Associated with the offering of food is the consecration of the tsok; the invitation to those to whom it will be offered; and the actual offering, which might have several subdivisions. There are confessions and fulfillment (kangwa), which help to restore broken samaya. If it is a Nyingma puja, a *phurba* (a ritual dagger) is used to liberate obstructors. While standard prayers, especially long-life prayers for the lamas, are recited, the participants also partake of the tsok offerings. Leftover food offerings are offered to the worldly protectors, and the siddhis (spiritual accomplishments) are received.

The concluding stages are more familiar. The deity and its mandala surroundings dissolve and reemerge, and there is the dedication of merit.

More elaborate pujas contain additional sections such as self-empowerment and fire offerings. This briefly introduces the main structure, but you must learn the details and meaning from a qualified lama after receiving empowerment.

No discussion of ritual would be complete without mentioning protectors. Most rituals have a section for protectors, which is usually recited between the mantra recitation and the tsok. Also, many pujas are specifically for the protectors—I've already mentioned the yearly Vajrakilaya ritual that is performed at my monastery in Nepal. In our retreat in Scotland, we did a daily protector practice for our main protector, the two-armed Mahakala, Dorje Bernag Chen, as well as a four-hour monthly practice and a one-week yearly practice.

There are two kinds of protectors—worldly and wisdom. Worldly protectors are powerful, unenlightened beings who have promised to aid practitioners. If you read the Buddhist sutras, you will notice that most sutra texts end with a chorus of many nonhumans who vow to protect the practitioners of that particular teaching. Also, in the life stories of great yogis such as Guru Rinpoche and Milarepa, we can read how they subjugated powerful spirits who came to disrupt their meditation and made them become servants of the doctrine.

Wisdom protectors are like yidams; they are emanations of the buddhas. In fact, some deities are regarded as both yidams and protectors. Vajrakilaya serves this dual function for the Nyingmapas; Yamantaka is both for the Gelugpas. They are generally, but not always, extremely wrathful and often in union. The majority are female. As is the case with the yidams, different people connect with different protectors; hence, the variety.

What is the function of these protectors and their associated rituals? Their job is to clear away obstacles for practitioners.

When we practice, we experience many kinds of obstacles. In general, these can be divided into the usual classifications of outer, inner, and secret. Outer obstacles are sickness, poor conditions, lack of leisure, and so on. Inner obstacles are difficulties with the tsa, lung, and tigle—the channels, winds, and essences of the "vajra body." (I'll be saying more about these in the next chapter.) Secret obstacles are subtle conceptualizations that obscure our buddha-nature.

When we practice, we purify eons of negative karma. Its ripening effect would be overwhelming if we were without any outside help. Luckily for us, every instant in the universe someone attains complete enlightenment, and these countless buddhas have nothing but the best wishes for us. Although not completely omnipotent in the way that some people imagine their gods to be, the buddhas are not without power. One way that power manifests is in the form of these protectors.

It is up to us to connect with that power. That is the purpose of the rituals. Generally, protector rituals are straightforward: we visualize the buddha, make offerings and recite their mantra, and imagine them somehow destroying or removing obstacles. Of course, even with these rituals, we will still have difficulties, but these practices should help lighten the load.

It's not always obvious what our obstacles are. We can think that being sick or poor is slowing our practice, but we may have some subtle attitude that is even worse. When in retreat, I was dreading a particular practice and becoming very negative about it. Right before our monthly Mahakala puja, I dreamed of a basketball team in white uniforms miraculously defeating another team dressed in black. During the subsequent ritual, I felt my negativity toward that practice dissolving, and I did it with an open mind. I was later pleased with the results.

In the beginning of our puja are the following lines:

Daypa dang ni damtsig gi
Palden gonpo chendren na

They mean something like, "With faith and commitment, the holy protectors are invited." This simple line said so much to me. There are all these enlightened beings out there who have vowed to aid me, and I yearn for their assistance. What do I need to invoke their help? Faith and commitment. Commitment here means keeping the vows of Vajrayana. When the vows are kept and there is the openness of faith, we can receive the blessing and assistance of these protectors.

We usually need an empowerment to do protector practice, and there is generally a daily commitment to make offerings, usually the offering of a *serkyem*. *Serkyem* means "golden cup" and is an offering of some grain, usually prepared with black tea or sometimes with wine or beer. The offerings are accompanied by a short liturgy. Exert yourself in keeping this commitment. I've been told the worldly protectors can get upset if you break it.

Also, never use these kinds of practices for your own power or to harm others. You may think other people are an obstacle, but don't use Buddhist ritual to harm them. In the first place, it probably won't work (you would be lacking the aforementioned commitment because of your attitude), and second, you would be creating bad karma and breaking many vows.

To return to the main discussion, what is the purpose of all these rituals? I've discerned five main reasons for doing group pujas: social relationships, accumulation of merit, reparation of broken samaya, symbolic or mythical meaning, and magic. The first three are easier to understand than the last two. The social and mythical explanations tend to be Western attempts to understand something foreign; the other three are the standard replies you might receive from your teacher.

When I complained about having to do so many pujas in retreat, rather than justifying them on their own terms, Lama Yeshe spoke of the social benefits: learning to get along, working together, and so on. In the moment, I thought it sounded trivial, but with time I learned that group activities give me a chance to step out of my rigidity and harmonize with others. It can be a powerful practice, and it is far from trivial.

We all have something to learn in this way. Even the various jobs during the ritual can be a teaching. One week we might be the loppon sitting majestically on a throne and maintaining the visualization; the next week, we are the lowly drummer. There are always people in the community with whom we don't get along; during rituals, we can try to work it out rather than avoiding them or being negative. Meditating with others can be very healing in this way. Even the chanting itself, learning to harmonize your voice with those of others, has a healing, symbolic effect. We are neither overwhelming others with our shouting nor retreating into a withdrawn silence. The proper chant becomes the proper stance and, as is usual in Buddhism, another opportunity to follow the Middle Way.

During the sequestering due to COVID it became more obvious to me how strong the need for community is. People really suffered from being continually alone! If we didn't have our rituals, what would we do as a community to provide the friendship and support people need?

Pujas are also intended as a means to accumulate merit. In Buddhism, there are two accumulations—the accumulation of merit and the accumulation of wisdom. When we're on our own, we can have better conditions for meditation, especially meditation on the nature of the mind. These practices mainly accumulate wisdom. To balance this, group practice mainly accumulates merit. Extensive offerings are made repeatedly, and it is believed that the merit is additive for the group. That is, ten people each accumulate ten times the merit by being in a group than if they were to do the puja on their own. The merit is shared equally, so if you are the choppon running around and not focusing on the visualization at all, the benefit for you is the same as for that quiet, meditative person in the back. The converse is, unfortunately, also true. If there is negativity, it too is shared.

Pujas repair broken samaya. As I've mentioned before, we take a whole collection of vows when we receive empowerment. Even when we try our best to follow them, we still break them all the time. What can we do to restore the vows, avoid vajra hell, and keep the stream of blessings flowing? Although there are innumerable vows we can break, they can all be reduced to losing pure perception, the view that all beings are deities, that the environment is a mandala, that all sounds are mantra, and so on. We lose pure perception of our teacher, our vajra brothers and sisters, our environment. The ritual is a way of reconstructing that purity. Of key importance is the tsok, where the main food offering is the meat and alcohol, foods that were considered completely impure in ancient Brahmanic India. If we see them with Western eyes, we miss the point. We take something that we regard as impure, and with our minds, we transmute it into something pure (perhaps we should offer Big Macs and Hostess Twinkies!). We then offer it to those in front of whom we made the original vow to maintain pure perception.

Almost all pujas have a section called the kangwa that takes place after the tsok has been offered to the invited holy guests. Lines are often chanted that end with *thug dam kang*. *Thug* means "enlightened mind," *dam* means "samaya" or "commitment," and *kang* means "fulfilled." So the general meaning is something like, "I have broken my samayas and hence my connection with your enlightened energy. Please accept these transformed offerings as my attempt to rectify and restore this transgression, and may your enlightened mind be satisfied with my effort." The kangwa is a very important part of a puja; it's where the reparation of samaya is accomplished.

When Westerners get together and try to make sense of this vast Tibetan system of ritual, our own feeble attempts usually focus on the symbolic meaning. I'm hardly an expert on symbolism, but I'll try to say a little. If you want to learn more about this way of viewing rituals, you can start with the works of Carl Jung or Joseph Campbell.

We use symbols and rituals all the time. Many gestures, such as shaking hands, are rituals. Forms of polite address ("Hello, how are you?") are ritualized. Moreover, symbols are everywhere—for instance, in the omnipresent Nike logo. Words are symbols too; in actuality, they're just black lines on white paper.

In a sense, symbols are keys to, as well as representations of, certain states of mind. Symbols are evocative, and what they invoke becomes identified with them. This is true with Nike, and it is also true of religious symbolism. Consider Chenrezig, the buddha of compassion. He is white with four arms, two outstretched, the other two placed at his heart. If you visualize yourself in this form, the actual imagery invokes compassion. You cannot help but get a glimpse or an intuition of what it would mean to have the love and compassion of a buddha. Or consider Manjushri's sword. Contemplating its sharpness and activity can also help you to understand and connect with the cutting-through quality of discriminating wisdom that it represents.

Just as a melody is a succession of notes, a puja is a succession of symbols. Strung together, they become a story. We can view this story as a myth or like a dream.

Myths are stories with which cultures express their deepest truths and most profound wisdom. They are usually transmitted to children before logical, representational thinking is fully developed so the children are able to let the wisdom inherent in the myths permeate their being.

Kyerim in general, and pujas especially, have story lines. In kyerim it can be as simple as the birth and death of a deity. In pujas, the story is more complex with the vanquishing of opponents, the feast, the achievement of spiritual accomplishment, and so forth. If we were as open to this mythical process as are children sitting around the fire at night listening to the village elders, it would be powerful indeed.

One day in retreat, feeling bored and alienated while sitting through another long puja, I thought, "What if I were dreaming this? What would it mean to dream that I was this wrathful deity vanquishing opponents?" I tried to place myself in a state similar to just waking up after a dream, where the barriers to symbolic meaning have yet to be rigidly erected. I had a powerful reaction. Instead of being wimpy or timid, I could feel myself with the actual courage, confidence, and strength to overcome the difficulties in my life. It was a moment of real insight into the ritual process.

I call the last main function of a ritual magical. You won't find

Tibetans using this term because of its association with black magic, which is practiced throughout Asia. If you inquire how rituals work, why waving an arrow with five-colored silk streamers helps to increase life, the answer will be *tendrel*. *Tendrel* is a word borrowed from the sutra tradition. There, it means "interdependent origination" and explains how everything arises due to various causes and conditions. The main teachings on tendrel are the teachings on the twelve links of interdependent origination.

When used in tantra in the context of ritual, this term can be translated the same way. However, the meaning is clearly the same as our word *magic*, which is the manipulation of appearances. Wherever magic is found, an integral part is always the use of a simulacrum, an image or representation of the object to be manipulated. One can recognize the use of simulacra in all tantric rituals. Tormas themselves are representatives of various offerings, and may even be flesh. Effigies are, of course, images of various beings. If one asks why manipulating these objects influences the object represented, the answer is tendrel. There is an interconnectedness between the image and the object that is more than symbolic. How things are interconnected in this way is a revelation of the omniscience of a buddha; there may not be an obvious connection.

When we dispel obstructing forces (gek) with mustard seed and gugal, there is no obvious link between the mustard seed and the gek. We can't say why mustard seeds function in such a way. We can't say that there's something symbolically evocative about mustard seeds that touches a part of us, making us feel strong enough to overcome any difficulty. All we can say is "magic."

One universal quality of magic is that it must be performed perfectly. That is, if one is making a magic potion, everything must be exact. The right ingredients must be gathered, prepared correctly, and the right magic words must be said. Only then will it work.

This principle also applies to our rituals. The tormas must have just the right shape; so must their butter ornaments. Mantras must be recited accurately. The music is not a creative expression; every note is prescribed by the lamas. Many of the jaling (an oboe-like

Indian horn) melodies in our retreat were written by either the Dalai Lamas or the Karmapas. And obviously the mudras must be done correctly. Most important are the visualization and the activation of the pride of the deity. Only when everything is done accurately can one expect to receive the benefits of the ritual, such as long life, wealth, or the vanquishing of obstacles.

Another aspect of tendrel is that in ritual we imitate the behavior of a deity, an enlightened being. Traditionally, we would even dress up like one. Now we simply speak, gesture, eat, and so on like the deity and imagine ourselves doing the other activities a deity does. Practice makes perfect!

These five functions of pujas and rituals are all interrelated. If you are having difficulties with the ritual, find the purpose that means the most to you and use it as a bridge to reach the others. It's perhaps best to leave the more Western interpretations behind and try to understand the ritual in its own terms.

Even with these five good reasons for participating, many of us still have difficulties with these rituals. These difficulties should be acknowledged and discussed.

The first reason for difficulty is the most obvious: rituals are almost always performed in Tibetan. In an earlier chapter I discussed the merits of learning Tibetan, but the vast majority of us will never have the opportunity to do it, so spending hours chanting a language we don't understand can be wearying. Also, the language barrier makes it difficult to actualize the benefits of many of the purposes of the ritual. It's hard to struggle with the transliteration, sneak glimpses at the English translation, and try to remember the meaning and visualization. The rationale for doing it in Tibetan refers to the fifth function mentioned earlier—magic. The ritual just isn't complete if it isn't correctly chanted, and that includes doing it in Tibetan. As the rituals are all composed by enlightened beings, the words are charged with power; one cannot say the same of the translation. It's as if the whole puja were one long mantra. The Tibetan is also written in meter, so it's more fun and powerful to chant; it's possible to chant it with the beat of the cymbals and drum.

Another main problem with ritual is cultural. We have very little in our culture that is similar to a puja, and many of us have lost our connection with our own rituals. We have also lost our connection with our great myths. Symbols don't speak to us easily.

Many of us, myself included, have difficulty relating to anything that isn't presented logically or linearly. The practices associated with rituals have generally been given to us without detailed explanations; as a result, we often assume that those explanations don't exist and the ritual is more a reflection of Tibetan culture than of Buddhist practice. Sometimes Westerners even say that the rituals are a reflection of the pre-Buddhist Bonpo culture and have been kept to appease ordinary Tibetans. Even if we would like to accustom ourselves to these practices, it can prove difficult to deprogram our modern perspectives. It's hard for us to enter a sweat lodge with the same openness as our forebears; our cynicism always seems to get in the way. The openness of faith and trust is what aids the effectiveness of rituals; if the trust is lacking, the practice doesn't seem to work, further inhibiting trust.

Tibetans are raised in a world of ritual and symbolism. It was one of the things I experienced strongly when I saw the movie *Kundun*. The magic and ritual were always there; they were a part of Tibetans' daily life the way technology is a part of ours. It's not something they have to learn or think themselves into. Tibetans don't have to talk themselves into ceremony any more than we have to talk ourselves into using a cell phone.

Sometimes the opposite situation is true. Some people come from a Catholic background that is full of ritual, some of it hauntingly similar to the rituals of Tibetan Buddhism. But for others, something about their early experiences may have left a bad taste, and when they encounter something in Tibetan Buddhism that seems similar, they feel turned off. When encountering Buddhist ritual, many people may not be able to let go of their previous negative associations.

One problem Westerners encounter in learning about Tibetan Buddhism is trying to discern what is *Tibetan* from what is

Buddhism, especially since much of what appears in Tibetan Buddhism doesn't appear in the other countries to which Buddhism spread. Because of the isolation of Tibet, its form of Buddhism was the last to reach the Western world, and by that time there was already an agreed-upon view of what Buddhism was. Are these rituals really the teaching of the Buddha, or are they a manifestation of Tibetan culture? We may find ourselves with the following attitude: "I regard as true, essential Buddhism those aspects of Tibetan Buddhism with which I feel comfortable. Those parts that make me nervous I regard as cultural. I can then dismiss everything toward which I feel resistance or that I do not understand." This argument is now being applied to more than just ritual; some people are questioning the principle of reincarnation and the importance of the lama in a similar way. Very neat.

It's really not so simple. Tibetan culture has been permeated by Buddhist insight and practice for more than a thousand years. Many of the things Tibetans do, right down to how they pour a cup of tea for you, are thoroughly grounded in Buddhist insight and compassion. We can understand these things if we take the time and make the effort. What we dismiss today might very well be discovered to be a manifestation of considerable wisdom tomorrow. As I have mentioned, Buddhist ritual is completely grounded in Buddhist philosophy, especially in the teachings on emptiness. We can even say that they are a natural expression of that understanding. So we should be cautious about what we discount without having made the effort to investigate deeper. That especially includes the world of ritual.

Other areas of resistance may be related to how Tibetan Buddhism is taught in this country. When lamas teach here, they talk about ngondro or other topics that are related to the theory and practice of ultimate truth. They only rarely talk about kyerim, and they never, to my knowledge, discuss ritual. I've never seen anything like a weekend seminar titled "Theory and Practice of Tibetan Magic" advertised in any of the Buddhist journals. With time, I am sure that the more extensive, profound commentaries on ritual practice will be available to sincere Western practitioners, and we will be able to understand what we are doing. Until then, they will remain a mystery.

Hence, we are not really prepared for the pujas when we encounter them. If we were attracted to ritual in the first place, we would have sought out a spiritual path that openly promoted a ritualistic approach to life. We were probably drawn to something else in Buddhism—perhaps the effortless simplicity of the most advanced practices. It can be disappointing to find that what we're expected to practice, especially in groups, is not what we have heard or read about.

Also, we haven't been instructed in the rituals themselves. The talk we went to hear was on relaxed awareness, not magic for life extension. When we come to do the magic part, we haven't been properly trained. After all these years, I still don't feel properly trained, and I find that I've picked up much of my understanding in pieces—some from lamas, some from outside sources, some from my own cogitation.

One lament I always hear, sometimes even within my own mind, is, "Can't we skip all this ritual stuff? I just want to sit." This is a question we should think about carefully, since we'll all ask it at one time or another.

Let's consider the common basis of all forms of Buddhism: the teachings on egolessness and the practice of meditation. That's where our interest is. But Vajrayana is supposed to be the esoteric, speedy path. If we neglect ritual, we are neglecting one of the components that make Vajrayana distinct and quick. It is taught that the Buddha said that there will come a time when people will no longer be able to gain realization through the sutra techniques. For these people, the Buddha provided a technique that would be more rapid based on three aspects: mudra, mantra, and samadhi. Aren't we those people? Can we really progress by relying merely on simple techniques? If we could, that would be best. For those of us who cannot, it behooves us to create some kind of working relationship with this vast system of Buddhist magic.

CHAPTER 17

Dzogrim and the Body

As you can probably tell by now, I'm a fairly intellectual person, the kind others would speak of as "being in his head." It's been amusing to me that my whole practice for these many years has mainly been body oriented. It wasn't something I chose; it happened somewhat automatically.

I began meditating earnestly in early 1975. In May, I attended a short mindfulness retreat taught by an English monk trained in Thailand. He taught us, through a series of techniques that gradually increased in subtlety, to be aware of extremely subtle sensations that with training could be felt in any part of the body. These sensations were soothingly blissful to experience. Time went quickly, and I had no problem gearing myself up to practice. These sensations and the accompanying bliss were very satisfying to me.

I knew these sensations didn't correspond to anything I had previously known. Also, they were like the tip of the iceberg; they were accompanied by a feeling that my body was hollow but full of moving energy. When this energy moved into a new area, I experienced sensations such as tingling.

I had previously read Hindu books about *kundalini*, the so-called serpent energy that moves up the spine through the body. I had seen pictures of the chakras, lotuses of various colors and sizes, oriented around a hollow central axis, with Sanskrit letters on them. It was a little too much for my skeptical scientific mind to accept, and I dismissed this whole tradition without a second thought. But here I was, experiencing processes reminiscent of those mentioned in the kundalini texts.

Three things happened at this point.

First, I became ill. This illness has lasted for years. It has always appeared to be linked in some way to a deepening involvement with these energetic processes. My health problems continued for decades. Second, I continued to experience inexplicable sensations in various parts of my body while meditating that have dominated my practice to this day.

Third, I developed a strong interest in the formal practice of meditation that uses the internal energies, especially in the systems of practice that have been developed in Tibetan Buddhism. I read everything I could find on the subject and did everything possible to learn these meditations from the lamas I met in the East and later in America.

These systems of meditations are generally classified as *dzogrim*, the stage of completion or perfection. Dzogrim is always juxtaposed with the previously discussed kyerim. It has several meanings. When doing a deity practice and completing the mantra recitation for that session, the environment, deity, and seed syllable all dissolve. One then rests in the resultant state. The practice of dissolution with the subsequent resting is one use of the word *dzogrim*.

The term also refers to an extensive system of teaching and practice that one engages in after completing a deity practice. It has two main divisions. "Dzogrim with signs" is the practice based on the body's energetic system. "Dzogrim without signs" is resting in the buddha-nature and is the same as mahamudra or dzogchen. We will discuss the former, dzogrim with signs.

A major tenet of the Buddhist tantric system is the belief in a vajra body, an energetic body that is somehow related to our grosser body of flesh and blood. The vajra body has three main components—tsa, lung, and tigle. *Tsa* (Skt. *nadi*) are the energy channels that run through the body. The most important is the channel that runs through the center of the body like a main tent pole. Two smaller parallel channels and numerous branches form the chakras. The functions of the chakras are explained in the commentaries and have little correlation to the meanings commonly ascribed to them in new age parlance.

Lung means "breath," "wind," or "air." It is the same as the Sanskrit *prana* and the Chinese *chi*—the subtle aspect of the breath that flows through the channels. *Tigle* (Skt. *bindu*) is harder to define. It literally means "drops" and refers to subtle energetic essences. We inherit the red tigle from our mother and the white tigle from our father at the time of conception. There is a strong connection between tigle and sexual energy. One analogy is that tsa are like channels, lung is like the currents that flow through the channels, and tigle is what is moved by the currents.

The main practice of tsalung is tummo. *Tummo* literally means "wrathful female" but is most often translated as "inner heat." Through posture, breath control, visualization, and some sense of the view, a great ecstatic heat that is extremely helpful for realization is generated in the body. The main exercise for tummo is *bumchen*, or "vase breathing," a kind of breath control. When performed as one's main practice, it is often accompanied by a set of physical exercises known as *trulkor*.

The bliss and heat generated from doing tummo has one primary purpose. It is a powerful means for stabilizing buddha-nature. Although the practice has many useful side effects—bliss, keeping warm in the cold, and miraculous powers—one should never lose sight of this connection with rigpa.

The principle involved here is the inseparability of mind and energy. Even as beginners we can be aware of the reciprocity between our breathing and our mental state. When the breath is rough, so is the mind. When the mind is serene, the breath is gentle and smooth.

This principle continues until enlightenment. Every mental state has a corresponding energetic configuration in the vajra body. Even the other realms have their energetic configurations; when energy flows in specific ways, we experience ourselves in vats of molten metal or enjoying the great pleasures of the gods. All our conceptual mental states and negative emotions come from our internal energy running amok. If we use these forceful methods to control our energy, the mind has no choice but to relax into its own nature. There is simply no fuel remaining for conceptualizations or obscurations.

Another explanation of the purpose of these practices is that since the nature of the mind is great bliss, to meditate on bliss puts us in a state that is closer to this realization. Because it is such a rigorous practice, tsalung utilizes the ambitious, active nature of some practitioners to reach a state of mind that is profoundly effortless and relaxed, rather than stifling that vitality.

From my years of study, I am convinced that when practiced properly, tummo is really a rapid path to enlightenment. Unfortunately, it is difficult to practice properly—the qualifications of a good tsalung practitioner are hard to attain. First, we must be able to sit in painful postures for long periods of time. Not much fun, but most of us can do this if we are willing. Second, we must be able to control our breath for long periods of time. This is something that develops over time. Third, we must have clear visualization of the deity and their channels. This also takes a long time to perfect. We must be willing to accept a lot a hardship, including abstention from sexual activity or release.

Acquiring the right external conditions may be difficult too. It should be cold and quiet. If we aspire to do trulkor, we need the appropriate room and gear, and we need to be far from any neighbors.

Kagyupas typically teach tsalung only to participants in three-year retreat. Some Nyingma centers are a little more relaxed, offering occasional courses in tsalung but with prerequisites. Many people can generate a small amount of warmth in the belly fairly easily, but the real experiences of tummo are difficult to attain. If you truly aspire to these practices, prepare yourself for a long period of diligence.

For those of us who would like to do some training that involves the body, what do we do? How are we to relate to our bodies as we practice? What does Tibetan Buddhism have to offer us if the traditional approach is beyond our present capabilities?

I've heard stories of beginners asking their lamas for some kind of introductory physical discipline to aid their meditation. The most frequent response is "prostrations." Prostrations do seem to have a yogic effect on the body in addition to their devotional benefits. Some lamas have introduced other beginning physical practices to their students—Namkhai Norbu Rinpoche with *yantra yoga*, Tarthang Tulku with *kum nye*, and several others. But in general, Western students are left without a physical side to their meditative practice that they find meaningful and effective.

Many practitioners use techniques from other systems, such as tai chi or hatha yoga. Alternatively, we might use more passive forms of bodywork, paying someone else to help us open up. My problem with this is that I always feel like I'm cheating by going outside the Tibetan system. On one hand, it's difficult for me to admit that there's a lack or shortcoming in the way that Tibetan Buddhism is offered to us here. On the other, I'm not completely sure of the benefits or effects of these other systems. My meditation teacher is a buddha; my acupuncturist decidedly is not. Do all systems nicely mesh, or can someone open me up in a way that will create obstacles to my Buddhist practice? These are important questions for most of us, since there is so much available to us here in America. We might be foolish to neglect powerful techniques already available in our culture; we might also be foolish to experiment with the wrong thing.

When through their diligence and devotion people apply themselves to practice, they might become aware of processes happening inside their bodies. It is easy to become fascinated by these experiences; it is also easy to overemphasize their importance. Not every sensation of warmth is tummo. That's where study can be useful. There's not much material available on the Tibetan view of the physical process, especially for beginners. But these processes are discussed at length in other systems that are accessible to us.

In the Chinese Taoist view, one tries to circulate one's chi in a loop up the back and down the front of the body. This is called the "microcosmic orbit" and is believed to be a great aid to meditation. It is the basis of both the internal martial arts and acupuncture.

In the Hindu system, a powerful energy called kundalini lies dormant at the base of the spine. Through practice and the transmission of energy from a master called *shaktipat*, this energy is awakened and begins to move up the spine, opening the chakras. This is also believed to be a great aid for meditation and is the basis of hatha yoga and other Indian meditations.

In the West, many people believe in body armoring, where negative patterns have become frozen into the musculature of the body. Releasing this armoring aids psychological growth while also easing stress and helping with its associated symptoms.

How do all these conflicting systems fit into the Buddhist tantric view? There are no simple answers to this kind of question because many of the lamas themselves are not sufficiently knowledgeable about other systems, and an accurate translation of the concepts and experiences is difficult. I've often tried over the years to question my teachers. What follows is what I have managed to piece together. Even so, do not accept it as the final word on the subject.

The Tibetan view is similar to the Hindu view. Both systems describe central channels, chakras, and so on. Hindu practice can be dangerous, however. With an inexperienced teacher, the energy can sometimes be awakened prematurely, which can produce unpleasant and negative physical or mental side effects. This is referred to as kundalini illness. Practices from the Hindu system that are often taught publicly require years of preparation from the Tibetan perspective.

The microcosmic orbit is not spoken of much in the Tibetan tradition. I've asked many lamas about it but have generally received only vague answers. Some of the visualizations that accompany mantra recitation seem to imply a connection—there is a circulation of light that resembles the Chinese version. I've never heard of any problems occurring when Westerners mix tai chi and Tibetan meditation. In fact, several lamas do it. Acupuncture, however, can be draining. When treated by the wrong person, you can feel very low in energy for quite a while after a treatment, so please be careful.

When I explained the Western belief of body armoring to my lama, he accepted it readily and felt that both Vajrasattva practice and the more advanced tsalung practices would deal with it. He had no problem with the concepts.

Several things can happen when the energetic processes start kicking in. At best, everything will happen smoothly. Blockages will open, and the mind will settle down. The practitioner might not even notice that a process is happening.

In a less gentle result, the practitioner might sway or feel warm during practice. Sometimes, they will feel inexplicable depression, anxiety, and restlessness.

Worse might be strong shaking or searing pain. If you read Krishnamurti's biography, there's a lengthy account of the years of agony he endured. Mentally, the mind can approach schizophrenia, although I've never seen it happen. I have seen people become mentally ill while practicing, but I'm not sure that it was related to an energetic awakening. I think those people were unstable to begin with, and their practice may have been more intense than their ego structure could handle.

Westerners are confronted with two choices. One is that we can devote ourselves exclusively to the Tibetan path. If it seems neglectful of our physical processes, we accept that as part of our path. We might prefer this to the danger of mixing paths.

The other option is to mix our practice with some other physical discipline. As I've mentioned, tai chi seems the safest. Gentle hatha yoga is also probably okay; just make sure that you're not dealing too strenuously with the kundalini energy and that you find a teacher you can trust. Western exercise, aerobics, jogging, weight training—it is unlikely that any of these will have much effect on your inner energy. It is also unlikely that they will hurt anything, and they will help to keep you healthy.

These days, hatha yoga, tai chi, and chi gong are often taught at Tibetan centers. It seems that at least some lamas have approved these practices for their students.

As the decades roll by, many new forms of physical practices have been developed. For example, Continuum was developed by Emily Conrad in Santa Monica, California, and is practiced extensively by Lama Drimed's students. There are many more, but I'm not familiar enough with them to comment.

Or you can try to learn tsalung. You'll probably find it difficult to receive the teaching and even harder to maintain it.

I've always found Western bodywork useful, although I've heard an occasional bad story. Cranial-sacral work has worked well for me, as have other forms of manipulations. If a part of the body is simply not in the right place, the energetic blockages will open only with the greatest of difficulty through practice alone. It is worth taking the risk of having someone who is skilled gently move things into place. Frankly, I can't imagine the difficulty of releasing these misaligned tensions without help, relying only on practice.

Sometimes medicine helps. I have had incredibly good results with homeopathy. It seems to work on a deep energetic level, and with the right remedy, deep tensions can be released. Probably the same is true of Asian medicinal systems such as Chinese, ayurvedic, or Tibetan. For all these, it's important to find a skilled doctor who is sensitive to the energetic aspects of their practice and is aware of the changes that can occur in meditators. Be careful and examine wisely your potential doctor, or any bodyworker for that matter. I've also had good results with acupuncture, but as I mentioned, it can be draining, especially with an inexperienced doctor.

The relationship between psychotherapy and meditation has been the subject of many books. Releasing psychological blocks can certainly have a profound energetic effect, if one is open on that level. In theory at least, it seems that once one has made a connection with the Dharma, therapy should become redundant. Meditation should do it all. I've seen it with myself and with my students. When I first started teaching, a student of mine was able to stop taking Prozac and to end a $400-a-month therapy regimen. Buddhist teaching and practice can be very powerful!

If you are currently going to a therapist, how do they feel about your interest in meditation? If your therapist isn't sympathetic,

I recommend finding a new one. If you don't have a close relationship with a meditation teacher, a therapist might be useful just for talking things out and discovering blind spots in your personality. They can also be helpful in the case of specific problems, such as raising children, that Buddhists don't discuss often. Once again, if you have serious problems, don't abandon professional help without consultation. How does your Buddhist meditation teacher respond to your seeing a therapist? If they object, are their objections reasonable?

There are many ways therapy can help. Some therapists are meditators and use their experience with the body's energetics as part of their treatment. Also, many people these days don't have much access to a good Dharma teacher, and their relationship with a therapist can fill in some of the gaps. In our culture, we are familiar with the view that our suffering results from childhood trauma and disappointments, making therapy more accessible.

It's important to stay healthy. It's also important to work on the energetic level. But remember two things: First, never separate your desire to improve your body from your quest for enlightenment. Perfect health never lasts. Your body is simply a vehicle for enlightenment. So although your various practices and disciplines should improve your health, that is not the point. The point is that a healthy body makes it easier to meditate.

Second, be careful whom you trust. An authorized Tibetan Buddhist teacher is part of a 2,500-year-old tradition. Even then, there can be problems. But where are the checks and balances with your yoga teacher or therapist?

Included within dzogrim are the practices of union. The tsalung practices are related with the second, the secret, empowerment; the sexual practices are related with the third, the wisdom empowerment. Because of our interest and because of the associations that have developed around the word *tantra* these days, a few words on sexual yoga and sexuality in general practice are appropriate.

You can probably go down to your local video shop or online and get a DVD on "tantra." The term seems to have come to mean the prolongation of intercourse through the use of techniques such as visualization, breath control, and so forth. While this may or may not be Hindu tantra, it certainly isn't Buddhism. In Buddhism, *tantra* is synonymous with the Vajrayana and does not refer to any one practice, especially a sexual one.

Buddhist sexual yoga belongs to the third empowerment practice. Thus, it is based on a certain degree of proficiency in the practices of the second empowerment, which are, in turn, based on a certain degree of proficiency in the practices of the first empowerment, and so on down the line to the practices of ngondro and the four thoughts.

I've been practicing Tibetan Buddhism for forty-five years. I have never received any usable teachings on sexual practices. I've only heard and read about them in brief. I have certainly never done them. Tibetan lamas think Westerners are sexually crazy. If you want to alienate a lama, try requesting teachings on the sexual practices.

If your interest or initial involvement in Tibetan Buddhism has been with the hope of learning these yogas, your chances are very, very slender. To be authorized to practice the path of union is another matter. Buddhist tantra is linear, step-by-step, and we have to start at the beginning.

Ladies and gentlemen, be aware of teachers or senior students who hit on you with a line about practicing tantra. Even if they're older students or have the name "lama," chances are they are only looking for sex. Do not be naive; do not allow the teacher to break their vows and go to hell. This misuse of the precious teachings is extremely harmful both to the perpetrator and to the overall reputation of Buddhism. Older students and teachers should be trustworthy; it's the very foundation of our path.

It's fine if we have desire; nobody is forcing us to be celibate. It's fine if we want to have a meaningful and supportive relationship. What is not right is deceiving yourself and others about your level of practice. If you do, you shame yourself, your partner, your teacher, and all of Tibetan Buddhism. There have been so many scandals; each one weakens our ability to trust our teachers and our tradition.

With that rather stern warning, how can we integrate our sexuality into our spiritual practice without going to dangerous extremes? Let us examine the options.

The first is celibacy. *Celibacy* is usually defined in the dictionary as meaning simply to be single; I think most of us use this term to mean a life where we abstain from any voluntary sexual activity. We could be living in the world, as hermits in retreat, or as ordained monks or nuns in a monastic environment. We could be perfectly celibate, having no release whatsoever; we could occasionally masturbate; or if we are men, we might experience release in our sleep.

There are many advantages to celibacy. The most obvious is that being free from the entanglement of relationships, and especially children, we have much more time to practice. Not only do we have the time, but our minds are also calmer since we are not thinking about our partner, children, or going out on Saturday night. In theory, that should get rid of most of our thoughts right there! Also, if we are skillful, that sexual energy will be available for practice. We will experience it energizing the body and as a source of bliss. We are fitting candidates for tsalung practice, where perfect celibacy is required. Others will respect us, and it will be easier to obtain sponsors and conducive conditions for practice.

The most obvious disadvantage to celibacy is if we are too full of lust to practice. Or even sleep, for that matter. Instead of feeling calmer, we become obsessed. The only things we can visualize are attractive people with whom we want to have sex. We are prone to making unwise decisions in that state.

Occasionally, masturbating works. I met someone who masturbated regularly through a three-year retreat. At the end, his lama was very pleased with his meditative accomplishments and even said he had attained some special powers. We can also learn to circulate the sexual energy upward, away from the genital area. This technique works better for some than others. It's also better to remove oneself as much as possible from anyone or anything that will give rise to lust. It was much easier for a heterosexual man to be celibate in the East, for example, where the women were always modestly dressed and certainly not available. There were no *Playboy* magazines, cable TV, or any other provocative media, although that's now changing.

There are many dangers to celibacy. Keeping the sexual energy in can help our practice, but it can also be overwhelming, causing many kinds of energetic imbalances. Lamas will sometimes tell their blocked-up students to have sex because they are having energetic problems with their practice.

We might have old emotional issues that make celibacy attractive to us, despite the obvious hardships. For those of us who tried to be celibate while still young, some of these issues were lurking in the background. We might have fears of sex, intimacy, rejection, and so on, all of which make celibacy seem appropriate. However, it doesn't work that way. We cannot maintain repression or denial and meditate at the same time. It's like trying to go east and west simultaneously. Eventually, all these old issues come out.

If you're seriously contemplating a celibate lifestyle, ask yourself if it's likely these issues exist. The only thing that will make them go away is confronting them, not running away from them. This doesn't mean you shouldn't be celibate, but you should know what you are getting into.

Another serious danger is that we can become emotionally cold from a lack of love as well as from the difficulty of maintaining the discipline. If this happens to you, try to find love in other ways, perhaps through your spiritual community or your devotion to your teacher. Nothing opens us up or puts us as close to our buddha-nature as love; the teachings all agree on this. If there is no love in your life, you are at a serious disadvantage in your practice. If you find your attitudes becoming rigid, this is also a mistake. I used to feel all noncelibate practitioners weren't serious or committed; now I recognize this attitude as simply a projection of my own unease.

Most of us will be sexually active laypeople. How can we use our sexual activity on the path? Obviously, we shouldn't use sex to hurt anyone, neither our partner nor an involved third party. People are very aware of these issues nowadays, so this much should be clear.

Fidelity is important, as is commitment. Don't use the need or desire to open yourself or to heal as an excuse to hurt your closest vajra brother or sister—your partner.

Anything done with a loving heart is virtuous. If you love your partner and give them pleasure as an expression of your care, that is a virtuous act. Its healing power is amazing. So many of us are stuck on the level of feeling unlovable, not being able to open to love, not being able to express love, and so forth. Lovemaking can then be a powerful practice for dealing with these old issues. Where our hearts are blocked, so will our meditation be.

Also, we can use a healthy sexual relationship to heal our relationship with our bodies or with our ability to experience pleasure. If we're not "in our bodies," sex can bring us back in; believe it or not, we have to get back in touch with the body before we can transcend it. If we're dissociated from our bodies due to experiences we have had in the past, this again will cause a limitation to our meditation. Sex provides us with a situation wherein we can be keenly aware and observant of exactly how far we have progressed.

If we have difficulty experiencing pleasure, how can we be open to the bliss of meditation? We will feel it is wrong to feel this kind of bliss when we are sitting and will subtly block and, therefore, limit and contract the experience. Sex is not necessary in any of these situations to deal with issues of love, dissociation, and pleasure. The healing can take place solely through practice. That would be best. But in the name of practice, we may also be avoiding dealing with these issues. If that's true, we may remain stuck for a very long time. Our sexual activity will bring all these problems undeniably to the surface.

Many of us feel some confusion about the relationship between pleasure and enjoyments, and true spirituality according to the Buddhist perspective. A major source of the problem is a confusion between pleasure, on the one hand, and attachment or desire, on the other. There's no question that in Buddhism attachment and desire are regarded as negative states. And what is it that we generally desire or to which we are attached? Pleasurable experiences.

Nevertheless, pleasure in and of itself is neither desire nor attachment. When we cling to pleasure, that is attachment. When we want to repeat it, that is desire. But the experience of pleasure per se is not desire or attachment. Therefore, it is possible to enjoy without these two.

A moment's reflection will reveal that not only are pleasure and attachment not the same, but they are antithetical in many ways. If we are enjoying the sunset or chocolate ice cream, clinging to the experience actually diminishes the pleasure. We are no longer experiencing it; rather we are starting to get lost in our thoughts, feelings, and anxieties about the experience.

Are there any spiritual benefits then to experiencing pleasure? The benefits are in the very abandoning of attachment. If we apply mindfulness to our enjoyment, we can let go of the clinging. This produces a kind of openness within the enjoyment that definitely has a spiritual component. Also, we can learn to let go of attachment in general. We see that it actually hampers our genuine experience rather than enhancing it. We can learn about deep patterns of attachment and clinging and use our pleasure to purify them. When we return to formal meditation, we will notice an improvement.

Another benefit of enjoyment is that meditation is also often enjoyable. Our attitudes about pleasure in general will be reflected in how we relate to pleasurable meditation experiences. The joy or bliss of practice is what keeps us going in the long run. Otherwise, meditation is a burden we take on because we hope for distant results. That's tedious and likely to lead to failure.

Many people who are drawn to spirituality have some kind of resistance to pleasure and assume that spirituality considers the pursuit of pleasure to be harmful to the path. In a sense the pursuit is indeed harmful; however, as I've mentioned, the pleasure itself is not. With this kind of attitude of resistance to pleasure, one will have difficulty accepting the pleasurable experiences of meditation without some kind of negative reaction. If we can recognize our negative patterns toward pleasure through our ordinary experiences, we can later meditate in a much purer manner.

Wilhelm Reich and his student Alexander Lowen explored the psychological aspects of pleasure in their exploration of the function of the orgasm. Although I've not discovered a spiritual component in their work, I feel they have mapped out a valuable area of growth. Most of us must make the journey from neurosis to sanity and mental health before real spirituality can begin. Our sexual activity and our attitudes toward it can give us valuable clues for making that trip.

It's normal for us to want to experience as much pleasure as possible in our sexual activity. What stops us? It's being too much "in our heads." The process of letting go of attitudes in order to experience a more satisfying orgasm is similar to the process of surrendering to deeper meditational experiences. Orgasms are, I'm afraid, no substitute for practice, but we can learn to recognize some of our habitual patterns regarding pleasure and apply what we have learned to our practice. Let's face it—most of us are not going to give up sex. Thus, if we are going to be sexually active, then it is important to use that activity as a way to aid our practice.

The body is always with us. Having a healthy relationship with it in the beginning and using it as an aid as we develop is a large part of our practice.

CHAPTER 18

The Path of Liberation

We started our exploration with some yearning for the truth, our buddha-nature. That yearning, based perhaps on some glimpse or intuition, led us to seek and hopefully find a teacher. Following the progression of this book, we will have found a teacher within the Tibetan Buddhist tradition, become involved in a center, received instruction, and begun a practice.

As we become more involved and diligent with our practice, we cannot lose sight of our original intention—to apprehend our true nature. Many of us become like tantric hobbyists. We learn everything we can about the lamas, the lineages, the practices, the rituals, and so on, but somehow we forget the big picture.

The big picture is recognizing and stabilizing buddha-nature. This is the whole point of Buddhism, tantric or not. As Guru Rinpoche has said,

> Do not resolve the Dharma,
> Resolve your mind.
> Resolving your mind is to know the one which frees all.
> Not resolving your mind is to know all, but lack the one.[1]

No matter how many lamas you've met, how many rituals you've mastered or mantras you've recited, it all boils down to one point—recognizing your buddha-nature.

The practices that deal directly with buddha-nature are called the "path of liberation." The practices that aid us in this recognition and stabilization are called the "path of skillful means." The path of skillful means includes such techniques as kyerim and tsalung, which we've already discussed. The practices of the path of liberation are mainly *shinay* and *lhagtong*, which are described in this chapter.

Practicing the path of liberation without skillful means can be slow. We might be attracted to the simplicity of the path of liberation; unfortunately, we don't have simple minds. However, to rely on skillful means without the path of liberation takes us nowhere since we lack the view. It is the combination of the two that gives Vajrayana its unique power. The combination is often symbolically depicted, sometimes by the two hands of the deity, sometimes by the deities in union. It's a point we should never forget.

Generally, these two paths are practiced concurrently, with the practitioner emphasizing one or the other over time. We might be doing a deity practice and at the end dissolve the visualization. At that point, we would apply the instructions we have heard on the path of liberation, either mahamudra or dzogchen. With time, the practices tend to merge as the path of skillful means approaches the path of liberation.

As I mentioned in chapter 16, many Westerners feel more drawn to the path of liberation. The rituals seem too foreign. Many lamas seem to concur; mahamudra and dzogchen, the two main systems of liberation, are widely and systematically taught these days.

Kagyu Samye Ling in Scotland, where I did retreat, has an annual program with H. E. Tai Situ Rinpoche teaching mahamudra step-by-step. He teaches it as a one-month retreat during the summer; the participants make a commitment to do two hours of mahamudra meditation a day for the rest of the year. Every year they meet and receive further instruction. The response has been highly favorable. Other Kagyu lamas are following suit with similar programs at their centers. There have also been a few attempts to teach dzogchen in America in this kind of systematic manner.

Mahamudra is the system practiced by the Kagyu and other Sarma schools; dzogchen is most widely taught in the Nyingma. There is no difference between them in view or in the result, which is complete buddhahood. The difference is in which practices they emphasize. Within both, you will find some distinction between a gradual and a sudden approach.

In the gradual system, the practitioner works their way through a series of practices aimed first at focusing the mind, then at recognizing its nature. The sudden path is obviously more direct. The buddha-nature is pointed out early in one's meditative career. The practitioner then takes this glimpse as the object of concentration for stabilization. Of course, both approaches have their proponents and their merit. In my opinion, without some initial calmness, trying to recognize or stabilize can be frustrating and agitating. However, if we wait until our concentration is flawless, we might have to wait a long time and never grasp the real meaning of Lord Buddha's teaching.

As I already stated, the main practices of liberation are shinay and lhagtong. *Shinay*, or *shamatha* in Sanskrit, literally means "calmabiding." *Lhagtong*, or *vipasyana* in Sanskrit, is often translated as "insight." When people speak of meditation, they are generally referring to shinay. There are many possible objects for shinay. You can visualize a buddha in front of you or a sphere of light in your heart. You can follow the breath, add the "vajra recitation" to the breath, or hold the breath in the vase as in the tsalung practices. You can take thoughts as the object or the absence of thoughts as the object. When the mind itself is taken as the object, it is called "formless shinay"; this can quite easily be confused with the insight of lhagtong. The absence of thoughts can be confused with emptiness, the mind's clarity with luminosity.

The benefits of shinay are twofold. Obviously, the pacification of the mind is a benefit in and of itself. We are no longer torn by emotionality and discursiveness but instead abide in a state of blissful, calm, spacious clarity. As I mentioned in the last chapter, the bliss will aid us in finding contentment in practice. The other benefit is that shinay prepares us for genuine insight. It is often said that insight happens in the space between thoughts. If there is no space, then there is little hope for any realization. Through our various practices, that gap should widen and become more frequent. Then, of course, we have a greater chance for insight.

There are also some dangers. Mistaking the experience of shinay for one of genuine insight is common. One needs a teacher and some study in order to avoid this pitfall. Also, the mind can become too spaced out. There are traditional stories of meditators remaining months or years in a noncognizing trance, wasting their time and exhausting their merit. That's probably not very common nowadays; what I see instead is people losing the ability to drive and nearly getting into accidents because they are engrossed in opening their minds but losing clarity, awareness, and mindfulness. Since I've been teaching, this is the only real danger I've noticed in my students. If you have a tendency to space out or be too open without boundaries, don't indulge like this in your meditation. Instead, you must emphasize the clarity and mindfulness and make certain you feel grounded, especially before operating dangerous machinery. When in doubt, don't mix activities like driving with your meditation.

The opposite is to have too much focus without any spaciousness. In that case, we're simply trying too hard. This can make us rigid and uptight and eventually lead to energetic imbalances and psychosomatic ailments.

Shinay is not only a practice; it is also the resultant state. Some teachings teach nine stages before the full attainment of shinay; the more meditative traditions usually teach three. Tsele Rinpoche, whom we first met in chapter 4, clearly explains these three:

> At first, the mind seems more agitated, with even more thought activity than before. Sometimes between thought activity, your mind remains still for a short while. Do not regard such thought activity as a defect. Although up to now your mind has always been thinking, you didn't recognize that. This point, of recognizing the difference between thinking and stillness, is the first shamatha experience, like the waterfall off a mountain cliff.
>
> After maintaining the practice like that, the thought will be mostly controlled. You become gentle and relaxed; both your

body and mind become totally blissful and you don't feel like engaging in other activities, but only delight in meditation. Except on rare occasions, you remain mostly free from any thought activity. That is the intermediate shamatha stage, like the gentle flow of a river.

Later on, after practicing with undistracted endeavor, your body is totally blissful, free from any painful sensation. Your mind is clear cognizance free from thoughts. Not noticing the passing of day and night, you can remain unmoved for as long as you are resting in meditation and you are unharmed by faults. The manifest disturbing emotions have subsided and you have no strong clinging to such things as food and clothing. You have conditioned superknowledges, and various kinds of visionary experiences occur. The manifestation of these numerous kinds of ordinary qualities is the final state of shamatha, which is like an unmoving ocean.[2]

It's encouraging to me to think that we only have to go one step on the path before we reach a state of blissful mind and body. It seems worth some exertion and hardship to attain.

If we wait for that oceanic final state before we begin lhagtong, we will probably have a long wait. But the calmer the mind, the easier the investigations that follow. Lhagtong begins with a series of questions for the student to answer, such as "What color is the mind?" or "From where do thoughts arise?" The student is guided in the direction of looking directly into the mind. The point here is not to analyze the question intellectually until a conclusion is reached but to gain experience through penetrating investigation. As we discussed in an earlier chapter, the student repeatedly reports back until receiving confirmation and attaining certainty.

Perhaps at no other stage of our practice is the teacher so crucial. Drungchen Kunga Namgyal states,

The purpose of having a spiritual mentor who knows the path to liberation is to have someone who knows how to remove the obstacles on the path and remove the veils of ignorance.

There are those who fail to speak to their mentor even though they have many things to ask. Due to both the conceit of having fine realizations or a sense of hopelessness, some conceal what is happening, thinking, "There's little reason to speak, for you don't tell the mentor about such things." Due to the mind being carried away as if by a hallucination, some think, "There is nothing even the spiritual mentor can do to help me in such things." Others think, "I must present an amazing report of realizations, not these specific questions that I have." All such attitudes are utterly useless.

Get answers to the questions you put to your mentor; then, after coming outside, it is you, the student, who maintains the training at the level of your own present practice. So keep that firmly in mind, and get ready to report.[3]

This process can take a while; even after rigpa has been glimpsed and acknowledged by your teacher, you can make subtle distinctions and entertain valid doubts.

With time, there's a shift from investigative lhagtong to resting lhagtong. That is, as doubts become clarified, one simply relaxes into rigpa; investigation becomes less necessary. It sounds nice to talk about relaxing into rigpa or into effortless meditation, but if the view has not been correctly ascertained, it can also be dangerous. Milarepa said this about effortless meditation:

Concerning the practice of non-correction, one should understand three things: If wandering thoughts and desire-passions are not corrected, one will fall into the lower realms. If bliss, clarity, and non-thought are not corrected, one will fall into the three realms of samsara. Only the immanent self-awareness needs no correction.[4]

Also, the investigative and resting meditations can be balanced into one practice. These are all techniques to be learned from one's teacher.

Realization of buddha-nature proceeds in clear, recognizable stages. The most common teaching is on the four yogas of mahamudra; you can find many books on this subject. Those of us who are not full-time contemplatives will probably have to be content with momentary glimpses. In time, these glimpses will increase in frequency, duration, and quality.

Many lamas say that this is the age of dzogchen. Indeed, these teachings are gaining popularity in America. They are being taught openly in a way that has never been done before. During one public teaching I received, the lama said that the teachings he was giving were given in Tibet only to those who had completed about fifteen years of retreat. I have never understood the rationale behind this tradition; many other Nyingma lamas have continued to keep the dzogchen teachings secret. When I asked Gyatrul Rinpoche about dzogchen being taught openly, he said that if there is one person in the audience who understands, then it is worth it.

There are many classifications of dzogchen, but the two most common are *tregchod* and *thogal*. *Tregchod* means "to cut completely"; by resting in the nature of the mind, we completely cut our delusion. *Thogal* is the more esoteric or secret of these techniques. It is a system of yogic practices involving posture and gazes that produces extraordinary results if the practitioner is able to conjoin them with the view. Thogal is the main practice that leads to the attainment of the rainbow body.

CHAPTER 19

Fruition

Our original inspiration has taken us along some unusual and profound paths. We have met great teachers; we have made commitments and sacrifices in our application of the teachings. We have found the pinnacle of Lord Buddha's teaching, the Vajrayana, especially the practices of mahamudra and the Great Perfection (dzogchen), and have started to apply ourselves with some diligence. What are the benefits, the fruition, of following such a path?

Perhaps I have given too many warnings in this book. It might seem that attempting to meditate is futile. However, once students have gone through some of the unlearning process and are more of a blank slate, they are much more likely to benefit from their meditation practice. And the benefits can be wonderful.

We can try to be clever about not having any goals or meditating to make a connection in future lives, but what will really keep us meditating is to have realistic goals and aspirations and make measurable progress toward them. If you look at Gampopa's *Jewel Ornament of Liberation*, you will notice that whatever topic he is presenting includes a discussion of the benefits of taking that topic to heart. I think we should be honest with ourselves and others about wanting the benefits of practice, check on how we are doing, and feel good about any accomplishments we realize. If, however, we are not making progress, we should investigate why and perhaps check with a teacher or older student.

What are reasonable experiences and transformations that a beginning meditator can expect?

First, calmness. What makes us "uncalm" is being distracted by sense objects and especially our thoughts and emotions. As I mentioned in chapter 9, it is unrealistic to believe that you can stop thoughts. However, through regular practice, thoughts will have less pull on your attention. They will still be there, but they will hook you less and less. The less they hook you, the calmer you will feel.

Within the stream of thoughts are more intense negative emotions. Buddhism puts them in five classifications: desire/attachment, anger/aversion (including fear), pride/arrogance, envy/jealousy, and dullness/ignorance. The latter would not be considered an emotion in normal Western thought or psychology, but it is in Buddhism since it is another way that the mind relates to the world, in this case by tuning it out in some way.

When we start meditating, we are often swept away by these emotions, but with time, they, like thoughts, have less pull on us. When that happens, not only do we calm down, but we do not make ourselves so miserable, as these five are the main causes of unhappiness in our lives. Our behavior changes, and all sorts of benefits follow.

For example, as our desire lessens, we might eat less or more healthfully and feel better. We might shop less and be able to save money for, say, retreats and teachings. We might also be able to avoid entering into unhealthy, destructive relationships.

As our fear decreases, we have less anxiety, and we sleep and function better. As our anger lessens, we have less conflict with others, get along better, and have more joyful and meaningful friendships. The same holds true for the other negative emotions.

Some degree of calmness will happen for anyone. My teacher has said that if one meditates half an hour a day for six months, there should be some noticeable change.

Many people will experience bliss. I have talked about bliss before, but it needs mentioning here. *Bliss* is a broad term for any kind of pleasurable experience in meditation. It can be more mental, like joy or mirth, or more physical, like a general sense of increased well-being, a tingling sense of pleasure, or a feeling that the body is lighter. People who take the body as an object of mindfulness or meditation are more apt to experience physical pleasure.

Let's face it—we all like to feel good! If our meditation has this effect, we will naturally want to continue it and meditate more. Some people feel guilty about feeling pleasure in their meditation, but that is an inappropriate response. Pleasure sustains meditators. Of course, if you get obsessed by bliss, crave it, and feel terribly disappointed when you don't experience it, that is an obstacle. But don't be too hard on yourself if you feel a little attached or encouraged by pleasurable sensations in your meditation. Bliss will make you want to meditate more, and then the other benefits can arise.

Next is clarity. The mind seems brighter or more transparent, like an autumn sky in the desert. We may feel more intelligent or articulate. Generally, clarity does not invoke the same level of attachment and craving that bliss does. Similar to clarity, the mind can feel more open, vast, or spacious. There can be fewer and fewer thoughts, and these seem gentler and less distracting. We feel less contracted inward on ourselves.

It's difficult to predict what you will experience, but the preceding examples are easily accessible and quite common. You probably won't have them every moment of your practice, but you should experience a gradual development of more positive experiences in terms of both frequency and intensity.

As I alluded to before, your meditation will begin to affect your behavior. As a matter of fact, this often happens before you even notice that your meditation has changed. I often say that the first sign of meditation is that others think you are less of a jerk.

Meditation makes us kinder, more thoughtful and considerate, and more loving. It also makes us less irritable and reactive. We do not respond negatively as frequently or as caustically, and as a result, our relationships all become smoother and more meaningful.

Meditation also provides a wonderful opportunity for emotional healing. Our retreat master in Scotland once said, "Lord Buddha taught that there were five negative emotions, but you Westerners seem to have invented a new one—guilt." He mentioned how hard his life had been, from the Chinese invasion, refugee status in India, and so forth, but noted he had always just let go and moved on. Westerners, in contrast, seem to have an idyllic life but are burdened by emotions they simply cannot let go of.

So not only do we have the five negative emotions, we have these darker ones like guilt, depression, self-loathing, and anxiety. They seem to be always "on," locked in our bodies and minds. It feels like we are carrying a hundred pounds of boulders on our backs at all times. (I talked about this in chapter 6.)

A skillful and brave meditator with a skillful teacher will have the confidence to face these negative states. They can often be experienced as different sensations in the body. For example, I've experienced depression as a heaviness in my chest and anxiety as a weakness in my lower back. By gently and lovingly placing my awareness in these spots, I sense some energetic release. Over time, the sensation dissipates and with it, the corresponding emotional pattern. I feel healed, freer, and profoundly grateful that such simple techniques exist and have such deep benefits. This is one of the most meaningful results of meditation and is accessible to anyone who is willing to give it a go.

Meditation can bring many useful benefits to the body and our relationship to it. We can heal ourselves of illnesses by purifying the underlying causes, whether karmic or energetic. If we remain ill, the practice of tonglen can be useful in transforming our illness into a vehicle for growth. One of the main signs that the mind is calming down is an increased lightness and suppleness in the body. This experience is even possible while doing the Vajrasattva part of the ngondro; in the texts, lightness is cited as a sign of success. This newfound suppleness can be your constant companion and a reminder of the benefits of meditation.

As I mentioned earlier, many of us are not "in our bodies"; we are "in our heads." Meditation, especially Vajrayana practices like deity meditation, can heal that sense of separation and alienation. Imagine yourself as a deity. The deity has a body, one with a fascinating form doing provocative activities. Visualizing the complete body of a deity spreads our awareness throughout our own bodies, bringing us out of our heads and into harmony with our bodies. This sense of oneness with the body accompanies the growing lightness and suppleness.

We become nicer people. Through the practice of lojong, we sincerely endeavor to be kinder. Through purification, our aggression and arrogance become pacified. By giving up self-images we no longer have such strong agendas with others and can, therefore, be more open and skillful when dealing with them. As we become kinder and more skillful, it will come back to us. People will like us better, and we will not get so embroiled in confrontations and disputes. It will be easier to get our way as we act more skillfully.

We will have fewer attitudes and judgments about other people and our environment. Because of this, we will get along with others better and easily adjust to any situation. We will be more flexible and able to adapt to seemingly contradictory roles in the family or at work because of not identifying too strongly with any of them. I always find it amusing how fussy so many "spiritual" practitioners are about food. Although there are many good reasons to have a sane diet, perhaps it's also good not to be so rigid and to learn to enjoy what's available.

One of the hardest things for me to give up is my negative attitudes toward others. I've realized that behind this is my own fear of social inadequacy; it's soothing to know others are floundering as much as you are and that you can get your friends to agree with your appraisal. But this kind of negativity, no matter how insightful it seems, is just a jealous and unhappy mind. Both lojong practice and the teachings on pure perception have helped me overcome this negativity, and I feel more open and loving for having done so.

Chapter 14 mentioned the subject of autonomy. Autonomy is not the same as having a big ego. It is more like having sound limits. In all kyerim practices, we generate a wheel of protection, or a vajra fence. It's obvious that our tradition believes in having healthy boundaries. All the problems that come with boundary issues are eliminated as the basic problem is addressed. People won't walk all over you. You will have a sense of your own strength and worth, and you will be able to say "no" when appropriate. Once again this can easily be understood in terms of the deity's pride. This practice is an invaluable technique of dealing with so many issues that plague the average Western practitioner.

Practice gives most people a sense of greater acceptance and humor in their lives. Self-condemnation is simply one more negative thought. As we see through these negative self-images, we become amused by our negativities rather than being repulsed. What an interesting display! How funny are these endless thoughts that pop into my mind every time I try to meditate.

Even a small glimpse of buddha-nature gives us a profound understanding of the Buddhist view. We no longer merely think, trust, or speculate; we know. That confidence is also invaluable; it's an anchor around which the rest of our lives can settle. We are never fooled quite as much by dualistic appearances as we were before.

Finally, a close relationship with a high teacher confers the benefits I mentioned in the beginning of the book. Having such a relationship also puts everything in one's life into perspective. There is no substitute for that kind of unconditional love, omniscient guidance, and great blessing.

As one practices longer and perhaps more diligently, naturally there are greater benefits. We simply enjoy meditating more. Both our bodies and our minds get used to it; they are both less restless. We are more confident, and our meditative experience is more rewarding.

We begin to develop the twin Buddhist qualities of compassion and wisdom. We become less selfish, think of others, and begin to have some understanding of emptiness.

As our understanding increases, our appreciation of the Buddhist teachings grows. At first, the teachings seem like various bits of information and belief that don't really fit together. But with time, these bits begin to form a more cohesive, larger picture. When this process happens, we can find ourselves amazed at the wonder of

Lord Buddha's teaching—how profound and how simple, how deep and how imminently useful and practical. A new book is like getting a box of chocolate.

With that comes some ability to explain the teachings and give helpful advice to others. Let's face it, most of our interactions will be with non-Buddhists, and we are their best chance at making a connection. But now we can say something that makes sense, and others may notice that we have changed. Some will be inspired to follow our example and start their own involvement with the Dharma.

One thing that's lacking in most people's lives these days is a sense of meaning, purpose, and value. Consumer culture and the American dream simply don't touch on those deep needs. As our practice deepens and the Dharma grows within us, so does our sense of purpose and meaning. Our lives still have their ups and downs, but those ups and downs take place within a context of awareness and understanding. This gives tremendous value to our lives—finding the Dharma is infinitely better than winning the lottery.

Lastly, we can face death with confidence. We may not be great meditators who can remain in a meditative state throughout the whole dying and rebirth process, but we have confidence that due to our faith and practice, we will die with the Dharma in our hearts and be able to continue our practice in the future.

Of course, most of us are not very advanced. But my teacher, Venerable Chökyi Nyima Rinpoche, has emphatically stated that if you practice and make continued gradual improvement to your state of mind, you will get a precious human birth in your next life and be able to continue on the path.

My wife works as a geriatric care manager; she arranges for the care of seniors as they age and then die. Through her and her work, I am very aware of how miserable people can be as they approach death. They often feel ripped off, as if dying was a big secret. They can be fearful, regretful, or simply bitter. What an awful way to end your life!

But that shouldn't be the case with us. We won't be surprised.

We will be prepared and have the necessary support to negotiate the transition.

Especially as tantric practitioners, even if we don't possess realization, we can still generate confidence concerning our approaching death. We can do a short phowa retreat that will almost completely assure us that we can be reborn in a pure land. We can do a practice like that of Amitabha that will also help us to cultivate the causes for rebirth in a buddha-field. Our devotion to our lamas makes us feel that their presence and blessing will help us when we die. The practice of tonglen can be a great aid in dealing with the suffering we most likely will experience as we approach death. I mentioned earlier the peace and joy that simple, older Tibetans transmit when one sees them in Asia, a condition that is so different from the gloom I have found in even a well-appointed senior citizen community here.

Part of the benefits of practice comes through the healing or purification that takes place in the transition from identifying with the ego to the development of egolessness. Many people are afraid to drop the ego; others misunderstand and do it incorrectly. Therefore, it's important to spend some time on this key issue.

In the West, the term *ego* is variously defined. My dictionary equates it to the self. In Freudian thought, the ego is contrasted to the id and superego as one of the components of the personality. We all have some general or intuitive understanding of what the term means. We can speak of people having big egos, weak egos, or healthy egos. None of these is exactly what ego means in Buddhism.

A more accurate term than *ego* might be *self-image*. The self-image is a mental event that contains a little picture of us. When someone insults us, we think, "How could they say that to *me*?" That "me," with all its associations, is self-image. Here, the "me" is someone special who couldn't possibly be reprimanded justly. In another circumstance, a different self-image may appear to us. After spending another lonely Saturday night, we think, "How could anyone ever like me?" All these different "me's" refer to the same person; however, the images are very different.

We have many of these images. Which image is activated at any given moment depends on the external trigger. What they all have in common is that they are mental events, things that appear in our minds. We have only one problem—we completely buy into these images. We identify with the various "me's" rather than regarding them in a detached manner as just another mental event. If we are able to observe their arising with detachment, the various self-images lose their power and slowly dissolve.

When we begin to do this, we may feel a considerable amount of fear and anxiety at first. The ego evolved as a way to deal with the chaos of being; dissolving it opens us to the fears that accompanied its original emergence. Letting go feels like death. Actually, it *is* death—what dies in the release is the same as what dies when we physically expire. But remember, in Buddhism the moment of death is also a moment of pure enlightenment for those who can recognize and use it. The fear and anxiety are simply more thoughts that we can let go. However, without the support of a teacher and a spiritual community, it can be difficult to walk through the fear.

When we let go of these images and their attendant fears, we begin to experience spaciousness. When we identify with the self-images, our minds are contracted; as we let go, our minds open up to their vastness, which approaches the true or absolute nature. With time, this vastness actually becomes inviting; it no longer makes us feel as if we are dying. We've experienced it enough to know that we can open up, survive, and be better off. Identifying with our self-image no longer feels safe and comfortable; it feels claustrophobic and stultifyingly boring. This is a major and important transition in our practice: when we reach this point, we "get it"; our progress will be smoother and our commitment stronger.

Many people fear egolessness because they fear they will become dysfunctional. But let's look at the lamas we know. They left Tibet as penniless, starving refugees, adapted first to Indian and then to Western culture, and are now engaged in an incredible range of truly beneficial activities. Hardly dysfunctional. What I recommend to people with this view is give up 10 percent of your ego, 10 percent of your thoughts. See what happens. Are you better or worse off? No one yet has said "worse." Having done this, you can trust that slowly giving up the other 90 percent will be beneficial.

Almost all of us associate *egolessness* with a state of nonassertive wimpiness because of the way this term is commonly used in the West. People who have that predilection are probably drawn to the Buddhist teachings due to this misunderstanding. We let people walk over us and say we are nonattached. We don't assert ourselves to get what we want because we think we have no desire. I was like this for decades, and I can assure you it is complete nonsense.

This attitude comes from confusing ego with self-image. The nonassertive personality has a strong self-image of being powerless and weak. They feel they will be crushed if they assert themselves. To compensate, they develop a philosophy that exhorts nonassertiveness and passivity, that confuses nonassertiveness with desirelessness. This is big ego. This is strong self-grasping. This is wrong—it is not good Buddhism. I've never met a wimpy lama. They are hearty, earthy people who enjoy themselves while actively engaging in the world and accomplishing a myriad of beneficial activities. They are never afraid of standing up for what they believe.

Here is one test you can give yourself: If there is something you want and you don't pursue it, is it because you truly have a different set of priorities, or is it that you simply feel unable either to pursue your desire or to succeed? If it is the latter, it is a highly defiled mental state that must be purified. It's wonderful to give up desires or not to retaliate when abused, but these should be choices made from a position of strength, not the limited responses of a crippled being.

A sense of weakness is a self-image to which we cling. It can and should be given up. When we give it up, we experience spaciousness and feel stronger. We don't have to become aggressive jerks; we simply want to reach a balance where we are free to act appropriately. This newly developed strength greatly encourages us in our practice. We feel much better because of it; we also have valuable resources for continuing on our journey.

Another typical mistake that was more common in the early days was to equate egolessness with a pre-egoic, childlike state. There's something to be said for the open, innocent, playful qualities of a child, but this line of thought becomes a rationale for indulgent behavior in the name of spirituality. Thinking, "I've transcended good and bad," while acting harmfully is obviously wrong thinking.

Similarly, some people never develop healthy boundaries because of their woundedness. As a by-product of this lack, they may be open to nonordinary states or experiences. They may feel quite developed. This is a very important point, because if people like this aren't careful, practice can make them schizophrenic. They already have the tendencies. It's great if you can talk with fairies; however, it's not the point of Buddhist practice, and you may find that by engaging in the Buddhist path, you have to abandon feeling you are special due to your ability. You may even lose that ability.

One thing I've noticed is how annoyed lamas become by people's "phenomena." They certainly don't feel that you are special if you have visions or amazing dreams. They want you to purify your five poisons. This kind of openness, derived from a lack of boundaries, may come from having a weak ego, not from egolessness.

The point is that our practice cultivates a strong, healthy ego (in the Western sense) as we dissolve our self-images (ego in the Buddhist sense). Although this appears contradictory because of the ambiguous use of the word *ego*, it is not. Why? Because the qualities of a healthy ego come from a deeper, more intrinsic part of the mind than the self-image. As the various self-images are discarded, positive qualities that are innate to our nature emerge. These qualities will give us a good, healthy ego, but they do so without reinforcing self-images that contract the mind.

Know that you can practice the Buddhist path of egolessness without becoming a vegetable! When practiced correctly, meditation will make you stronger, more confident, and better able to deal skillfully and compassionately with the world.

Everything I've written about the benefits of meditation in this chapter was written with ordinary, lay practitioners in mind. Not monks or nuns, not yogis or yoginis, not unusually gifted practitioners. The point I want to make perfectly clear is that you may never get to enter into long retreat. You may be hopelessly neurotic.

You may never even vaguely approach the profound experiences that we so often read about in books. Nevertheless, there is a world of inconceivable value for you in the practice of Vajrayana Buddhism, just as you are. Much of that value comes from Vajrayana's uniqueness and the profundity of its many techniques, but also from non-Vajrayana practices mastered in Tibet. Find an authentic teacher, practice intelligently and diligently, and these benefits will be yours.

Conclusion

As I mentioned in the preface, I originally wrote this book more than twenty years ago. Soon after, I went through a long period of depression, when I felt a tremendous sense of failure as a practitioner as well as a growing sense that Tibetan Buddhism wasn't working in the West. I needn't go into why I came to that conclusion, but in the last ten years or so I've become more optimistic. Because we as individuals are all part of the larger picture of the spead of Buddhism to the West, I would like to end this book by bringing previous discussions into a larger perspective.

When I first went to Asia to study, I found myself and most of my companions fascinated by the topic "the Dharma in the West." For me, it was almost like a puzzle to be solved, and somehow we older students were going to be the ones to solve it.

But that was silly. First, there isn't one right approach that suits all Westerners. Some of us easily fit into an Asian mold, while others rebel against it. We all have different interests and proclivities, different lifestyles and resources.

Second, Buddhism is Buddhism. It needn't and shouldn't change. It is perfect as it is.

Third, as younger lamas have learned Western languages and Western culture, they have learned to communicate Buddhism more and more in a way that seems free from cultural bias and speaks directly to us in a way that is meaningful and accessible. When I first studied Buddhism, it was more like studying chemistry, something foreign that needed to be mastered. Now it seems immediate and touches my heart.

Besides these young lamas, I see a lot to be optimistic about. As the years pass, originally nutty people are becoming warm, kind, and serene. I lack the abilty to know what people are experiencing, but I do find that many take delight in practice and devote more and more of their time to it. It must mean it is working! There are more good Western Dharma teachers, and it is easy to forsee the time when much of the Dharma will be transmitted by people like ourselves.

Since I originally wrote this book, my teacher's activity has spread like wildfire. He's building retreat centers, a translation center, a university, and a large temple in the West. He wouldn't be doing this if he felt we weren't ready for it.

Buddhism has always changed when it has moved from one country or culture to another. America couldn't be more different from Tibet, and we may feel that those differences imply a vastly different spiritual path. We can sit around and speculate, but if we try to change it ourselves, even with the best intentions, it becomes "Bruce-ism" or "Mary-ism," no longer Buddhism. This is an extremely important point. We may be accustomed to a great deal of freedom in many areas of our lives, but a spiritual path has its own coherent logic and its own lineage of blessing and transmission. Imagine telling your surgeon, "It's okay to cut me up, but I don't want you to cauterize such-and-such veins." That would be simply crazy. Yet Westerners seem quite happy to do that with Buddhism. "I like this part, but I don't like that. Let's throw it away. It's not really Buddhism." That results in there no longer being a lineage of blessing and transmission. It has been killed by our good intentions.

Only enlightened beings can really change Buddhism. We can see that now in His Holiness the Dalai Lama as he tries to address some of the cultural problems of Westerners. I read one of his discussions with gay Buddhist leaders in which they were trying to gain acceptance even though the traditional teachings condemn their sexual practices as nonvirtuous. He has the wisdom, power, and authority to change matters like these; we don't. Chögyam Trungpa Rinpoche was also quite an innovator; but he was also an enlightened being.

I see now that many of the younger, English-speaking lamas are writing books that address some of the issues that I went over in chapter 6. This will undoubtably lead to saner, warmer Western practitioners who will be prepared to progress through the Vajrayana Buddhist path. I find this exceptionally encouraging—we are being seen, guided, and cared for by highly realized beings. The works of Tulku Thondrup on love and healing have been especially inspiring and life-changing for me.

With time, Westerners will become enlightened. They may not radically transform Vajrayana; they may simply be able to teach in a more easily understandable form. There is an internal logic to Vajrayana that becomes clearer the more one studies it. We would like to think the parts with which we have difficulty are an expression of Tibetan culture and of no use to us here. In truth, they are an expression of the deepest insight and understanding into ultimate truth. I imagine that, with time, we too will change a little. Our children will grow up with concepts that seemed strange and alien to us now. Buddhist ideas have already begun to infiltrate our culture, making it easier for Westerners to approach the real thing.

Nonetheless, some changes may be inevitable. There will most likely be a moving away from ritual to formlessness in practice. This has already been predicted, but as I just mentioned, I fear that if it goes too far, many of the benefits of tantra will be lost.

Fewer people will become ordained; there will be a greater emphasis on lay life. The great danger, of course, is that there won't be enough people developing the depths of meditation to maintain the tradition. In that case, we will always be dependent on foreign teachers. Also, many of the outer forms, such as the details of rituals that only full-time practitioners have the time to learn, may be lost. So many of those who are now ordained have such a difficult time. They aren't supported by the laity and must often work. They are not able to isolate themselves from the distractions and temptations of worldly life, and they often end up doing more center work than actual formal meditation. These days, ordination may often not be a good option for someone who wants to lead a contemplative life.

With the emphasis shifting to the laity, aspects of the layperson's life will become more respected vehicles for growth and transformation. Romantic relationships are now emerging as such a focus. Work and child-raising are others. Situations that give rise to negativity are also situations in which we can learn about ourselves as we never could in a traditional cloistered environment. They always provide opportunities to step out of the ego and act mindfully, lovingly, and skillfully.

The profound insights of Tibetan Buddhism will become integrated with more ideas from Western disciplines. We are already seeing this in many ways. Dream researchers acknowledge Tibetan Buddhists as the experts in the field. Cognitive scientists have an annual meeting with the Dalai Lama. Many Buddhists are therapists, and the meeting between Western therapeutic thought and Buddhism has been compared to the meeting of Christian and Greek thought centuries ago. Buddhists will now converse with the contemplatives of Western religions and with physicists on the nature of the universe.

In the past, Buddhism always spread through royal patronage. When the king converted, the kingdom converted with him. The king became the main patron of the monastic system. This will not be the case in the United States. There are no kings. Buddhism will always have to compete with a healthy Christianity, scientific skepticism, and mindless materialism. As Buddhism grows, we Buddhists may start to experience animosity from one of these groups, which may lead to a kind of persecution or at least to an adaptation of defensiveness on our part. But as I've visited the older, more established centers and met with many of the older, more accomplished Western practitioners, I have no doubt that Tibetan Vajrayana Buddhism has already truly and deeply established itself here in our country and in the West.

We will also need to have a relationship with democracy. We are no longer practicing in kingdoms where matters of governance are beyond our control. Are Buddhists always liberal, as many people assume, or is there a meaningful way to embrace a conservative view? Some of us will be drawn to activism, believing that the world's problems are too immediate to justify a retreat into meditation. Others will see meditation as the only solution to these problems.

I am often asked about a Buddhist approach to environmental problems. I answer that if we look at the root of these problems, there are two causes: too many people on the planet, and almost all of them want too much stuff. The root of these is desire. And who are the world's experts on desire, its effects, and its remedies? Of course, us. We Buddhists can serve a very powerful role in Earth's future through sincerely following the path.

I don't believe there is one "Western Buddhism" just like there has never been one "Asian Buddhism." After all, there must be a billion of us. Buddha-nature can and will unfold in myriad ways that we may now be unable to envision.

Systems and Stages of Practice

The teachings of Tibetan Buddhism are unbelievably vast. There are so many categories and lineages that it can be quite daunting for a beginner to try to sort it all out. But it's also essential—knowing the context of a teaching will make it much more meaningful for you. You might sometimes come across contradictions between the teaching you're receiving now and others that you have previously heard or read about; such apparent contradictions can only be resolved by understanding the differences between the various systems represented. The three different methods to introduce students to the mind's nature (presented in chapter 7) can be seen as examples of this. In some sense, these three presentations can seem contradictory, and it would be confusing to try to study a little of each approach. Similarly, different kinds of behavior, such as drinking or sexual activity, are evaluated differently in different teachings.

When you study them all, it starts to make sense. Teacher A prohibits the drinking of alcohol. Perhaps they are speaking from a Hinayana point of view. Teacher B allows students to drink a little because they feel it relaxes people in social situations and permits them to open up and bond with each other—this person could be teaching from a Mahayana perspective. When you understand the "big picture" of Tibetan Buddhism, you realize how truly amazing it is and how incredibly realized the lamas must be to have grasped it all. Also, how kind they are to provide you with a teaching that's just right for you. Instead of feeling confused and overwhelmed by the vastness and complexity of the Tibetan system, we are actually incredibly fortunate to find a path that can be adapted to our exact needs.

Let's begin by looking at the basic divisions and subdivisions of Tibetan Buddhism. I'm not going to explain what everything means here; I'm only presenting the outline to give you an overview. More traditional teachings and books can fill in the details. You might find all the different names and lists boring or confusing; however, with time you may refer to this outline for clarification. Also, you may find sources that seem to contradict what I'm saying, but it shouldn't be a big deal. I will use many of the more commonly used Sanskrit or Tibetan Buddhist terms; if both the Sanskrit and Tibetan terms are used often in common conversation among Buddhist practitioners, I'll use both. Be flexible; even the broad divisions are not rigid, and the same terms may be used in different contexts.

First, the three *yanas*, or "vehicles": Hinayana, Mahayana, and Vajrayana. Hinayana translates as the "lesser vehicle," Mahayana as the "greater vehicle," and Vajrayana as the "adamantine vehicle." The *vajra* is an indestructible weapon of the gods; here, it refers to the indestructible buddha-nature. The word *vehicle* is intended to convey the meaning "spiritual path."

Hinayana can be subdivided into Shravakayana (the path of the listeners) and Pratyekabuddhayana (the path of the solitary realizers). Together, Hinayana and Mahayana can be called the Dharma of the sutras; Vajrayana is the Dharma of the tantras. Vajrayana is regarded both as a subdivision of Mahayana and as a separate vehicle.

Sutra and *tantra* are often used to refer both to spiritual approaches and to the texts or teachings of the Buddha that discuss these approaches. If you wanted to learn more about Mahayana meditation, you would read a sutra; if you wanted to know about Vajrayana, you would study a tantra. We believe that both the sutras and the tantras are the actual words of Buddha. Table 1 shows a chart of the various vehicles.

Paramitayana (the path of the six perfections) and Bodhisattvayana are synonyms of Mahayana. Tantra and Secret Mantra are synonyms for Vajrayana.

Vehicle	Subdivisions	Approach/Text
Hinayana	Shravakayana	Sutra
	Pratyekabuddhayana	Sutra
Mahayana		Sutra
Vajrayana		Tantra

Table 1. The Divisions of the Vehicles of Tibetan Buddhism

People usually fall into one of the yanas, depending on their approach to practice. The yana system of Tibetan Buddhism does not travel well to other Buddhist traditions—in fact, the term "Hinayana" is considered pejorative when applied to other traditions. We might say that the sutra teachings are shared teachings with Theravada, while Zen is mostly Mahayana. However, the point of our discussion is not to compare different forms of Buddhism but specifically to understand Tibetan Buddhism as a whole. The three-yana approach is taught within Tibetan Buddhism; the lesser yanas serve as a foundation to the Vajrayana. This is not meant as a put-down of other Buddhist traditions by the Tibetans. Here in America, Trungpa Rinpoche emphasized the three-yana approach and felt that his students had to work their way up through each vehicle. Some experience and understanding of a lower vehicle was considered necessary before a higher one would be introduced.

Many lamas encourage their students to practice all three yanas simultaneously—Hinayana with body, Mahayana with speech, Vajrayana with mind. In this approach, the yanas are not seen as mutually exclusive or contradictory; rather, they are interpreted as governing different aspects of one's spiritual life, as shown in Table 2. To continue this explanation, we have to talk about the lineages, since their subdivisions differ.

As I mentioned earlier, there are four main lineages, or orders, of Tibetan Buddhism. The Nyingma is the oldest; it can be called the Old Translation School. The other three can be grouped into the New Translation School or, in Tibetan, Sarma. Originally monks wore red hats; when the Gelug, the youngest order, was founded, they switched to yellow hats. You'll see this in the older Western books about Tibetan Buddhism—they talk about the Red Hat Lamas and the Yellow Hat Lamas. This division is hardly ever used anymore.

Don't forget, many lamas will know more than one lineage and will teach from these differing perspectives as they feel appropriate. Kagyupas especially are equally well versed in the Nyingma teachings. My training has been in the Nyingma and Kagyu, and this book reflects my attempt to present a framework for their wisdom. A technical note: the -pa at the end of many of these words means "one who" or "practitioner of." Thus, a Nyingmapa is one who follows the Nyingma teachings. The suffix -pa is generally masculine; -ma is the feminine.

The Nyingmapas divide all the Buddha's teachings into nine yanas, or vehicles. There are also corresponding terms used by the Sarma traditions, as shown in Table 3. Again, this is not the place to explain the nine yanas in detail. I'm just trying to show you how all the pieces fit together.

In general, the Outer Tantras refer to the practice of the peaceful deities, who are usually without consorts, such as Tara, Manjushri, or Chenrezig. The Inner Tantras contain the wrathful deities and the deities in union such as Chakrasamvara and Vajrakilaya. A particular deity might have an Inner Tantra and an Outer Tantra representation; for example, the white, four-armed form of Chenrezig is an Outer Tantra practice; when Chenrezig appears as red with a consort, he's called Gyalwa Gyamtso, whose practice is from among the Father Tantras (in the Kagyu system). The most profound methods of Tibetan Buddhism, such as the tsalung (the meditations on the winds and channels of the body) and thogal (an advanced dzogchen practice) are contained within the Inner Tantras.

Not many of the tantras have been translated. The sadhana, or liturgy, for a particular practice may be available, but there are many other parts to the tantra. There are numerous rituals to accomplish various goals such as long life or an increase of wealth, an overview of the practice with more general teachings, and the more advanced practices. When you have a particular yidam, or meditational deity,

Vehicle	Door	Focus of Practice
Hinayana	Body	Moral discipline
Mahayana	Speech	Helping others through one's words
Vajrayana	Mind	Maintaining rigpa or pure perception

Table 2. The Vehicles as Related to Different Aspects of Practice

	Nyingmapa	Sarmapa	
Sutra	Shravakayana Pratyekabuddhayana Bodhisattvayana		Shravakayana Pratyekabuddhayana Bodhisattvayana
Outer Tantra	Kriya Tantra Carya Tantra Yoga Tantra		Kriya Tantra Carya Tantra Yoga Tantra
Inner Tantra	Maha Yoga Tantra Anu Yoga Tantra Ati Yoga Tantra	Father Tantra Mother Tantra Nondual Tantra	Maha-anuttara-yoga-tantra

Table 3. The Divisions of the Nyingma and Sarma Lineages

you aspire to work your way through all its associated practices, not only the mantra recitation. It's a lifetime's work. Commentaries written by accomplished masters give many of the most valuable details, such as what to visualize while reciting the mantra, how to begin and end retreat, the signs of success, and so on. Unfortunately, most of these texts have not been translated into English.

The practices for a particular deity are divided into two stages. The practices for visualizing a deity while reciting its mantra are called *kyerim*, which has been variously translated as "creation stage," "development stage," or "arising yoga." Kyerim was the topic of chapter 15. When one has stabilized the practice, one moves on to dzogrim (discussed in chapter 17), the stage of completion or perfection where advanced yogic techniques are practiced. Different tantras emphasize different dzogrim practices; Hevajra emphasizes tummo, or heat yoga, while Guhyasamaja practice stresses a breathing practice called the vajra recitation. The term *dzogrim* can be applied to elaborate yogic practices or to simply resting the mind in buddha-nature after a period of mantra recitation. This dual use of the term can be a little confusing.

Remember the four empowerments? They are derived from the Inner Tantras and cover the different subdivisions in practice. The vase empowerment permits you to practice kyerim; the secret and wisdom empowerments permit you to practice dzogrim; and the fourth, or word, empowerment permits the practice of dzogchen, or mahamudra. Among the Inner Tantras, the different levels of tantras emphasize different practices, as shown in Table 4: the Father Tantras, or Maha Yoga, emphasize kyerim; the Mother Tantras, or Anu Yoga, emphasize dzogrim; and the Nondual Tantras, or Ati Yoga, stress the mahamudra and dzogchen. So, if you aspire to practice tsalung meditations, such as inner heat, you will seek instruction on a Mother Tantra deity; if you aspire to the Great Perfection, or dzogchen, an Ati Yoga Tantra will be best for you. You'll find this overview more useful as you learn more about what the different entries mean.

Another useful subdivision that you should know is between the path of skillful means and the path of liberation. This is also a division within the Inner Tantras. The path of skillful means contains the more elaborate deity practices, such as tsalung, while the

Empowerment	Stage	Meditation	Emphasized by
Vase	Kyerim	Kyerim	Maha Yoga and Father Tantras
Secret	Dzogrim	Tsalung	Nyingmapa Anu Yoga
Wisdom		Union	Sarmapa Mother Tantras
Word or fourth		Mahamudra and dzogchen	Ati Yoga and Nondual Tantras

Table 4. The Tantras and Their Correspondence with the Four Empowerments

Path of Liberation	Path of Skillful Means
Preliminaries	Preliminaries
Shinay	Kyerim
Lhagtong	Tsalung and union
Mahamudra and dzogchen	Mahamudra and dzogchen

Table 5. The Path of Liberation and the Path of Skillful Means

path of liberation contains the simpler practices of shinay and lhagtong, calming the mind and gaining insight. These practices were explained in chapter 18. Many Westerners don't feel comfortable with the complexity of the path of skillful means; they are drawn to the simplicity of the path of liberation. Both paths start with the preliminaries and end with mahamudra and dzogchen; they diverge, however, in the middle (Table 5). In reality, serious practitioners will practice a combination of both.

What is the normal sequence of practice for a typical practitioner? In the Kagyu, Sakya, and Nyingma systems, first comes the ngondro, the preliminary, or foundational, practices. The ordinary or common preliminaries are the contemplations of the four thoughts that turn the mind (see chapter 11), which give the practitioner the motivation and energy to throw themself into the practice. Next come the uncommon, or extraordinary, preliminaries that consist of refuge and bodhichitta (chapter 12), Vajrasattva practice and mandala offerings (chapter 13), and guru yoga (chapter 14). These purify obscurations, accumulate merit, and gather the blessings of the lama and their lineage. These four extraordinary preliminary practices are common to all four schools in Tibetan Buddhism. In the Gelug tradition, however, the practitioner can engage in as many as nine preliminaries, the aforementioned four, plus another five, which include Dorje Khadro fire puja, the purification practice of Samayavajra, and several others. Upon completion of the ngondro, one is given a deity practice to do (chapters 16 and 17). After that are the yogas associated with the energy systems (chapter

18). Meanwhile, the practitioner studies and applies the teachings directly related to buddha-nature, that is, mahamudra and dzogchen (chapter 19).

This is a typical progression in Vajrayana. It is important to accomplish each step before moving on to the next. In the Gelug, the largest of the traditions, practitioners often engage in the ngondro and deity practices during their academic career; it's generally not considered necessary to complete the ngondro before engaging in deity practices. After that, the sequence is the same as the other lineages.

Vajrayana is vast. It's an incredible system containing an amazing collection of techniques for rapid transformation. This appendix has presented the bare outline of how those teachings fit together and correlate. As you receive empowerments and teachings and begin your practice, this framework will help you integrate all this material and, with time, help reveal the underlying simplicity of all the subdivisions. *Vajra* refers to buddha-nature, and Vajrayana is the path that constantly points to our buddha-nature and helps us realize it. All these different techniques serve only that purpose.

Notes

Chapter 1

1. Tulku Urgyen, "Re-enlightenment," in *The Dzogchen Primer*, ed. Marcia Binder Schmidt (Boulder: Shambhala, 2002), 45.
2. Tulku Urgyen, "The Basis: Buddha Nature," in *The Dzogchen Primer*, ed. Marcia Binder Schmidt (Boulder: Shambhala, 2002), 26-27.
3. Khenchen Thrangu, "Buddha Nature," in *The Dzogchen Primer*, ed. Marcia Binder Schmidt (Boulder: Shambhala, 2002), 24.
4 Arya Maitreya and Acarya Asanga, *The Changeless Nature* (Eskdalemuir: Karma Drubgyud Darjay Ling, 1985), 30.
5. Arya Maitreya et al., *Buddha Nature: The Mahayana Uttaratantra Shastra with Commentary* (Boulder: Shambhala, 2012), 124.
6. Arya Maitreya and Acarya Asanga, *The Changeless Nature* (Eskdalemuir: Karma Drubgyud Darjay Ling, 1985), 30.
7. Je Gampopa and Khenchen Thrangu, *The Jewel Ornament of Liberation* (Delhi: Zhyisil Chökyi Publications, 2003), 12.
8. Ibid.
9. Ibid.
10. Arya Maitreya et al., *Buddha Nature*, 32.
11. Ibid., 155.

Chapter 2

1. Longchenpa, *Kindly Bent to Ease Us, Part One* (Berkeley: Dharma Publishing, 1975), 78.
2. Ibid., 76
3. Tsang Nyon Heruka, *The Life of Marpa the Translator* (Boulder: Prajna Press, 1982), 92.

Chapter 4

1. Tsele Rinpoche, *Empowerment* (Kathmandu: Rangjung Yeshe Publications, 1994), 15.
2. Ibid., 31.
3. Ibid., 32.
4. Ibid.

Chapter 6

1. "Scientism," Wikipedia, last modifided October 17, 2020, https://en.wiki pedia.org/wiki/Scientism.
2. Dzogchen Ponlop, *Emotional Rescue: How to Work with Your Emotions to Transform Hurt and Confusion into Energy that Empowers You* (New York: TarcherPerigee, 2017), 48.

Chapter 8

1. Longchenpa, *Kindly Bent to Ease Us, Part Two* (Emeryville, CA: Dharma Publishing, 1976), 58.

Chapter 14

2. Jamgon Kongtrul, *The Torch of Certainty* (Boulder: Shambhala Publications, 1977), 123.
3. Ibid., p. 128.
4. Chökyi Nyima, *Sadness, Love, Openness: The Buddhist Path of Joy* (Boulder: Shambhala Publications, 2018), 93.

Chapter 15

1. Bokar Rinpoche, *Chenrezig: Lord of Love* (San Francisco: ClearPoint Press, 1994), 11.
2. Jamgon Kongtrul, *The Oral Instructions of Padmakara*, unpublished translation by Peter Roberts (Oxford, 1989), 6.

Chapter 18

1. Dudjom Rinpoche, *A Dear Treasure for Destined Disciples: Pointing Out the Great Perfection*, from *Crystal Cave* (Kathmandu: Rangjung Yeshe Publications, 1990), 119.

2. Tsele Natsok Rinpoche, *Lamp of Mahamudra* (Kathmandu: Rangjung Yeshe Publications, 1988), 39.

3. Karma Chagme and Gyatrul Rinpoche, *A Spacious Path to Freedom* (Boulder: Snow Lion, 1998), 97.

4. Garma C. C. Chang, *Teachings of Tibetan Yoga* (New Hyde Park, NY: University Books, 1963), 42.

About the Author

If you would like more information on Bruce's teaching schedule, please visit his website, lamabruce.com, or his Facebook Community Page, Lama Bruce Newman, https://www.facebook.com/LamaBruceNewman/.